INSTITUTIONAL TRUST AND ECONOMIC POLICY

INSTITUTIONAL TRUST AND ECONOMIC POLICY

Lessons from the History of the Euro

Dóra Győrffy

Central European University Press
Budapest–New York

Published in 2013 by

Central European University Press

An imprint of the
Central European University Limited Liability Company
Nádor utca 11, H-1051 Budapest, Hungary
Tel: +36-1-327-3138 or 327-3000
Fax: +36-1-327-3183
E-mail: ceupress@ceu.hu
Website: www.ceupress.com

400 West 59th Street, New York NY 10019, USA
Tel: +1-212-547-6932
Fax: +1-646-557-2416
E-mail: martin.greenwald@opensocietyfoundations.org

ISBN 978-615-5225-22-2

Library of Congress Cataloging-in-Publication Data
Gyorffy, Dóra.
 Institutional trust and economic policy : lessons from the history of
the euro / Dóra Gyorffy.
    pages cm
 Includes bibliographical references and index.
 ISBN 978-6155225222 (hardbound)
 1. Trust. 2. Euro. 3. European Union countries–Economic policy. I.
Title.

 BF575.T7G96 2013
 338.501'9–dc23

                        2012048145

Printed in Hungary by
Prime Rate Kft., Budapest

Contents

List of Figues   ix
List of Tables   xi
Preface and Acknowledgments   xiii

1.   Introduction   1
1.1.   The controversy over trust   2
1.2.   Research questions   3
1.3.   Methodology and research design   4
1.4.   The concept and measurement of trust   6
1.5.   The argument in a nutshell   10
1.6.   Summary of chapters   11

2.   Institutional Trust and Individual Decision Making   13
2.1.   Theories of expectations   14
2.1.1. Rational expectations   14
2.1.2. Austrian and Post-Keynesian approaches to expectations   19
2.2.   The concept of uncertainty   22
2.3.   The role of institutions in reducing uncertainty   24
2.4.   Compliance and legitimacy   28
2.4.1. Tax compliance   30
2.5.   Institutional trust and individual planning   31

3.   Institutional Trust and Policymaking in the EMU   35
3.1.   Unique and recurrent decisions: the rationality of
       policymakers   36
3.2.   The de-politicization of money in the EMU   37
3.2.1. The collapse of Bretton Woods and its turbulent aftermath   38
3.2.2. The creation of the Single Market   39
3.2.3. Learning monetary cooperation: lessons from history   40
3.2.4. A technocratic approach to the de-politicization of money   41
3.2.5. Self-imposed commitments for sound money   42

3.2.6. Tensions within the arrangement—the role of fiscal policy   43
3.3.   Policy choices within the euro-zone: the role of trust   44
3.3.1. Fiscal policy, growth, and trust   45
3.3.2. The difficulties of reform   50
3.3.3. Implications for fiscal consolidation   51
3.3.4. Implications for adjustment within the EMU   53
3.4.   Prospects after the euro—hypotheses   55

4.   Fiscal Developments in the EU-15, 1992–2007   59
4.1.   The EMS crisis—the start of the convergence period   60
4.2.   The working of the EMU fiscal rules   63
4.3.   Motives for change: internal commitment vs. external anchor 65
4.4.   Institutional quality in the EU-15   75
4.5.   Approaches to fiscal consolidation   76
4.6.   Virtuous and vicious cycles at work: Sweden vs. Portugal   82
4.6.1. Institutional conditions   82
4.6.2. Fiscal policy and growth following the EMS crisis   84
4.6.3. The political economy of fiscal reforms   91

5.   The Maastricht Process in the CEE-10   95
5.1.   An environment of distrust   96
5.1.1. Paternalism and rule of law under communism   96
5.1.2. The heritage of transition   98
5.2.   The role of external constraints in an environment of distrust 101
5.2.1. International financial markets   102
5.2.2. The EU as an anchor   103
5.2.3. The Maastricht process as an anchor   104
5.3.   Institutional quality and exchange rate choice   106
5.4.   The impact of distrust on economic policy in the CEE-10   117
5.4.1. Fiscal policy in the CEE-10, 2002–2007   118
5.4.2. Credit developments in the CEE-10, 2002–2008   120
5.4.3. Assessment   125
5.5.   Reforms without trust: Hungary vs. Slovakia   126
5.5.1. Roots of distrust   126
5.5.2. Vicious cycles in Hungary   128
5.5.3. From isolation to star performer: reforms in Slovakia   137
5.5.4. The political economy of reforms in a low-trust environment 143

6.	**Financial Crisis in the EU-25**	147
6.1.	The origins of the subprime crisis	148
6.2.	The crisis in the EU	149
6.3.	Consequences of the crisis in the EU-25	151
6.3.1.	Growth	152
6.3.2.	Public debt	154
6.3.3.	Unemployment	155
6.3.4.	Assessment of crisis performance	156
6.4.	Surprising cases: Ireland and Poland	159
6.4.1.	Ireland	160
6.4.2.	Poland	167
6.4.3.	Implications for the theory	173
7.	**The Relevance of Trust for Economic Outcomes**	177
7.1.	Summary of findings	177
7.2.	Differences between East and West in the EU	180
7.3.	Institutional trust and economic consequences	181
7.3.1.	High-trust countries in the euro-zone	183
7.3.2.	High-trust countries outside the euro-zone	184
7.3.3.	Low-trust countries in the euro-zone	185
7.3.4.	Low-trust countries outside the euro-zone	186
7.4.	Factors moderating the role of trust	188
7.4.1.	Initial level of development	188
7.4.2.	International financial market pressures	189
7.4.3.	Overconfidence	190
7.4.4.	Economic ideas	190
7.4.5.	Leadership	192
7.5.	Implications for policy	193
7.5.1.	The future of the euro-zone	193
7.5.2.	Accession of CEE countries to the euro-zone	194
7.5.3.	The political economy of policy reforms	195
7.6.	Conclusions	196
	Bibliography	199
	Index	217

List of Figures

2.1. A stylized model of institutional trust and individual decision
      making   32
3.1. Virtuous cycle between trust and growth   48
3.2. Vicious cycle between lack of trust and low growth   49
4.1. Fiscal deficit in Belgium and Spain 1995–2007   67
4.2. Fiscal deficit in Finland, Netherlands, Ireland, Sweden, Den-
      mark 1995–2007   69
4.3. Fiscal deficit in Greece, Italy, Portugal 1995–2007   71
4.4. Fiscal deficit in Austria, France, Germany, Luxembourg, UK
      1995–2007   72
4.5. Quality of governance in the EU-15 (1996)   75
4.6. Change in primary expenditures in the EU-15 1992–2007   77
4.7. Social benefits other than social transfers in kind in the
      EU-15 1992–2007   78
4.8. Change in total revenue in the EU-15 1992–2007   78
4.9. Sources of fiscal consolidation in the EU-15 1992–2007   80
4.10. Public debt in the EU-15 1992–2007   80
4.11. Growth rates in Portugal, Sweden, and the EU-15 1995–2007   87
5.1. Views on the old regime in the CEE-10   99
5.2. Convergence in the CEE-10   101
5.3. Preferences regarding the introduction of the euro (2006)   105
5.4. Quality of governance in Estonia, Slovakia, and Slovenia
      (2004)   107
5.5. Fiscal balance in Estonia, Slovakia, and Slovenia 1995–2007   109
5.6. Quality of governance in Bulgaria, Latvia, and Lithuania
      (2004)   110

5.7. Fiscal balance in Bulgaria, Latvia, and Lithuania 1995–2007   112
5.8. Quality of governance in the Czech Republic, Hungary, Po-
      land, and Romania (2004)   114
5.9. Fiscal balance in the Czech Republic, Hungary, Poland, and
      Romania 1995–2007   115
5.10. Social benefits other than social transfers in kind in the CEE-
      10 2002–2007   119
5.11. Sources of fiscal consolidation in CEE-10 2002–2007   119
5.12. Public debt in the CEE-10 2002–2007   120
5.13. Credit to private sector in the CEE-10 2002–2008   121
5.14. Public and private debt in the CEE-10 in 2007/2008   122
5.15. Public and private debt in the CEE-8 in 2007/2008   122
5.16. Current account balances in the CEE-10 2002–2007   124
5.17. Trust in public institutions in Hungary (2006)   127
5.18. Trust in public institutions in Slovakia (2006)   127
5.19. Unemployment, GDP growth and inflation in Slovakia
      2003–2008   141
6.1. Change in GDP in the EU-25 2007–2011   153
6.2. Public debt in the EU-25 2007–2011   154
6.3. Unemployment in the EU-25 2007–2011   156
6.4. Irish inflation and ECB policy rate 1999–2010   162
6.5. Irish housing prices 1970–2008   163
6.6. Wage costs and current account in Ireland 1995–2010   165
6.7. Selected macroeconomic indicators in Poland 2005–2011   169
6.8. Housing loan balance in Poland 2002–2009   171
7.1. GDP per capita PPS in high-trust euro-zone countries
      (1998–2010)   183
7.2. GDP per capita PPS in Denmark, Sweden, and the UK
      (1998–2010)   184
7.3. GDP per capita PPS in low-trust euro-zone countries
      (1998–2010)   186
7.4. GDP per capita PPS in CEE-7 (1998–2010)   187

List of Tables

3.1. Structural reforms: sources of resistance, solutions and the
     role of credibility   51
4.1. Growth, unemployment and fiscal balance in the EU-15
     (1991–1994)   62
4.2. The motive for fiscal change: internal commitment vs.
     external anchor   65
4.3. Average change in selected indicators by country groups
     1992–2007   81
6.1. Summary of crisis performance in the EU-25   157
7.1. Trust and the euro: surprises to the theory   182

Preface and Acknowledgments

Distrust is a palpable experience for all who live in Central and Eastern Europe. Untrustworthy governments and endemic corruption characterize the political class, while law avoidance and lack of civic involvement is a feature of the masses. In such an environment maintaining an attitude of distant cynicism is a sort of survival tool for those still interested in politics. Understanding the consequences of this state of affairs for economic policy is the major objective of this book.

My interest in trust originates from following Hungarian economic policies in the past decade. During this period an atmosphere of permanent electoral campaign produced short-sighted policies, which eventually made the country the first victim of the subprime crisis in the European Union. As distrust towards policy-makers grew, the inability to implement long-term oriented measures became increasingly evident. In my earlier book (Győrffy 2007) through exploring the roots of fiscal profligacy, I found that the relation between trust and economic outcomes is more than a moralistic narrative: in the old EU member states satisfaction with democracy proved to be a strong predictor of fiscal performance during the decade following the introduction of the euro.

The recognition for the potential influence of trust on economic policy however presented more questions than answers. What are the precise mechanisms through which trust exerts influence on economic outcomes? Why have some post-socialist countries been more successful in mitigating the consequences of distrust than others? At the time of a global financial crisis it is also natural to wonder whether trust can help our understanding of the roots of the crisis as well as the tasks to build more resilient economies. The research presented in this book focuses on these questions.

During the years of research and writing I have received support from several sources. First and foremost, I am deeply grateful to my former doctoral advisor, long-time friend and mentor László Csaba, who encouraged me to undertake this project and helped me through every stage from conception to completion. His enthusiasm was crucial in overcoming my recurrent feelings of inadequacy, when it appeared that I would never be able to organize my thoughts.

The project was greatly helped by a three-year Bolyai Fellowship between 2007 and 2010 from the Hungarian Academy of Sciences. Being a recipient of this fellowship allowed me to research questions, which interested me the most.

Many of the ideas presented in this book were first discussed at the annual economic policy roundtable conferences, which started in 2007 at the University of Debrecen. I am indebted to the organizer of this roundtable, László Muraközy, for always inviting me and giving insightful feedback on my presentations and papers. Over the years the event became a wonderful place to exchange ideas and opinions on the state of the world economy and Hungary within it. I was greatly inspired by the presentations and discussions with the other members of the roundtable including the late László Antal, István Benczes, Lajos Bokros, László Jankovics, Júlia Király, József Péter Martin, Éva Palócz, István György Tóth and Ádám Török.

During the period of writing up the manuscript, I was privileged to be a fellow at the Collegium Budapest through its last semester as a participant of a joint program with the Volkswagen Foundation on new European democracies. I am grateful to Mihály Laki for suggesting the opportunity. At the Collegium I had the chance for regular discussions with János Kornai, whose work has always been an immense source of inspiration for me and crucially shaped the way I approach social science problems. His kindness and support for my ideas gave me confidence about the research. I also had inspiring conversations with Menachem Fish about science, theology and rationality, which helped me see beyond my immediate questions. In such an intellectually stimulating environment many of my preconceived notions on trust changed, and the end result turned out to be something different than I expected.

The publication of this book was made possible by Central European University Press. I am indebted for the support and insightful comments of the two reviewers, Joachim-Jens Hesse and Alexander Lascaux. The quality of the text was greatly improved by the editorial team and I am grateful for the help I received from Virág Illés, Linda Kunos and Nóra Vörös.

Finally, I would like to thank my family for being a constant source of love and support for me and allow finding an (almost) healthy balance between life and work.

All remaining errors are mine.

Budapest, February, 2013

CHAPTER 1

Introduction

When trust is present, we hardly notice it. It is only the disruption caused by its loss that makes us aware of its significance. In the economic sphere no other time has shown this more clearly than the period following the collapse of Lehman Brothers in September 2008. The normal functioning of the interbank market was suddenly suspended, and the global financial system froze. While the intervention of public authorities around the world helped to avoid the worst consequences, four years after the collapse, the system has been unable to return to pre-crisis normality.

This book does not attempt to give another interpretation to the above events. Instead, it tries to go back in time and consider the role played by trust during the run-up to the crisis. Unlike the majority of the literature, its focus is on the European Union, which ended up struggling with the consequences much longer than the United States, the source of the cataclysm. Examining the roots of the subprime crisis from a perspective of trust can also provide new insights to the decades-long debate on the relevance of trust to economic outcomes.

In the following I will provide an overview of the research. The next section gives a brief summary about the main themes of the controversy in the economics and political science literature on trust and its consequences. Then I will turn to the major questions of the research followed by a discussion on methodology and research design. The concept and operationalization of trust is the subject of the fourth section. In the last two sections I will present the argument in a nutshell and provide a brief overview of the chapters.

1.1. The controversy over trust

The concern about the consequences of declining trust can be considered a global phenomenon and is not limited to the post-Socialist region. Starting from the 1990s, a steady decline of trust has been documented extensively in the developed world both at the interpersonal level and toward government.[1] Following the subprime crisis these tendencies are likely to accelerate even further (Tonkiss 2009, Uslaner 2010). Such developments naturally raise the question of consequences.

Declining trust might lead to suboptimal economic outcomes through a variety of ways. Interpersonal trust can help to resolve coordination failures, facilitate the sharing of information, as well as improve individual incentives for cooperation (Durlauf and Fafchamps 2005, 1652). Trust in government matters through contingent consent, which means that the government can rely on the cooperation of the citizens even if the costs of cooperation exceed the individual benefits (Easton 1965, 273, Gamson 1968, 43, Levi 1998, 88). The beneficial influence of trust on economic outcomes has received substantial support in empirical research. Interpersonal trust has been associated with higher level of economic growth (Fukuyama 1995, Knack and Keefer 1997, Whiteley 2000), while trust in the government is conducive to liberal economic policies (Hetherington 2004) as well as increased redistributive spending (Rudolph and Evans 2005).

While the research on trust has a clear normative appeal, its findings have not gone unchallenged in the literature. O'Neill (2002, 9) questions whether there is more to the "crisis of trust" narrative than a culture of suspicion—indicating that distrust toward pollsters is contradicted by the many instances when citizens actively trust suppliers of public goods. Hardin (1999) claims that distrust is actually the proper attitude toward government, since we do not have the relevant information for placing trust in a reasonable manner. Inglehart and Wenzel (2005, 259) also considers the decline of confidence in public institutions as a positive development since it reflects a more critical attitude toward authorities and hierarchies, which is a sign that self-expression values[2] are becoming more important in society. Their ideas are supported by the EBRD (2011, 43) *Life in Transition* survey, which shows that some authoritarian re-

---

[1] On the U.S. see Hetherington (1998), Patterson (1999), as well as Putnam (2000). For other countries see the references cited in Newton (2008, 244–245).

[2] Self-expression values include social toleration, life satisfaction, public expression and an aspiration to liberty. They stand in contrast to traditional values emphasizing survival.

gimes in the post-communist region display exceptionally high trust in their presidents, governments, and political parties.

On the question of consequences Durlauf and Fafchamps (2005) note that while trust has been declining since the 1950s in the U.S., the period coincided with significant economic growth.[3] They also question the possibility of drawing causal inferences from growth regressions, which are generally used to assess the effects of trust on economic outcomes, and claim that such results are always open to criticism on the omission of relevant control variables. In his overview of the literature, Fehr (2010) takes a similarly critical stance on whether we can assign a causal role to trust for economic outcomes since the trust variable might simply capture the consequences of formal and informal institutions. Such doubts can also be supported by the experiences of Central and Eastern Europe, where in spite of the generally low level of trust, most countries have been able to catch up considerably with Western Europe in the past two decades. Thus even if trust is indeed declining, whether it matters at all remains an open question.

1.2. Research questions

In the context of the above controversy the present research starts from the assumption that trust matters for economic outcomes but accepts that a causal link is very difficult to verify through cross-country regression analysis. Thus the first objective of this research is to explore whether a causal link can be established between trust and economic outcomes through other methods. Instead of searching for a direct connection, I will examine the question in an indirect manner and focus on the influence of trust on decision making over economic policy. Analyzing how the presence or absence of trust shapes policies might provide a causal link between trust and economic outcomes.

Economic policy is by its nature contextual, which means that its objectives and methods differ widely across regions and time periods. Consequently in order to answer the above question the research will apply the theoretical considerations about trust to economic policies associated with the euro in the old member states (EU-15) and in the new post-socialist

---

[3] The linear relationship between trust and growth has also been challenged by others—Berggren, Elinder, and Jordahl (2008) found a negative relationship between trust and growth while Roth (2009) argues for a curvilinear relationship.

member states (CEE-10) prior to the subprime crisis. Such an analysis allows not only the assessment of the theory but also raises further questions for the research: How can the concept of trust help our understanding of the roots of the subprime crisis in the EU? If it is a useful concept for this objective, what are the implications for the future of the eurozone?

The examination of concrete cases makes one sensitive to the complexity of the real world and the presence of factors which might modify the link between trust, economic policy, and outcomes. Understanding the conditions under which the influence of trust prevails is the third objective of the book. Gaining an answer to this question might also give low-trust countries policy-relevant insights on possible paths for mitigating the consequences of distrust.

1.3. Methodology and research design

In order to address these issues a qualitative case-oriented approach is taken. The reason for this choice comes from the type of questions I aim to answer: for the identification of causal links as well as the establishment of scope conditions, case studies—especially tracing historical processes—are particularly suitable (Durlauf 2001, George and Bennett 2005, Mahoney 2010). The policy-oriented nature of the questions provides further justification for case studies, since these allow the kind of interdisciplinary and comparative analyses, which are almost inevitable in studying the public sector (Hesse 2007, 14).

Similarly to statistical approaches, case studies "attempt to develop logically consistent models or theories, they derive observable implications from these theories, they test these implications against empirical observations or measurements, and they use the results of these tests to make inferences on how best to modify the theories tested" (George and Bennett 2005, 6). The design of the research adheres to these requirements. First, a theoretical framework will be developed on the possible mechanisms through which trust affects economic policies. Second, the hypotheses drawn from the theory will be assessed empirically. Finally, the possible deviation of the empirical evidence from the theoretical predictions will lead back to the reconsideration of the theory.

The most critical aspects of case studies are case selection, confirming bias, and the potential for generalizability. Selection bias occurs when cases are selected on the dependent variable and thus identifying a shared feature of the cases might be mistaken for causal relation (Geddes 1990). The confirming bias means that cases are chosen in order to confirm the theory (Flyvberg 2006, 221). Generalizability refers to the fact that findings from a small, non-representative sample cannot be applied automatically to a larger sample (George and Bennett 2005, 30–31). This research tries to deal with the above problems in a variety of ways.

Most importantly I draw on a relatively large sample of 25 countries from the European Union—the EU-15 and the CEE-10 countries. Such a sample provides almost laboratory conditions for testing a theory on trust and economic policy. The common framework for economic governance—primarily for monetary and fiscal policy—represents an external anchor to which domestic policies can be compared. In spite of the similar conditions for decision making, the 25 countries exhibit considerable variety in their economic performance both before and after the subprime crisis. The similar framework conditions and the different performances give ample opportunity for comparison across countries and the assessment of the theoretical propositions. These opportunities are further enhanced by the presence of post-Socialist countries, which have to deal with a very different heritage than the old member states. Searching for processes of convergence or divergence within and between the two groups allows assessing the theory in a relatively controlled setting.

Within the sample I use both cross-case and within-case analyses. Cross-case analyses serve the purpose of assessing hypotheses drawn from the theory through examining outcomes. Such analysis can provide an initial assessment about how the theory fares in a given sample as well as serve as a structured method for the selection of cases for within-case analysis. The objective of within-case analysis is the examination of processes and developments over time in order to uncover the causal chain behind the outcomes. The major advantage of this exercise is to consider the particular real-life context, within which the causal mechanisms prevail. With the careful selection of cases it is also possible to explore the conditions that foster or hinder the working of these mechanisms.

In order to enhance the potential for exploring causal links and scope conditions, the book presents within-case analyses in the context of three paired comparisons. First, a high-trust and a low-trust country (Sweden and Portugal) are selected from the EU-15 in order to illustrate the working of the theory and show the causal links between trust and decisions over economic policy. Second, two low-trust countries with different economic polices (Hungary and Slovakia) are examined in order to identify the scope conditions for the theory. Third, I examine the outcome of economic policies in the 25 countries following the subprime crisis and contrast the experiences of the two major surprises to the theory (Ireland and Poland). Finding an explanation for the cases, which seem to challenge the theory, provides a chance to refute the theory or identify further scope conditions.

The outcome of the research is the discovery of patterns, rather than laws in the sense of natural sciences.[4] In social processes future developments are uncertain and very often it is not even possible to foresee all potential outcomes. In the attainment of a certain outcome numerous factors might be at play interacting with one another and their individual contribution is far less easily separated than in a laboratory. One factor might be decisive in one setting, while inconsequential in other cases. Identifying some of the factors that foster or prevent the manifestation of certain tendencies associated with the level of trust is the second aim of the project.

1.4. The concept and measurement of trust

When considering the influence of trust on decisions over economic policies, the first problem the researcher faces is defining the concept itself. As the relevance of trust has increased for social sciences, the concept itself has become the matter of substantial debate. Problems of measurement pose a second critical issue, which is subject to even greater debates. As the two questions can not be separated, in the following I will first delineate the kind of trust I am interested in then explain the reasons for the chosen way of measurement.

Based on a cross-disciplinary analysis of trust, there seems to be an underlying agreement on the basic definition of trust. According to Rousseau et al. (1998, 395), trust is commonly understood as "*a psychological state comprising the intention to accept vulnerability based upon positive expectations of the intentions or behavior of another.*" When taking such risks both *rational and non-rational motives* are at play: having information on the other party and knowledge of her incentives contribute to the rational assessment about whether to trust or not, while subjective percep-

---

[4] Kornai (1992, 13) argues that the aim of social sciences is to discover "regularities" rather than universal, immutable laws. He argues that "any regularity is generated by a recurrent constellation of circumstances that produces behavioral patterns, decision routines by economic agents, political and economic mechanisms, and trends in economic processes that are susceptible to explanation." A similar position is represented by Elster (2007).

tions and the relevance of moral sanctions comprise the non-rational aspects of trust (Tonkiss 2009, 199).

In the literature a basic differentiation exists between *horizontal and vertical trust*—trusting other people and trusting institutions. Horizontal trust comes in two forms: *generalized and particularized trust*. The differentiation reflects out-group and in-group attitudes of trust—generalized trust means that most people, including those outside one's social group, can be trusted, while particularized trust means that only people within the group can be trusted (Uslaner 1999, 126–127). From the perspective of aggregate economic outcomes, it is generalized trust that matters, since this form of trust makes anonymous exchange possible.

There has been considerable debate in the literature about the origins of generalized trust and its relation to vertical trust. Cultural theorists (Almond and Verba 1963, Putnam 1993) claim that institutional trust is an extension of generalized trust, which is determined by participation in various associations and conveyed through early life socialization. Research on institutional trust has largely refuted this theory[5] and shown that a reverse causality exists—vertical trust strongly influences generalized trust as institutions substitute particular knowledge of the other party (Offe 1999, Mishler and Rose 2001, Rothstein 2005, Rothstein and Stolle 2008, Rothstein 2011).

According to Offe (1999, 73–75) institutions generate trust through enforcing the values truth-telling, promise-keeping, fairness and solidarity, which contribute to trust. Such an outcome is not the result of a single institution but rather the joint effect of a set of institutions. Truth telling and the provision of information are ensured for example by the freedom of the press, public court proceedings and accounting standards. Promises are enforced by contracts and independent courts. Equality before the law and equal political rights foster a sense of fairness. Finally, state redistribution toward the less fortunate generates the feeling of solidarity. The success of institutions in these endeavors can give rise to *moralistic trust*, which claims in a normative sense that most people should be trusted. This is a variety of the Golden Rule, which requires "you do unto others as you would have them do unto you" (Uslaner 2008, 103). Not attributing the intention of exploiting trust to the other party follows from this rule. According to Uslaner (2008, 117) moralistic trust is the real foundation for generalized trust.

Whether institutions are able to perform the above roles is likely to have important consequences not only for general trust but also for poli-

---

[5] See Rothstein (2011, 149) for a summary of the empirical evidence on this issue.

cymaking. In the research the analysis will focus on the influence of institutional trust on economic policy. In line with Offe (1999, 71) institutional trust will be understood in the sense that *the institution fulfills a legitimate function and operates in the interest of the common good*. In political science this is sometimes referred to as legitimacy. In choosing to use the concept institutional trust I follow the distinction made by Rosanvallon (2008, 3–4), who claims that legitimacy is a strictly procedural term based on free and fair elections, while trust is far more complex. It implies an expansion of legitimacy into a moral dimension (integrity of policymakers) and a substantial dimension (concern for the common good).

Measuring the kind of institutional trust that is the focus of this research poses serious challenges. The most often used measure for institutional trust is done through surveys, which try to explore public trust in different institutions such as the government, courts, police, political parties, etc. The output of such surveys is an assessment, which might reflect the performance of these institutions, but most likely also include a great deal of subjectivity, which often comes not only from short-term reactions to the most recent events, but also from different expectations about what and how these institutions should deliver. In countries, where more is expected in public services, better performance might still result in lower satisfaction rates. As it has been already cited from O'Neill (2002) a basic attitude of suspicion might not imply that active trust is not given— responding to a poll and saying that doctors cannot be trusted is not the same as not going to hospital when someone gets ill.

Given the above problems with subjective assessments of trust, in the research I will not try to defend one particular measurement of institutional trust. Instead I will approach the concept in two ways. For cross-case analysis, I will rely on the World Governance Indicators (WGI), while for the case studies I will make a qualitative assessment of trust.

What are the World Governance Indicators?

The makers of the indicators Kaufmann, Kraay, and Mastruzzi (2010) define governance as "the traditions and institutions by which authority in a country is exercised. This includes (a) the process by which governments are selected, monitored and replaced; (b) the capacity of the government to effectively formulate and implement sound policies; and (c) the respect of citizens and the state for the institutions that govern economic and social interactions among them" (6). They construct two aggregate indicators for each area on the basis of 31 data sources for 213 countries. The resulting six indicators are the following (7):

- *Voice and accountability* refers to "capturing perceptions of the extent to which a country's citizens are able to participate in selecting their government, as well as freedom of expression, freedom of association, and a free media."
- *Political Stability and Absence of Violence/Terrorism* refers to "capturing perceptions of the likelihood that the government will be destabilized or overthrown by unconstitutional or violent means, including politically motivated violence and terrorism."
- *Government effectiveness* refers to "capturing perceptions of the quality of public services, the quality of the civil service and the degree of its independence from political pressures, the quality of policy formulation and implementation, and the credibility of the government's commitment to such policies."
- *Regulatory quality* refers to "capturing perceptions of the ability of the government to formulate and implement sound policies and regulations that permit and promote private sector development."
- *Rule of law* refers to "capturing perceptions of the extent to which agents have confidence in and abide by the rules of society, and in particular the quality of contract enforcement, property rights, the police, and the courts, as well as the likelihood of crime and violence."
- *Control of corruption* refers to "capturing perceptions of the extent to which public power is exercised for private gain, including both petty and grand forms of corruption, as well as 'capture' of the state by elites and private interests."

The scores range between -2.5 and 2.5. The makers of the index make the assumption that the overall world average of governance quality does not change over time, which implies that values should be used for comparing relative positions rather than as absolute measures of quality.

There are several advantages of using the WGI for cross-case analysis. The cross-country comparability is very useful to illustrate the broad trends, which I aim to explore. Even more importantly, the WGI provide a complex assessment of the institutional environment, rather than focusing on one particular institution. Since trust in society is influenced by a set of institutions working together, the index can be viewed as a good approximation of the underlying institutional quality.[6] While it is not a direct measure of trust, I make the assumption that quality institutions are eventually recognized by the public and become trusted. This assumption can be supported by evidence from the research on the determinants of institutional trust, which show that good governance is the most important determinant of legitimacy and satisfaction with democracy (Gilley 2009, Teorell 2009, Wagner, Schneider, and Halla 2009).[7] Taking this approach can also be justified by

---

[6] The difficulty of separating the various dimensions of governance is one of the major criticisms against the index. See Langbein and Knack (2008) as well as Thomas (2010).

[7] The relation among these concepts will be elaborated further in the next chapter.

the already noted consideration that policymakers can only improve the institutional framework and cannot directly change the assessment by citizens.

Although for the purposes of cross-case analysis the World Governance Indicators are suitable, a more nuanced view of institutional conditions and trust is necessary for the case studies and the establishment of causal links. This is due to the fact that in the research I recognize the subjective reality of trust since perception rather than objective facts are considered as the main drivers of action. Consequently I also recognize the fact that the same institutions might generate different levels of trust in different countries. Furthermore very different events or histories can shape the prevailing level of trust, which cannot be standardized across countries.[8] Using a case-study approach fortunately allows a context-specific assessment of trust, which means that a qualitative narrative can be given about the critical country-specific factors, which contribute to high or low level of trust in a given setting.

1.5. The argument in a nutshell

The central proposition of the research is that the presence or absence of trust gives rise to virtuous or vicious cycles in the economy. Trusted institutions are conducive to rule-compliance, which in turn contribute to the reduction of uncertainty and allow long-term planning by agents. In such an environment the selection mechanism on the outcome of these plans is generally perceived as fair, thus failure of individual plans induces revision of the plans rather than calls for the revision of rules. In contrast, in a low-trust environment widespread evasion of rules implies a high level of uncertainty, which necessarily leads to shorter time horizons in decisions for both agents and policymakers. Given their difficulty of planning and the perceived unfairness of rules, agents aim to receive partial treatment and tangible benefits from authorities, while policymakers on their part try to address the immediate concerns of the electorate in order to gain support. Political business cycles, lax regulations on credit, and the prevalence of boom-bust cycles are some of the symptomatic phenomena of such an environment.

In the European Union mainly the Southern member states can be considered as illustrative examples of the consequences of lack of trust and the subprime crisis strongly exposed their vulnerabilities. Several Central

---

[8] This is a recognition for the role of collective memory in the shaping of institutional trust, as elaborated by Rothstein (2005), 148–166.

European countries also exhibit similar cycles and confirm the predictions of the theory. However, the example of those CEE countries that have succeeded in conducting responsible policies in spite of low level of trust, as well as the example of those EU-15 countries that developed a credit boom in spite of high level of trust, point to the limitations of the theory and the need to consider other factors in assessing outcomes, including financial market influences, current fashions in economic theory, as well as political leadership.

1.6. Summary of chapters

Chapter 2 provides the theoretical basis for the book and tries to explain how the decision making of individual agents is shaped by the presence or absence of institutional trust. In order to answer this question, the chapter explores existing theories on the major elements of trust: expectations, uncertainty, institutions, and rule compliance. Building primarily on the broadly understood institutionalist school of economics, it proposes a theoretical framework showing how trust creates virtuous and vicious cycles in law-abidance, which critically influence the possibility for economic agents to have realistic long-term plans.

Chapter 3 focuses on the question of how the prevailing time horizon in society can be expected to influence decisions over economic policy. In the context of the creation of the Economic and Monetary Union (EMU), a differentiation is made between unique and recurrent decisions. It is hypothesized that while in the case of unique decisions other factors than trust play a role, for recurrent decisions pressures from the societal level have to be taken into consideration. Based on this distinction the chapter develops several hypotheses for expected economic policies and performance within and outside the euro-zone.

Chapter 4 assesses the validity of the theoretical propositions through the examination of fiscal consolidations between 1993 and 2007 in the EU-15. Research on this area has shown that expenditure-based consolidations are more likely to prove sustainable than consolidation based on increasing revenues. The main hypothesis of the chapter is that high-trust countries are more likely to implement expenditure-based consolidations than low-trust regimes. Sweden and Portugal serve as representative cases for the theory in order to illustrate how decisions on consolidation are made in high- and low-trust regimes. Their cases also indicate the economic consequences of the different policy choices.

Chapter 5 examines the economic policies of the CEE-10 countries. Following accession to the EU the next step of integration is the introduction of the euro. Given the strict conditions of accession, it is hypothesized that the level of trust is a decisive factor in the ability to fulfill the requirements and introduce the euro. After recognizing the deviations from this prediction, the chapter examines the contrasting cases of Slovakia and Hungary—in spite of a lower level of trust, Slovakia has been able to introduce the euro, while Hungary, a former leader of transition, has been steadily falling behind in terms of fulfilling the criteria. Their cases serve to establish the scope conditions for the theory.

In Chapter 6, the consequences of the subprime crisis are analyzed both in the EU-15 and the CEE-10. The main question is whether the evaluations of performance prior to the crisis remain valid following the crisis. While the chapter answers with a qualified yes, critical exceptions are identified: in spite of its low level of trust, Poland has fared rather well during the crisis, while high-trust Ireland developed a credit boom and needed a bailout due to the crisis. These cases necessitate serious qualifications to the theory.

Chapter 7 will summarize the findings and answer the original question of the research about how and when trust matters in economic policymaking and economic outcomes. Potential applications to policy conclude the book.

CHAPTER 2

Institutional Trust and Individual Decision Making

The main objective of this chapter is to theorize how the process of individual planning is influenced by the presence or absence of trust in the institutional environment.[1] This is a necessary first step to understand the major question of the book: how institutional trust affects the making of economic policy.

In order to build a theory on the role of trust in individual decision making, it is useful to start from the definition of trust given in the introductory chapter: "a psychological state comprising the intention to accept vulnerability based upon positive expectations of the intentions or behavior of another." Based on this definition, trust can be seen as an expectation concerning an uncertain future. Acting on this expectation implies taking risk. Whether it is worth taking the risk depends on the perceived trustworthiness of the other party. In the case of institutional trust, the trustworthiness of the institution is likely to strongly depend on whether others hold the institution in respect and comply with its rules.

Starting from the above premises the chapter aims to build a theory of institutional trust through integrating existing theories on the various elements of trust: expectations, uncertainty, institutions and compliance. The central argument of the chapter is that institutional trust affects individual decision making primarily through influencing the time horizon of plans. The presence of institutional trust makes long-term planning

---

[1] Through focusing on individual plans the chapter follows the traditions of Austrian economics, which places individual plans into the center of economic analysis. Austrians justify their stance with the assertion that human action should be understood as purposeful behavior, thus a causal explanation of action has to start with purpose (Mises 1949, Lachmann 1971).

possible as it is conducive to general compliance with rules and thus to the reduction of uncertainty. Lack of trust in contrast increases the tendency towards short-term planning given persistent uncertainty due to lack of compliance.

The structure of the chapter is the following. The next section discusses the dominant rational expectations paradigm and explains why it is inadequate to address the concept of trust as defined in the previous chapter. Then alternative approaches to expectations will be presented focusing on the Post-Keynesian and Austrian schools. Uncertainty is a central concept in both schools; its various forms will be discussed in the following section. The role of institutions in reducing uncertainty will be examined in the third section followed by a discussion on their quality as a critical factor in whether they are able to fulfill their objective. The literature on tax compliance is used to illustrate the theoretical claims. Finally I will organize these building blocks into a theoretical framework, which provides an answer to the question of how individual plans are affected by the presence or absence of trust in the institutional environment.

2.1. Theories of expectations

2.1.1. Rational expectations

Mainstream economic thinking on expectations is dominated by the rational expectations paradigm, thus it is a natural starting point for approaching the question of how trust matters in individual decisions. In the following I will briefly discuss the main features of the theory, its major applications, as well as the reasons for its success. Then I will turn to its particular relevance for trust, explain why it is inadequate to capture the concept and integrate this explanation into the context of broader criticisms against the theory.

The theory of rational expectations was first elaborated in an article published in *Econometrica* by John F. Muth in 1961. In the article Muth develops a model, which asserts that "expectations, since they are informed predictions of future events, are essentially the same as the predictions of the relevant economic theory" (Muth 1961, 316). The reason for this hypothesis is that if there were a better prediction, economic agents would have a strong incentive to obtain the model, as it would imply unused profit opportunities on the markets. The main assumptions of the theory—that agents build all available information into their expectations and that their average forecast is the same as that of the relevant economic model—do not imply either perfect information or perfect foresight. As Gerrard (1994) explains, the theory instead has two other properties: unbiasedness and orthogonality. Unbiasedness means that while the expectations of economic agents might differ, there is no systematic error in their forecasts. Orthogonality means that since all past and present information has been built into the expectations, errors are due to random factors.

The theory became the foundation for theories calling for the withdrawal of the state from the economy through two major applications: efficient market hypothesis and the policy ineffectiveness proposition. The *efficient market hypothesis* claims that after profit-driven market players make their best guesses on stock market prices, stock prices equalize according to their expected returns adjusted for risks. This implies that changes in prices reflect unpredictable random factors, which no one can know beforehand, and thus prices follow a random walk (Fama 1970). The main conclusion from this theory is a strong favor of market forces over policy intervention—unrestrained market processes lead to the best prediction of future prices, and even if bubbles were possible, there was thought to be no way policymakers would know it better beforehand than market actors (FSA 2009, 40). The *policy ineffectiveness proposition* was developed by Sargent and Wallace (1976) and states that governments cannot manipulate the economy to produce higher output and employment, as rational economic agents with foresight know that expansionary efforts will be followed either by higher inflation or higher taxes. *Real business cycle theory*, developed by Lucas (1977) as well as Kydland and Prescott (1982), also advises against governmental interference as it claims that business cycles are natural market phenomena responding to exogenous shocks in the real economy, and thus monetary or fiscal measures only hinder these adjustments. Finally, the particular ineffectiveness of fiscal policy is also supported by the theory of *Ricardian equivalence*, which states that debt-financed tax cuts cannot reach their objective of increasing consumer spending as such cuts will be saved to pay for future tax increases, which are necessary to pay off the debt (Barro 1974).

In the 1970s the rational expectations paradigm brought revolutionary changes in macroeconomics, which was due to two factors: first, it could be modeled very well, second, it was almost immediately successful in economic policymaking. According to Chari (1999) rational expectations theory was a significant breakthrough in modeling expectations for three reasons: 1. free parameters associated with expectations disappeared from the models as expectations were not inputs but outputs of theorizing; 2. it is consistent with individual profit maximization as it excludes obvious profit opportunities; 3. given 1 and 2, it is the only compatible treatment of expectations with the equilibrium point of view. In the policy arena the theory is widely credited to have contributed to the disinflation process of the 1980s—alongside with monetarism. The leading theorists of rational expectations (Robert Lucas, Jon Taylor, Stanley Fischer, Thomas Sargent, Neil Wallace, Edward Prescott, etc.) successfully argued that instead of the earlier stop-go cycles in monetary policy, when decisions were aimed at manipulating output and employment levels, credible and transparent decision making allows a disinflation process without the excessive costs that Keynesian theories predict.[2] The main reason is that any systematic macroeconomic policy is anticipated by economic agents and thus governmental interventions cannot play a stabilizing role but instead enhance the cycles.

The theory has major application to the issue of institutional trust through emphasizing the need for formal constraints on governmental discretion given the problem of *time inconsistency*. The concept was formulated by Kydland and Prescott (1977), and it means that a decision, which is optimal at time t, will not be optimal at time $t + s$ under new conditions. As the public is aware of this incentive structure, the government loses its ability to influence people's decisions that results in suboptimal outcomes such as higher inflation. In order to solve this credibility problem two solutions have been proposed: *reputation-building* (Barro and Gordon 1983) and *delegation to an independent institution* (Rogoff 1985). The worldwide spread of central bank independence is one of the most successful applications of these ideas.

The theory of credibility fits well with the understanding of trust as the outcome of rational calculations based on objective facts. The most basic form is *deterrence-based trust*, which means that "one party belies that the other will be trustworthy, because the costly sanctions in place for breach of trust exceeds any potential benefits from opportunistic behavior" (Rousseau et al. 1998, 398). Another example is *calculus-based trust*, which refers to the expectation that the other "intends to perform the action that is beneficial" not because of sanctions but rather because of the presence of credible information about her intentions and competence

---

[2] On the contribution of academic advances to the American disinflation process see Goodfriend (2007), 18–24.

(Rousseau et al. 1998, 399). These types of trust reflect the view of trust as "encapsulated interest," which expects trust when the other party has good reasons not to abuse this trust (Hardin 1999, 26).[3]

While such an understanding might be legitimate for modeling purposes, in a real-life context one cannot abstract away from the subjective elements in trust. As James (2002) emphasizes, such approaches to trust remove the issue of vulnerability from the definition, which is the very essence of trust. Vulnerability comes from subjective perceptions as well as non-rational choices (Tonkiss 2009, 199). The disregard of these issues also forms the basis for general criticism against rational expectations theory. A brief overview of these criticisms can help to understand better, why the claim that the theory is inadequate to understand trust, is not simply a matter of definition but has crucial real-life relevance.

The question of how agents process all the relevant information and how they know what is relevant has been a major criticism against the rational expectations paradigm. The theory assumes that agents share the same model as economists and arrive to the same conclusion as the econometric tests. However, as Sent (1997, 327–328) recounts in her article, even Thomas Sargent, one of the major proponents of the rational expectations hypothesis, recognized this to be a very problematic assumption: it turned out that the model attributes more knowledge to agents than possessed by the econometrician—while he was just learning how the theories could be tested, in the model the assumption was that agents have somehow already solved this problem.

The second issue is how agents come to know the underlying model of the economy and whether such a model exists at all. Given that the basic assumption of the model is that agents do not make systematically biased decisions and errors are due to random factors, one of the major questions regarding the theory is how agents learn the true underlying model of the economy (O'Driscoll 1979, 158–159). However, an even deeper problem is how the model can assume that one true model of the economy exists. As Davidson (1982, 185–187) explains, the implicit assumption behind Muth's claim about the correctness of averages of expectations is that the economic future is ergodic, which means that the underlying stochastic processes are unchanged, in other words "none of the basic parameters of the system vary with the historical time." In contrast, once we recognize

---

[3] This kind of trust is often examined in game theoretical models, which regard the phenomenon in the context of cooperation in a prisoner's dilemma. For an overview of this literature see James (2002).

with Hicks that "all economic data is dated," we have to conclude that the future is non-ergodic, in which future statistical averages can systematically vary from present statistical averages (Davidson 1982, 193). This implies that even the incorporation of learning into the models as attempted by Sargent (1993) does not solve this problem as the underlying model is subject to change. This idea is also elaborated by Lachmann (1971, 46), who claims that "the real world is a world of continuous unexpected change, in which targets are moving rather than fixed. This means that even while men are gaining additional knowledge by learning from earlier mistakes, at the very same time some of their existing knowledge is continuously becoming obsolete."

The problem of knowledge at the individual level is exacerbated once we consider the problems of the theory at the macro level. Models based on the rational expectations hypothesis assume that "there is a communism of models. All agents inside the model, the econometrician, and God share the same model" (Evans and Honkapohja 2005, 566–567). This implies a modeling strategy based on the representative individual, which in turn allows modelers to disregard aggregation problems (Kirman 1992, 134). However, once we admit individual differences in objectives and expectations, the theory cannot disregard either interactions among heterogeneous agents and the emergent properties of the system—as Kirman (1992, 118) argues "there is simply no direct relation between individual and collective behavior." Interaction among agents might introduce systematic biases into the expectations, which is denied by rational expectations—as economic agents have to form expectations about the expectations of others rather than simply assess economic fundamentals.[4] Herd behavior during the latest financial crisis is an obvious example for this issue.

The theoretical criticisms against rational expectations are underlined by the meager empirical evidence for the paradigm. The questionable application of the theory to real-life context has been apparent from its inception since the econometric evidence did not confirm its hypotheses.[5] After these results, rational expectations theorists gave up strict statistical standards and

---

[4] The phenomenon of speculating about the action of others rather than fundamentals and its possible problems was recognized already by Keynes (1936, 158).

[5] Thomas Sargent admitted this in an interview saying that: "after about five years of doing likelihood ratio tests on rational expectations models, I recall Bob Lucas and Ed Prescott both telling me that those tests were rejecting too many good models" (Evans and Honkapohja 2005, 568).

used calibration methodology for the verification of the models.[6] However as Frydman and Goldberg (2007, 113–119) recounts, even after three decades the theory has been unable explain the movement of prices in the foreign exchange market, one of the largest markets in the world. The failure of the paradigm to understand the real-world has become especially important following the subprime crisis. As Krugman (2009) argues, the failure to forecast the approaching crisis was not even the major problem for the profession—the outright denial that a crisis of such magnitude is possible even in theory is much more embarrassing. The dominance of rational expectations played a central role in this denial—after memories of the Great Depression faded, economists fell back "in love with the old, idealized vision of an economy in which rational individuals interact in perfect markets, this time gussied up with fancy equations."

Based on the above discussion, it becomes evident why there is a need to start from different theories of expectations in order to understand the problem of trust. This is not simply a matter of definition, but rather the recognition for the subjectivity of knowledge and interpretation, which cannot be disregarded if we want to understand the real world. In the following I will turn to theories, which accommodate subjectivity in expectation-formation.

2.1.2. Austrian and Post-Keynesian approaches to expectations

While the rational expectations paradigm starts from axiomatic assumptions about the market in approaching expectation formation,[7] alternative approaches focus on observations about human psychology in the forma-

---

[6] In the same interview Sargent justifies this choice in the following manner: "There was a danger that skeptics and opponents would misread those likelihood ratio tests as rejections of an entire class of models, which of course they were not. ... It was a sensible opinion that the time had come to specialize and to use a sequential plan of attack: let's first devote resources to learning how to create a range of compelling equilibrium models to incorporate interesting mechanisms. We will be careful about the estimation in later years when we have mastered the modeling technology" (Evans and Honkapohja 2005, 569).

[7] As discussed in the previous section the theory is built on the assumption that there are no obvious profit opportunities in markets in equilibrium. The problems of assuming market equilibrium are not discussed in this book—for a thorough critique of the equilibrium assumption see Kornai (1971), who calls equilibrium theory a mere intellectual experiment rather than a theory describing reality. In his most recent work he describes capitalism as an "economy of surplus" versus socialism as an "economy of shortage" (Kornai 2011). Austrian theorists have also been traditionally against the notion of equilibrium; see Shackle (1972) as well as Lachmann (1976).

tion of their theories. This is particularly important for Post-Keynesian theorists, while Austrian scholars give more weight to the evolutive processes in expectation-formation.

A Post-Keynesian theory of expectations generally starts from Keynes' idea of animal spirits, defined as "a spontaneous urge to action rather than inaction, and not as the outcome of a weighted average of quantitative benefits multiplied by quantitative probabilities" (Keynes 1936, 161–162). Several critics have associated this concept with the assumption of irrationality in human decision making.[8] While the recognition of the irrational in the formation of expectations is certainly part of this concept, followers of Keynes have attempted to give a more nuanced definition to the idea. In the interpretation of Dequech (1999, 418) the concept of animal spirits can be split into three components: uncertainty aversion, uncertainty perception, and spontaneous optimism. While these factors are necessarily subjective, uncertainty perception generally has a factual basis and involves some knowledge about the environment. In contrast, uncertainty aversion and spontaneous optimism are individual attributes, which do not have a factual basis.

Besides knowledge about the environment and animal spirits, the third critical factor determining the state of expectations is creativity, which can be defined as "innovative imagination, that is, as the ability to imagine a future that is, at least in some respects, radically different from the present" (Dequech 1999, 422). The idea originates from G. L. S. Shackle, a student of both Hayek and Keynes. He compares the formation of expectations to the creation of a mosaic from disconnected facts (Shackle 1972, 428):

> Expectation is of course an application of general principles to particular facts; but those facts are so much the creation of the individual observer depending on a unique personal history and experience; they are so much a matter of interpretation, of the character of their setting or background, that any objectivity ascribed to them must be largely illusory. Even if the supposed facts could be taken at their face value, their pathetic insufficiency as grist for the mill of reason appears insistently when we consider what questions the expectation-former needs to answer. The 'facts' at best are like a few pieces of colored stone or glass intended for a mosaic, and the task for expectation is to design the mosaic as a whole from the suggestion offered from these few disconnected fragments.

While Post-Keynesian theories focus on the various elements of expectation formation, Austrian theorists emphasize the process involved in shap-

---

[8] For a survey of the critics see Marchionatti (1999), 416–417.

ing and reshaping expectations. The starting point in this area is Hayek's theory of knowledge, which implicitly addresses the problem of expectations. Hayek's central insight into the problem of knowledge is that individual experiences should be viewed as sensory inputs ordered by the abstract rules of the mind, which are results of centuries of evolution.[9] In the interpretation of Butos and Koppl (1997) this has four implications for Hayek's view on expectations. 1. All knowledge is fallible interpretation. 2. An individual's knowledge and expectations derive from a mental classificatory apparatus. 3. This apparatus is an adaptive mechanism, which is regularly modified based on a "goodness of fit" criterion. 4. Knowledge and expectations are endogenous to the environment.

The emphasis on process and continuous revision of knowledge in light of the empirical evidence receives a central place in the works of Ludwig M. Lachmann, who was a student of Hayek at the same time as Shackle. In his understanding "expectations are not economic results in the sense in which prices and output quantities are. No economic process *determines* them. A 10 per cent rise in the price of apples may just as well give rise to an expectation of a further rise as to that of a future fall. It all depends on the circumstances accompanying the rise, and different people may give these circumstances a different interpretation" (Lachmann 1978, 20). Later he states that "expectations are thus phases of a never-ending process, the process by which men acquire knowledge about each other's needs and resources" (24).

The emphasis on continuous revision of interpretation in light of the empirical evidence makes Lachmann's theory of expectations compatible both with the work of Keynes and Hayek. In forming expectations psychological factors cannot be excluded as these are critical in the interpretation of a given situation. However, as experience validates or invalidates an expectation, a learning process takes place that makes expectations endogenous to the environment. Still, this does not imply a return of rational expectations and the denial of psychological factors in expectation-formation—as it has been discussed already, in a non-ergodic world knowledge is continually gained and becomes obsolete. Uncertainty thus has a central role in the formation of expectations in both schools. However, uncertainty comes in different forms and degrees, and our understanding of the concept plays an important role in approaching the question of expectations. This is the subject of the next section.

---

[9] Hayek's theory of knowledge is most explicitly exposed in Hayek (1952).

2.2. The concept of uncertainty

When discussing uncertainty, a general starting point is the differentiation
by Frank Knight (1921) between *risk* and *uncertainty*. Risk is "a quantity
susceptible to measurement," while uncertainty is a non-quantitative concept (19–20). This means that in the case of risk the probabilities of possible future events are known at the time of decision such as in the case of
tossing a die. According to Knight, risk is not true uncertainty as it can be
"reduced to certainty by grouping cases" (232).[10] Keynes also interpreted
the concept of uncertainty in a similar manner when he defined it as the
absence of probabilistic knowledge: "The sense in which I am using the
term is that in which the prospect of a European war is uncertain, or the
price of copper and the rate of interest twenty years hence, or the obsoles-
cence of a new invention, or the position of private wealth owners in the
social system in 1970" (Keynes 1937, 123–124).[11]

As Dequech (2000, 45) shows, the concept of uncertainty can be further differentiated as *ambiguity* and *fundamental uncertainty*. In his understanding "ambiguity usually refers to a situation in which there is uncertainty about probabilities and this uncertainty is due to lack of information." He cites the Ellsberg paradox, when people are offered to gamble
on the color of balls in two urns—experiments show that people generally
prefer choosing from the urn about which the ratio of different color balls
is known. In these problems ambiguity influences the perception regarding the tradeoffs in the gamble. These types of situations however cannot
be considered as cases of genuine uncertainty since all possible states of
the world are known and information about probabilities exists at the time
of decision even though it is hidden from the agent.

Fundamental uncertainty in contrast implies that the future cannot be
known even in principle—not even the possible outcomes least of all their

---

[10] Among the Austrians, Mises (1949) makes a very similar distinction between class and
case probability. Class probability means that "we know or assume to know, with regard
to the problem concerned, everything about the behavior of a whole class of events or
phenomena; but about the actual singular events or phenomena we know nothing but
that they are elements of this class" (107). An example for this is lottery. Case probability in contrast means that "we know, with regard to a particular event, some of the factors which determine its outcome; but there are other determining factors about which
we know nothing" (110). According to Mises this kind of probability is relevant when
dealing with human action—even a football game falls into this category, where past
results of two teams are not determining future results (111)

[11] For a further overview about the question of probability and uncertainty see Lawson (1988).

probabilities. The reason for such radical uncertainty is that some information simply does not exist at the time of making the decision—the future is yet to be created by agents' choices with their intended and unintended consequences (Dequech 2000, 48). This idea was most explicitly elaborated by Shackle (1972, 3), who emphasized that human choices based on imagination shape the future and not deterministic forces: "What does not yet exist cannot be known. The future is imagined by each man for himself and this process of imagination is a vital part of the process of decision." This is particularly important in the case of a crucial decision, which Shackle (1955, 6) defines as "one where the person concerned cannot exclude from his mind that the very act of performing the experiment may destroy forever the circumstances in which it was performed."[12] Lachmann (1978, 22) provides further support for the presence of fundamental uncertainty by emphasizing that we live in a world of continuous change, where "today's knowledge may be out of date tomorrow, hence no longer a safe guide to action." As it has been discussed in the previous section, in such a world even prices are not a safe guide to action—while they transmit some information, they require interpretation, which is bound to be imperfect. However, Lachmann argues that instead of the uniqueness of crucial decisions, which are in fact extremely rare, differences in particular situations should be emphasized that make probabilistic decision making meaningless in individual cases (Lachmann 1978, 26–27).

Acceptance of fundamental uncertainty often evokes the criticism of *nihilism*. In a famous quote Lucas (1981, 224) claims that the rational expectations hypothesis is useful in situations in which the probabilities of interest concern a fairly well defined recurrent event, "which are situations of risk in Knight's terminology. In cases of uncertainty economic reasoning will be of no value."[13] However, once we accept Davidson's claim, which was discussed in the previous section about a non-ergodic world, such a position strongly limits the applicability of economic analysis to real-world issues.

---

[12] The idea of reflexivity in the works of George Soros gives a similar importance to creating rather than discovering the future. According to Soros (2006) this makes social sciences very different from natural sciences, where there is a clear delineation between agent and the observed event—at least prior to the discoveries in quantum physics.

[13] Lucas' position is shared in a paradoxical sense by Shackle as well. In an interview he recounts that given the pervasive uncertainty of the future, statistical results hold for the observed period but cannot be considered similar to the gravitational constant of physics. He accepts this to be a nihilist position: "I've been saying for almost forty years that economics isn't a science, and we ought not to call it a science" (Ebeling 1983, 7).

A way out of the above dilemma is the recognition of *different levels of uncertainty*. This means that even if the precise extent of uncertainty is not known beforehand, at least we can compare situations with more or less uncertainty—have some knowledge about how ignorant we are regarding outcomes (Dequech 2000, 55). Keynes (1936) uses the concept of confidence, which means "how highly we rate the likelihood of our best forecast turning out quite wrong" (148). In Shackle's works a similar concept is surprise value, which can be interpreted as a possible measure of the level uncertainty defined as follows: "surprise is what we feel when an expectation has gone wrong, has proven in the event to have been ill-founded and false" (Shackle 1955, 56). For other authors in the Post-Keynesian and Austrian camps, the degree of uncertainty about the future is strongly influenced by the institutional environment.

2.3. The role of institutions in reducing uncertainty[14]

Although the accusation of nihilism in the sense of Lucas is an often voiced claim against Keynesian fundamental uncertainty, there is plenty of ground in the works of both Keynes as well as his followers to refute this accusation. In Chapter 12 of the *General Theory*, Keynes mentions two important methods to deal with uncertainty. The first is a psychological convention that in case of radical uncertainty we make the assumption that "the existing state of affairs will continue indefinitely" even if we know from experience that this is highly unlikely (Keynes 1936, 152–153). The second method refers to various institutional arrangements that stabilize the prospective yield of long-term investments: long-term contracts in the case of buildings, monopoly privileges in the case of utilities and the existence of the state, which undertakes investments based on social advantages rather than on the basis of commercial yield (163). These considerations however do not completely eliminate uncertainty as Keynes notes that this method of calculation works only "as long as we can rely on the maintenance of this convention" (152). Consequently Carabelli and De Vechi (2001, 282) argue that for Keynes rules do not eradicate the need for personal judgment on the basis of

---

[14] In the following I do not aim to provide even a brief account of institutional economics but only underline some of the main questions of these schools based on the works of some of their representative thinkers. For thorough overviews of institutional economics see for example Hodgson (2004) and Chavance (2009).

individual circumstances, and "even following a convention has to be rationally justified."

Following rules in order to reduce uncertainty is even more pro-nounced among Austrian thinkers,[15] most importantly in the works of Hayek. He argued that in a world of uncertainty rules make rational action possible: "the problem of conducting himself successfully in a world only partially known to man was thus solved by adhering to rules, which had served him well but which he did not and could not *know* to be true in the Cartesian sense" (Hayek 1973, 18). In his conception rules are "'products of human action but not of human design' in which the experience gained by the experimentation of generations embodies more knowledge than was possessed by anyone" (Hayek 1973, 119). This is particularly true in the case of spontaneous orders, such as morals, religion, law, language, money, and market. Formulated laws also serve the purpose of reducing uncertainty and coordinating individual expectations but only if they adhere to the idea of the *Rule of Law*, which means that laws are pro-spective, general, impartial and equally applied—most importantly they constrain the coercive powers of the government. In other words, they determine the rules of the game rather than its particular outcome (Hayek 1944, 75–82). If rules fulfill these conditions they should be strictly followed—"for the Rule of Law to be effective it is more impor-tant that there should be a rule applied always without exceptions, than what this rule is" (Hayek 1944, 83).

While Hayek expresses an unshakable belief in the Rule of Law, con-siderably stronger than Keynes,[16] he also considers the possibility of insti-tutional change, when existing rules do not provide satisfactory answers

---

[15] While Post-Keynesianism and institutionalism can be relatively easily linked together, Austrian scholars are somewhat more reluctant to take the institutionalist path. Accord-ing to Gloria-Palermo (1999) the Austrian emphasis on subjectivism and fundamental uncertainty makes it necessary for Austrian economics to develop a theory of institu-tions explaining "the influence of institutions on the process of individual plan forma-tion and revision" (34). However, given their strict methodological individualism, which means that "all social phenomena (their structure and their change) are in principle ex-plicable only in terms of individuals—their properties, goals and beliefs" (39), Austrian thinkers are uncomfortable with analyzing the influence of institutions on individuals. Still, Austrian theorists made important contributions to the theory of institutions.

[16] A major criticism against his views is that they might be compatible with evil laws as well such as slavery, segregation, apartheid (Tamanaha 2004, 71). Furthermore, as we shall see in the case of North, the naïve belief in Darwinian evolution seems to imply a theological stance to develop efficient laws—however inefficiencies in legal systems can persist; this is evident once we look at less developed societies.

(Hayek 1976, 15). He has two conditions that validate exceptions to existing rules. First, if there is another rule which is also valid at that time and can be shown to be superior to the first rule (24). Second, the question has to be asked about the potential of generalization—what would happen if all would act the same in the given situation (28). This is very different from the views of Keynes, who focuses on individual interests concerning the decision about whether to follow a particular rule.

Hayek's ideas are further elaborated in the works Lachmann, who represents most forcefully fundamental uncertainty among Austrians. Unlike Shackle, he did not believe himself a nihilist and developed a sophisticated theory of institutions, independently of the reviving institutionalist school. Lachmann's theory of institutions starts with a paradox: in spite of the fundamental uncertainty and open-endedness of the world, how can a relatively stable order exist in society? To answer this question Lachmann calls attention to institutions, which he defines as the following: "an institution provides a means of orientation to a large number of actors. It enables them to coordinate their actions by means of orientation to a common signpost. If the plan is a mental scheme in which the conditions of action are coordinated, we may regard institutions as orientation schemes of the second order, to which planners orientate their action plan. ... They are nodal points of society, coordinating the actions of millions whom they relieve of the need to acquire and digest detailed knowledge about others and form detailed expectations about their future action" (Lachmann 1971, 49–50).

Similarly to Keynes and Hayek, Lachmann also notes that institutions cannot completely eliminate uncertainty—as new knowledge emerges, institutions also have to change. In addressing the problem of stability and change, Lachmann (1971, 68) differentiates between primary and secondary institutions—the stability of the former is the condition for the flexibility of the latter. The system can react to the evolving new needs through changes in the secondary institutions. Primary institutions should be concerned only with the most necessary coordination of interactions, since only in this manner can they provide the necessary freedom for the execution of various plans—and one can never tell in advance, which of these plans will succeed in an open-ended world.[17]

---

[17] Lachmann's ideas about primary and secondary institutions tie in closely to the Freiburg tradition of ordoliberalism, founded by Walter Eucken, and the research program of constitutional political economy, represented by James Buchanan. Both of these schools accept that unhampered markets do not exist and in order for markets to work, strong

At a time when the institutionalist agenda was not fashionable (Hodgson 2004, 380–395), the heterodox schools were important avenues for institutionalist thinking. The insights of Post-Keynesian and Austrian economics regarding uncertainty and institutions are important forerunners to the ideas of the new institutionalist school. This is most evident from the works of Douglass North.[18]

In building his theory of institutions, North (2005, 16–17) also opposes the rationality postulate and calls attention to uncertainty and non-ergodicity in the sense discussed by Post-Keynesians. He defines the role of institutions as the following: "the major role of institutions in a society is to reduce uncertainty by establishing a stable (but not necessarily efficient) structure to human interaction. … From conventions, codes of conduct, and norms of behavior to statute law, common law, and contracts between individuals, institutions are evolving and, therefore, are continually altering the choices available to us" (North 1990, 6).

While institutions can be used to reduce uncertainty, North (2005, 2) also recognizes that they are also subject to change, thus uncertainty cannot be perfectly eliminated. A theory of institutional change and stability is thus important to understanding expectations. Unlike Hayek, North views rules not as accumulation of knowledge over generations and a guide to efficiency, but rather the imprint of actual power relations in society. Once these relations change and bargaining strength of players change, institutions also need to change (North 1990, 86). In his later work North (2005, 42) writes: "conformity can be costly in a world of uncertainty. In the long run it produces stagnation and decay as humans confront ever new challenges in a non-ergodic world that requires innovative institutional creation because no one can know the right path to survival." However change is always gradual and incremental, past institutions are important inputs into the formation of new institutions: "path dependence will occur because the direction of the incremental institutional change will be broadly consistent with the existing institutional matrix … and will be governed by the kinds of knowledge and skills that the entrepreneurs and members of organizations have invested in" (North

---

procedural rules are needed that guide market transactions. In these schools the state has an important role as guardian of the legal order. For a brief summary of the ordoliberal schools see Chavance (2009), 42–44. For a broader overview see Vanberg (2001).

[18] Similarly to other non-mainstream approaches, new institutional economics is a diverse school—even a partial review of its contributions is beyond the scope of this chapter. Dequech (2006) provides a comprehensive overview about the treatment of uncertainty by the various schools that go under the heading of new institutionalism.

2005, 62). North also addresses the question of stability asked by Lachmann, and sees it "accomplished by a complex set of constraints that include formal rules nested in a hierarchy, where each level is more costly to change than the previous one" (North 1990, 83).

The recognition about the role of institutions in reducing uncertainty has not remained at the theoretical level but has been emphasized in policymaking circles as well. In its extensive report on institution-building, the World Bank (2002, 8) identifies three major channels, which make institutions critical for markets: providing information on market conditions, goods, and participation; defining and enforcing property rights and contracts; and increase or decrease in competition on a certain market. These are complemented by checks and balances in the political sphere, which ensures that the state can credibility commit itself to respect the rules.

Overall we can see that the role of institutions in reducing uncertainty is relatively uncontroversial both in theory and practice. At the same time we also know that uncertainty is a pervasive feature of the environment in less developed countries, which means that we do not know enough about why institutions work well in some countries and why they fail in others.[19] The question of what makes institutions work will be examined in the next section.

2.4. Compliance and legitimacy

It is somewhat of a truism that institutions can fulfill their role if people see them to be useful and legitimate and adjust their behavior to them. Unless compliance is general, institutions might increase the level of uncertainty through adding an additional unknown variable to expectation-formation—whether other people will be guided by existing institutions. This naturally leads to the question why and when people obey the law.

In his overview about rule compliance, Hurd (1999) differentiates three different motives for following the law: coercion, self-interest, and the legitimacy of the rule. He claims that the most efficient is the third, when internal convictions rather than external pressure create obedience. Physical coercion is not only expensive but also leads to resentment and resistance to the law and authorities (384–385). Self-interest is somewhat

---

[19] According to North (1990, 54) "the inability of societies to develop effective, low-cost enforcement of contracts is the most important source of both historical stagnation and contemporary underdevelopment in the Third World."

better in motivating voluntary compliance, but in the long-term it is likely to fail since it encourages continuous cost-benefit analysis about following the rule—once it appears too costly, there seems no reason to obey.[20] In contrast, rule compliance based on legitimacy does not calculate and obedience becomes habitual—in this case breaking the rule has psychological costs and thus requires special consideration (388).

Once we accept Hurd's argument, the next question is what generates legitimacy. According to Tyler (2006, 25) the legitimacy of the law can come from two sources: the legitimacy of authorities and the content of the law, which reflects one's moral convictions. In creating voluntary compliance the former is considerably more effective, since the latter can just as easily serve as the basis for resistance. This implies that in order to understand compliance we need to understand the sources of legitimacy. In answering this question on the basis of survey evidence, Tyler found that *procedural justice*, including *impartiality, efforts to be fair*, and *consideration of opinions* are more important for legitimacy than whether outcomes are favorable or not (128–129).

Tyler's results are paralleled by Rothstein and Teorell (2008, 169), who claim that for creating legitimacy the output of the political system is far more important than the act of voting. In evaluating the output side they also focus on procedures and emphasize the importance of impartiality, which they define as following: "when implementing laws and policies government officials shall not take into consideration anything about the citizen/case that is not beforehand stipulated in policy or the law" (170). Such a definition not only rules out all forms of corruption, "but also practices such as clientilism, patronage, nepotism, political favoritism, discrimination and other forms of 'particularisms'" (171). It is also a broader concept than the Rule of Law, because it applies "to spheres of state action other than those directly governed by law" (182).

The importance of procedural justice and impartiality for compliance with institutions receive strong support from research on tax compliance. According to Hellman and Kaufman (2004, 102) "tax compliance is a broader indicator of the subversion of public institutions as it reflects both

---

[20] It is important to note that Hurd does not accept references to enlightened self-interest, since if everything can be considered self-interest, then the concept becomes empty (Hurd 1999, 386). In his definition of self-interest the individual does not accept moral responsibility for others, which means that her relations are purely instrumental. This does not exclude cooperation, but it does imply that the relationship in itself is not valued, only the benefits it yields.

the firm's willingness to contribute to the development of public institutions as well as the effectiveness of the state's capacity to collect taxes and punish cheaters." The next section gives some of the most relevant findings of this literature.

2.4.1. Tax compliance

Why people pay their taxes has long been a central theme in compliance research. Unlike cases of pure coordination—such as driving on the right side of the road—following rules in the field of taxation can be only a second-best strategy for the individual: she can do better by deviating from the rule (Goldman 2006, 453). While taxes cover the provision of important social goods, individual cheating does not necessarily affect these goods while offering large benefits for the cheater. At the same time if many act this way, all will be worse off than with the compliance of all.

In the world of pure rational choice the temptation to free-ride and the low probability of getting caught would predict that people cheat on their taxes as much as possible. Indeed Andreoni et al. (1998, 822) underline that the major puzzle of the research on tax compliance is that most people actually pay their taxes.

In order to explain the puzzle, Feld and Frey (2007, 104) develop the concept of a psychological contract, which implies "a complicated interaction between taxpayers and the government establishing a fair, reciprocal exchange that involves giving and taking of both parties." This psychological contract is composed of "elements of gain (redistributive justice) and participation (procedural justice)." Such a relationship "presupposes that taxpayers and the tax authority treat each other like partners, that is, with mutual respect and honesty." The authors provide an extensive survey of studies, which empirically support their theory. From the survey they conclude that people are willing to pay their taxes "even if they do not receive a full public good equivalent to tax payments as long as the political process is perceived to be fair and legitimate" (102).

The above theory is indirectly supported by evidence from Central and Eastern Europe. Based on data from 6500 companies in 26 transition countries, Hellman and Kaufmann (2004) find that those firms which feel that they have disproportionately small influence on regulations directly affecting them have a negative view of public institutions, are less likely to pay taxes, and more likely to engage in corrupt practices. Paying taxes or paying bribes appear to be substitutes.

The contract theory of taxation is also supported by insights from psychological theories. In order to explain tax compliance, Braithwaite (2009) takes a much more complex perspective on identity than the rational choice approach of mainstream economic theory. Looking separately at the moral self, the status-seeking self, and the democratic collective self she is able to address the various factors that facilitate compliance. Individuals have to reconcile their moral self, which tries to be a good, law-abiding citizen, with the status-seeking self, which tries to be a winner above all and might feel threatened by taxation. If the authority is held in respect by the individual and the community, it has a status-ascribing capacity affirming the person as an honest law-abiding citizen (256). At the same time, a broader view about how democracy is working also plays an important key role in the paying of taxes—disillusionment with the system breeds legal cynicism and undermines moral obligation (261). Based on data from Australia, the author finds strong support for these propositions.

The above findings from tax compliance research strengthen the argument from the previous section that compliance and thus the success of institutions in reducing uncertainty is strongly dependent on the perceived quality of institutions. Elements of such quality include perceptions on the fairness of the exchange, fairness of procedures, and respectful treatment by authorities.

2.5. Institutional trust and individual planning

Integrating the discussion from the previous sections into a causal chain makes it possible to understand the basic question of the chapter—how institutional trust[21] affects the formation of individual planning. The line of reasoning goes in the following order: institutions → uncertainty perception → expectations → plans → outcomes. The iterative interactions among the main concepts are represented in Figure 2.1.

---

[21] As explained in the introductory chapter I conceptualize institutional trust as an extension of legitimacy in the sense discussed in the previous section. The reason I use the concept of institutional trust instead of legitimacy is to differentiate it from the narrow interpretation of legitimacy focusing on the procedure of assuming power.

Figure 2.1. A stylized model of institutional trust and individual decision-making

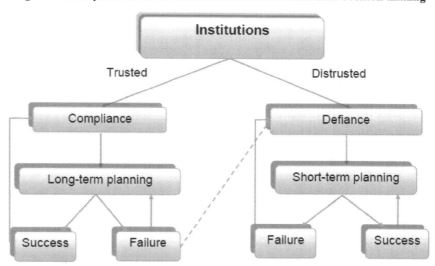

The model shown by Figure 2.1. is naturally stylized and involves a number of abstractions. First, it relies on a dichotomous view of institutional trust, which is a continuous variable in reality. Similarly, the success or failure of plans is not always clear cut and depends on the subjective criteria for evaluation. Finally, whether someone is planning for the short or the long-term is the factor of multiple variables including age, objectives, psychological disposition, etc.[22] With these considerations in mind the model should be understood as a way to underline certain basic tendencies within high- and low-trust environments. By taking a dichotomous perspective on institutional trust, it tries to illustrate the major implications of the theory in a *ceteris paribus* manner.

The starting point for the model is fundamental uncertainty, where institutions represent the main source of knowledge about the future. If institutions are trusted and rules are followed, uncertainty can be substantially reduced. In such an environment the success of individual plans starts a virtuous cycle, where the institutional framework is continuously reinforced, uncertainty is manageable and thus long-term planning becomes possible with a reasonable chance for success. If plans fail, agents are likely—at least initially—to look for problems with their plans and

---

[22] For an overview of factors that influence time preference see Frederick, Loewenstein, and O'Donoghue (2002).

revise them rather then blame the rules of the game. Naturally, with repeated failures and revisions, the rules themselves might be questioned; this is represented by the dotted line on the figure. However, it is important to underline that in an environment of trust, the first reaction from the agent in the case of failure is to revise her plan rather than question the rules.

The situation is very different when institutions cannot be trusted for reasons of corruption, favoring special interest groups or disregarding the common good. While the list could be continued, the result is the same for all these problems: people are unlikely to obey these kinds of laws and assume that others feel the same way. In such an environment circumventing the rules for personal gain becomes a strategy for survival.[23] Consequently rules cannot serve their purpose, and fundamental uncertainty remains a pervasive feature of the environment. In an uncertain environment the outcome of long-term plans is unpredictable, thus plans are likely to focus on short-term, relatively certain outcomes.[24] If plans fail, it is likely to reinforce the lack of trust in the system and agents will try new—and often dishonest—ways to cope with the environment. The major difference with the high-trust case however comes in the case of success—being able to navigate in an environment of distrust through corruption, personal connections or other ways do not translate into trust in the institutions but rather creates a stake in maintaining such channels of influence.

The feedback effects in the model ensure that in the absence of external intervening factors, we can expect virtuous or vicious cycles in the

---

[23] Although success might be possible even if rules are followed, the perception about the need to break the rules to get ahead is sufficient to maintain alienation from the laws. This has been analyzed empirically by Csepeli et al. (2004, 222), who found that in contrast to Western Europe, in Eastern Europe perceptions on success are much less associated with talent and hard work than with dishonesty. Several years later a survey in Hungary found very similar results—82 percent of the respondents agree with the statement that "in this country it is impossible to get rich through honest means," while 75 believe that "if one wants to succeed, she needs to break some laws" (Bernát 2009, 30).

[24] Prospect theory developed by Kahneman and Tversky (1979) has revealed the importance of certainty effect in human decision making: people value rewards, which are certain, to larger and uncertain future rewards even if their expected utility is the same. Risk aversion in choices involving sure gains and risk seeking in choices involving sure losses are important implications of this finding. Later studies have also found that uncertainty has a dramatic effect on the discount rate of future prospects as it includes a large risk premium in addition to time preference (Frederick, Loewenstein, and O'Donoghue 2002, 382).

institutional environment depending on the level of trust. The major factor that generates these cycles is the perception of agents on whether to comply or not with the rules. In an environment where institutions are trusted, people who do not comply are expected to be caught and punished. Successful planning thus necessitates compliance with rules. In contrast, in a low-trust environment success is associated with breaking the rules and weak institutions are seen as unlikely to punish trespassers.

* * *

The main objective of this chapter was to develop a conceptual framework to understand how the presence or absence of institutional trust affects the formation of individual plans. It has been shown that the dominant rational expectations paradigm is more of a theoretical construction than a theory to understand a world characterized by novelty and fundamental uncertainty. It has been also shown that this kind of uncertainty does not necessarily involve nihilism, and can be analyzed through understanding the nature of institutions and the formation of expectations. Non-mainstream schools have developed important insights regarding these questions.

Through integrating theories about uncertainty, institutions, and compliance with rules, I argued that *ceteris paribus* uncertainty primarily affects the time horizon of individual plans—while in an environment of institutional trust, complying with rules and long-term planning can lead to success with a reasonable chance, in an environment of distrust plans are likely to concentrate on short-term and relatively certain rewards as well as involve the use of illegal practices. In the absence of major shocks, we can expect self-reinforcing cycles in both cases.

Politicians who expect to gain votes during elections cannot remain impervious to the prevalence of the above cycles. In the next chapter I will attempt to develop hypotheses of their likely reactions concerning concrete decisions over economic policy: the introduction of the euro.

CHAPTER 3

Institutional Trust and Policymaking in the EMU

In the previous chapter a theoretical framework was proposed on how trust or distrust in the institutional environment affects the plans of individuals in society. It has been argued that *ceteris paribus* the presence or absence of trust primarily influences the time horizon of decision making: long-term orientation is realistic only in a high-trust environment, where the institutional structure is capable of fulfilling its role in reducing the uncertainty of the future.

The major objective of this chapter is to develop hypotheses about how the time horizon of individual plans is reflected in decision making over economic policy. The focus on the Economic and Monetary Union (EMU) provides an excellent ground for assessing the hypotheses given the divergent outcomes within a jointly adopted, self-imposed external framework.

The central claim of this chapter is that the presence or absence of institutional trust is a critical input in recurrent economic policy decisions, which determine whether a country can flourish within the euro-zone. At the same time institutional trust was less relevant in the elite-led bargaining process, which resulted in the creation of the institutional framework of the common currency. The differentiation between the two types of decisions helps to understand the inherent tensions within the EMU. While high-trust countries are expected to benefit the most from the euro given the long-term orientation in their economic policies, the weakness of low-trust countries is enhanced by the euro as their short-term orientation is incompatible with the arrangement. The different performance prospects within the euro-zone have represented a built-in challenge for EMU economic governance from its beginnings.

In order to show the above, first I will consider when and to what extent policymakers are expected to respond to the length of time horizon prevalent in society. After distinguishing between unique and recurrent decisions I will show how such distinction helps to understand the different motivations of policymakers in the act of committing themselves to the rules of the common currency and in their adherence to this commitment. In the following section I will provide an overview of the major factors, which led to the creation of the euro. Afterwards I will discuss the relevance of trust for fiscal policy and structural change, which strongly determine a country's performance in the euro-zone. At the end of the chapter I will summarize these ideas in testable hypotheses about expected economic performance following the establishment of the euro.

3.1. Unique and recurrent decisions: the rationality of policymakers

I concluded the previous chapter with the claim that politicians cannot remain impervious to the time horizon of individual decision making. Once we assume that politicians are rational and motivated by a desire to maintain their political support, we can make the claim that low-trust regimes are characterized by short-term economic decision making.

There are strong grounds for applying the rational choice framework to policymaking in democracies as politicians have a high stake in obtaining the necessary information for decision making over issues, which affect their reelection potential (Tsebelis 1990, 33–36). Such considerations are particularly important in the case of iteration, when learning processes eventually reveal the correct means for the desired end.

At the same time, similarly to the previous chapter, we also have to recognize that the world is constantly changing and thus policymakers also have to face unique situations and make decisions, which fundamentally change the conditions in which they were made. Their reversal is either impossible or very costly. In such situations fundamental uncertainty is a critical feature of the context, which also excludes having a clear ordering of preferences. According to Kornai (1970, 151) the natural reaction of policymakers to such cases involves hesitation, learning and collecting information—as well as frequent shifts in preference ordering. The shifts can occur for a number of reasons including persuasion from other parties, the reinterpretation of past experience or changes in structural constraints.

The above processes are particularly likely to prevail if a decision affects multiple levels and involves international and domestic consequences. According to the theory of two-level games in such situations the objective of policymakers is to "maximize their own ability to satisfy domestic pressures, while minimizing the adverse consequences of foreign developments" (Putnam 1988, 434). At the same time, as Dyson (1994, 12) asserts, these games also have the character of processes, in which there are significant sunk costs, socialization and learning effects, which influence the final outcome just as much as initial preferences.

When considering the creation and the functioning of the EMU the distinction between unique and recurrent decisions have to be kept in mind. In the following I will show how the creation of the euro and the self-commitment to sound finances can be considered as a unique, crucial decision, while the economic policy choices associated with it have the characteristics of recurrent decisions. The contradiction between the two types of decision making has implications not only for the performance of individual countries within the euro-zone but also leads to significant tensions within the euro-zone as a whole.

3.2. The de-politicization of money in the EMU

For centuries money has been the symbol of national sovereignty and power. The strength of a government is reflected in the value of its money—economic actors are willing to accept money in a transaction if they have the confidence that other actors will accept it in future transactions. The insignia of the authority serves to generate confidence (Goodhart 1989, 34). Where such confidence is present, money can serve its essential public good function in reducing transaction costs in an economy through its roles of unit of account, means of payment, and store of value (Spahn 2001, 15).

Authority over monetary matters and the exchange rate is also an important economic policy tool. While Keynesians and monetarists have long debated the extent to which money can affect real aggregates such as output or employment, imperfect information and the potential for inconsistent decision making imply that changes in monetary aggregates can have real effects at least in the short-run (Goodhart 1989, 292). This makes monetary policy useful in the case of an unexpected shock to the economy as well as for the stabilization of the business cycle. In the case of external imbalances exchange rate adjustment provides a relatively painless method to restore the current account balance.[1] Mundell (1961)

---

[1] This is naturally true only in the short run. In the long-run the possibility for regular devaluation not only triggers conflicts with trading partners but might also entrench an inefficient economic structure.

has long shown that lacking such a tool can impose significant costs on an economy unless other mechanisms of adjustment, such as mobile labor, are present.[2]

Prior to the creation of the euro, authority over money has not been given up without a political union. The historically unprecedented process of creating a currency without a state involved both symbolic and real costs for the participants. It was also surrounded by considerable uncertainty given earlier failures with cooperation over monetary matters. The major questions to be answered in relation to the euro are the following. First, why did these countries give up their decision making power over money? Second, how can the credibility of the newly created money be guaranteed? Answering these questions helps to understand the motivations of policymakers behind this unique decision.

3.2.1. The collapse of Bretton Woods and its turbulent aftermath

When the Rome Treaty was signed in 1957, there was no mention of a monetary union—at the time the Bretton Woods regime guaranteed stable monetary relations. The system depended on the commitment of the U.S. to convert dollar to gold at fix parity (35 dollar/ounce), while other countries pegged their currencies to the dollar. By the late 1960s the commitment of the U.S. to maintain convertibility was increasingly questioned—the costs of the Vietnam War as well as a mounting trade deficit greatly increased the quantity of dollars in the world economy, while the U.S. gold stock was slowly declining (Spahn 2001, 137). As it became clear that the U.S. could not meet its obligations, the market price of gold soared to well over 40 dollars/ounce. As efforts to negotiate devaluation failed, in August 1971 the convertibility of the dollar to gold was suspended by Nixon.

Following the collapse of Bretton Woods, international monetary relations were characterized by exchange rate volatility. The U.S. remained dominant in the system, but with the loss of its anchor function it was free to devalue as its domestic interests dictated. In the early 1970s a sharply weakening dollar caused concern about competitiveness for the EC countries, while after 1979 the interest rate hikes led to the weakening of European currencies and ensuing concerns about inflation. Efforts in the 1980s to increase monetary cooperation and stabilize exchange rates including the Plaza Accord in 1985 and the Louvre Agreement in 1987 failed. As a

---

[2] Mundell's work is the founding article of the theory of optimal currency area. I will return to this issue in section 3.3.4.

result, there was an increasing conviction among European leaders that the dominance of the U.S. is harmful to their interests and stronger European cooperation on exchange rate matters was seen as necessary to counter this dominance (Dyson 1994, 47–48, McNamara 1998, 125).

3.2.2. The creation of the Single Market

Besides the increasing resentment about the dominance of the U.S. in the international monetary system, a parallel development, which pushed towards a common currency, was the creation of the Single Market in 1986. While it was one of the main objectives of the Rome Treaty, a major factor behind its creation was the lesson learned from the oil crises in the 1970. As inflation and rising unemployment hit the region at the same time, the role of monetary policy to affect real developments in the economy was questioned not only in theory but also seen in practice (Dyson 1994, 234, McNamara 1998, 129). These experiences were not limited to the core states of the EC—countries in the Southern periphery also learnt the limited use of anti-cyclical monetary policies in the case of structural problems (Csaba 2007, 187–188).

Following the disillusionment from Keynesianism, by the 1980s the solution to the competitiveness problems of the European economy was seen not in old-fashioned demand-management ideas, but rather in strengthening markets. The Single European Act in 1986 envisioned a single market in goods, labor, capital and services by 1992. Monetary union was a natural follow-up to this program for two reasons. First, the possibility of devaluation could be viewed as a tax imposed on imports thus contradictory to the objectives of the Single Market. Second, the free movement of capital and exchange rate stability was a shared objective, and as independent monetary policy became impossible, it was thus no longer considered a great sacrifice (Hall 2005, 141).[3]

---

[3] This can be explained by the open-economy trilemma, which states that a country cannot have simultaneously free flow of capital, independent macroeconomic policy to support full employment, and a fixed exchange rate. Only two of the three goods can be targeted, which means that the loss of the third good is the price to be paid for the other two. For example, if the exchange rate is fixed and capital can move freely, any change in the interest rate provokes capital inflow or outflow. The idea of trilemma comes from the Mundell–Fleming model, which showed that in a world of perfect mobility of capital the choice of the exchange rate regime critically influences the effectiveness of monetary and fiscal policies in influencing employment and output. See Mundell (1963) as well as Fleming (1962).

3.2.3. Learning monetary cooperation: lessons from history

While developments in the world economy as well as increasing integration pushed European states towards greater monetary cooperation, the particular shape of this integration was strongly influenced by lessons from history.

The euro was not the first attempt in creating a monetary union—immediately after the collapse of the Bretton Woods system, the Werner Plan aimed to create a common currency by 1980. Its most visible aspect was the so-called "snake in the tunnel": a ±2.25% band to the dollar, within which six European countries decided to maintain a ±1.125% band with each other. With multiple realignments, the failure of the arrangement to ensure exchange rate stability became evident by the mid-1970s. Given the different responses to the inflationary pressures due to the oil crisis, maintaining a pegged exchange rate became extremely difficult. The crisis exposed sharply the major underlying tension of the arrangement: there was no agreement among participating countries about how the costs of adjustment will be distributed between strong currency countries and weak currency countries (Dyson and Quaglia 2010, 181–182). The need for economic convergence prior to fixing parities and the desire for a more symmetric monetary system were probably the most important lessons from this effort.

As the Werner Plan failed, a more pragmatic approach was taken with the introduction of the European Monetary System (EMS). It focused on stabilizing exchange rates through a bilateral parity grid based on the ECU (European Currency Unit), which was a basket of currencies comprising of national currencies weighted according to the member countries' economic and trading power. The EMS fell short of a plan for a common currency since the ECU was never planned to be used either for reserve purposes or for circulation, while the Bundesbank prevented plans on joint management of reserves. Germany also declined to commit to unlimited intervention if the arrangement would come under pressure (Dyson 1994, 110–111).

While its creators tried to design the EMS as a symmetrical system, the German mark was clearly the anchor in the system—both as a reserve currency and as the currency with the largest weight in the ECU. This arrangement implied that other member states were forced to follow the monetary policy of Germany. On the one hand, it had the advantage of importing credibility and the system functioned rather well throughout the 1980s. On the other hand, once internal and external commitments came into conflict for Germany, the built-in tensions of this arrangement became manifest. The problem emerged already in the early 1980s, when France faced repeated speculative pressure and had to follow Germany's austere interest rate policy (Hall 2005, 144). The real challenge came with the unification of Germany when the inflationary pressures due to the transfers to the East required higher interest rates, while to help other members of the EMS fighting with a global downturn would have necessitated low rates (Spahn 2001, 162). Germany eventually chose its domestic interests, which caused the EMS crisis in 1992.[4]

The major lesson from both the Werner Plan and the EMS was that without a common currency, a simple fixed exchange rate regime is bound to remain asymmetric and privilege the anchor currency country. Such asymmetry can be reduced only by common decision making over monetary policy.

3.2.4. A technocratic approach to the de-politicization of money

Given the credibility of the mark and the reputation of the Bundesbank in fighting inflation, Germany was hardly interested in giving up its currency and entering into a joint arrangement with countries characterized by financial profligacy. However, German unification took priority over these considerations—in return for not vetoing unification, France was able to convince Germany to go along with the creation of a monetary union (Dyson and Featerstone 1999, 758, Hall 2005, 145).

The design of particular institutional arrangements of the common currency was delegated to technical committees of central bankers, which basically accepted Germany as a model (Dyson and Quaglia 2010, 343). The Delors Plan in 1989 was strongly influenced by the preferences of the Bundesbank. It suggested a detailed roadmap to the euro with a particular emphasis on economic convergence prior to the irreversible fixing of the exchange rates.

In the run-up to the euro, policymakers often played the strategy of tying hands—while Germans could point to their domestic constituency for imposing strict institutional constraints on their partners, Southerners could use the international scene to force through domestic fiscal adjustments (Dyson and Featherstone 1999, 45). As a benefit Germany could silence fears about unification and promote European integration, while Southern countries could obtain credibility from the common currency.

---

[4] This will be discussed more in depth in the next chapter.

3.2.5. Self-imposed commitments for sound money: the economic governance of the EMU

The eventual economic governance framework that was created for the common currency reflected the belief that an institutional straightjacket can lock in ideas of "sound money" and guarantee the credibility of the newly created currency.

The most important elements in ensuring the credibility of the new currency are the institutional arrangements for decision making over monetary policy. Article 105 of the Maastricht Treaty (MT)[5] states that "the primary objective of the ESCB shall be to maintain price stability." The ESCB (European System of Central Banks) is composed of the European Central Bank (ECB) and the national central banks. Article 107 guarantees the independence of monetary decision making through asserting that "the Community institutions and bodies and the governments of the Member States undertake to respect this principle and not to seek to influence the members of the decision-making bodies of the ECB or of the national central banks in the performance of their tasks."

The MT also prohibits the explicit bailout of member states, which was also viewed as a necessary factor in ensuring that the objective of price stability remains the primary objective. Article 104 states that "overdraft facilities or any other type of credit facility with the ECB or with the central banks of the Member States (hereinafter referred to as 'national central banks') in favor of Community institutions or bodies, central governments, regional, local or other public authorities, other bodies governed by public law, or public undertakings of Member States shall be prohibited, as shall the purchase directly from them by the ECB or national central banks of debt instruments."

Finally, the creators of EMU also recognized that even in the absence of a need for bailout, fiscal profligacy in member states can undermine common monetary policy. The accumulated public debt is a liability for other member states—the debt is paid either through artificially low interest rates and high inflation or overly high interest rates, which might be required for the maintenance of price stability (Fatas et al. 2003). These concerns lay behind the Maastricht criteria, which made entry into the euro-zone conditional upon having a lower than three percent general government deficit and a lower than 60 percent or steadily declining public debt. Given the possibility for abuse once within the euro-zone, in

---

[5] Text available: http://www.eurotreaties.com/maastrichtec.pdf.

1997 member states signed the Stability and Growth Pact (SGP) initiated by the German finance minister, Theo Weigel. The original SGP[6] was based on the political commitment of the member states to keep their budget "close to balance or surplus" over the economic cycle. For this purpose member states are required to submit to the Commission annual stability or convergence reports depending on whether they have introduced the common currency or not. The Commission has the right to issue an early warning to a member state if it expects that the deficit or debt is going to breach the threshold. If a country does not correct the imbalances within a certain period, the excessive deficit procedure is initiated that can end in a fine without consolidation.

The Maastricht criteria and the Stability and Growth Pact implied important constraints on fiscal policy. At the same time they regulated the outcome rather than the roots of the problem of overspending. As fiscal policy is at the heart of democratic politics and represents the major tool for a government to implement its agenda, it was rightly seen that the EC has no role in regulating the particulars of collecting and spending public resources.

3.2.6. Tensions within the arrangement—the role of fiscal policy

With the institutional structure guaranteeing the independence of the ESCB in monetary policymaking, the de-politicization of money was concluded. The outcome was the result of the structural changes in the world economy, the progress in European economic integration, as well as changing views about monetary policy as a useful tool for economic policy. The institutional arrangements reflected the sound money paradigm, which became dominant following the stagflation in the 1970s. Countries that eventually did not introduced the common currency—Denmark, Sweden and the UK—were primarily driven by concerns over losing their sovereignty as well as skepticism of a politically imposed currency rather than by questions over the validity of the sound money paradigm.[7]

In spite of the shared conviction of the elites about the benefits of sound money, the arrangement was not without tensions. For those countries that introduced the euro, the loss of monetary policy meant that alter-

---

[6] The legal documents are available on the ECOFIN website: http://www.europa.eu.int/comm/economy_finance/about/activities/sgp/main_en.htm.

[7] On the case of the UK see Gamble and Kelly (2002), on Denmark see Marcussen (2002), on Sweden Lindahl and Naurin (2005).

native methods of adjustment had to be working, while fiscal policy assumed an enhanced role in cyclical stabilization and support for economic growth. Such expectations could easily come into contradiction with the fiscal rules of the EMU—especially in those countries where the sound money paradigm was not internalized through historical experiences such as the hyperinflation in Germany. If sanctions would not work as planned, which proved to be the case, breaching the rules could be expected. The irreversible nature of the arrangement further increased the dangers of free riding on the credibility provided by the responsibility of other member states.

The major tension within the EMU arrangement is that fiscal policy is much more difficult to depoliticize than monetary policy. While as part of a unique decision over monetary policy a self-commitment to discipline was declared by EU governments, decisions over fiscal policy have remained entrenched in domestic politics. They are also recurrent rather than one-time decisions, which means that policymakers are likely to act within the constraints represented by the prevalent time horizon in society, which in turn affect their motivation to comply with the self-imposed constraints. The mechanisms behind these claims are discussed in the next section.

3.3. Policy choices within the euro-zone: the role of trust

For the countries choosing the euro, the unique decision is followed by the normal tasks of governance, where the promotion of economic growth is generally high on the agenda. In the euro zone, monetary policy is not a tool anymore, thus decisions focus on fiscal policy as well as structural change. At the same time, given the recurrent nature of such decisions it is expected that policymakers cannot insulate themselves from the prevalent time horizon in society, which is largely a function of trust in the institutional environment. The major objective of this section is to describe some of the mechanisms through which trust may affect economic policies. First I will discuss its relation to fiscal policy through assessing its role in the various dimensions of fiscal policy quality from a growth perspective. Then I will consider through what channels it affects the prospects for policy change followed by an application to fiscal consolidation and structural reforms. The specific applications to the performance in the euro-zone will be discussed afterwards.

3.3.1. Fiscal policy, growth, and trust

In standard neoclassical thinking fiscal policy has no role in the growth rate of an economy. Based on the model created by Solow (1956), long-run growth is entirely determined by exogenous technological progress, which defines the steady-state path of the economy. Solow created his model in response the Harrod–Domar model, which asserted that growth is a function of savings and the productivity of capital—thus the state is able to raise the rate of growth at will through increasing savings and investment. Showing the problems with this line of thinking and the transitional nature of forced growth was the major contribution of the Solow model.[8]

The next generation of growth models challenged the policy ineffectiveness proposition drawn from the Solow model. Theories of endogenous growth assert that the increase in human and physical capital productivity through technological improvements makes GDP growth possible and these factors can be influenced by policy. In endogenous growth theory fiscal policy can positively influence growth through the following channels (Gemmel 2001, 2–3):

1. *Production externalities*: public investment or education may enhance private sector production.
2. *Productivity growth*: fiscal policy may influence innovation, for example through investment in basic research.
3. *Factor accumulation*: fiscal policy may affect investment into physical or human capital either through indirect incentives or direct public investment.

Recent research on fiscal policy and growth incorporates the above theoretical considerations and aims to assess the problem in an explicitly policy-oriented framework through focusing on the various dimensions of fiscal policy quality influence growth.[9] The major dimensions of fiscal policy quality as classified by Barrios and Schaechter (2008) are the following:

---

[8] Solow (1956, 93–94) was well aware of the limits of his own model—in particular he notes uncertainty as missing from his theory even though it is impossible to think seriously about investment without taking it into account.

[9] This research is mostly European-conducted in the European Commission and the European Central Bank. Given the importance of fiscal policy in members of the euro-area, the explicit policy-orientation is not so surprising.

1. *Size of the state*: overly high redistribution can become a hindrance to growth since it is usually accompanied by high tax rates, monopolistic provision of services and disincentives to employment and savings. While there are clear exceptions to this perspective, most importantly the Scandinavian countries, empirical evidence on the basis of samples from EU and OECD economies appear to confirm the conventional wisdom—most studies find a significant negative relationship between the level of redistribution and growth.[10]

2. *Fiscal deficits and sustainability*: high deficit and debt levels lead to weak growth as government debt crowds out companies from the credit market, while investments are also reduced by expectations about higher future taxes. With large fiscal imbalances there is a tendency towards greater pro-cyclicality,[11] which results in greater volatility that is in turn negatively associated with growth (Fatas and Mihov 2003).

3. *Composition and efficiency of expenditure*: state spending increasing human and physical infrastructure might be growth enhancing but only if they can be provided in an efficient manner. At the same time social transfers are generally regarded as non-productive expenditure. The latter not only fail to contribute directly to increased private sector output, but they can serve as important disincentives on labor market participation and thus through decreasing the supply of labor, they have negative effect on growth prospects.

4. *Structure and efficiency of revenue systems*: if the system of taxes introduces large distortions in market incentives, it can have a significant negative effect on growth rate. Such distortion might be a high tax wedge or steep progressive taxation, which provide disincentives to employment and investment into human capital. On this basis it is generally preferable to tax consumption than labor or

---

[10] For a survey of the results of recent empirical studies see Barrios and Schaechter (2008, 11) as well as Afonso et al. (2005, 23). At the same time as Muraközy (2012) emphasizes in his extensive overview, the size of the state is primarily the outcome of long-term historical processes, rather than the matter of discretionary policy choices. Consequently the relevance of debates on the optimal level of redistribution is rather limited.

[11] The reason is that if governments do not accumulate reserves during good times, they will be forced to implement stabilization measures during recessions, when credit channels freeze for untrustworthy borrowers. Furthermore as trust in sustainability evaporates, higher interest rates undermine the potential benefits of expansionary fiscal policy during the management of a recession (Spilbergo et al. 2008, 7–8).

profit since such taxes have a wider base than other taxes, and they do not present disincentive against employment, savings, or investment. Reports on competitiveness based on surveys from business actors underline the importance of stability and predictability of the tax systems, which makes business calculation possible. The efficiency of tax administration is similarly important as an efficient administration is able to minimize the tax burden on economic actors.

5. *Fiscal management framework*: the primary objective of numerical rules, independent fiscal councils, and procedural rules over the planning, implementation, and execution phase of budgeting is to decrease the opportunity of budgetary actors to implement measures that serve narrow interest groups rather than the public good. Such rules contribute not only to the reduction of fiscal imbalances but also have a positive effect on all other dimensions of fiscal policy quality as they make decision making more efficient.

6. *Market efficiency and business environment*: studies on competitiveness place great emphasis on the time and costs of obtaining various licenses and complying with administrative regulations. Expensive and overly complicated regulations are harmful to growth for several reasons. They encourage corruption, which distorts competition and thus decreases the productivity of the economy. Higher administrative costs also decrease investments leading to less employment opportunities, which imply not only unused resources but also a narrowing of the tax base and thus the necessity for higher tax rates. While cutting back these regulations might bring savings, if the budget needs income from administrative fees, simplifying administration cannot be expected (Török 2007, 1072).

The critical underlying factor of all these dimensions is the integrity and efficiency of public administration. A high-quality public administration is able to constrain the demands of interest groups for increasing expenditure and able to raise the amount of taxes needed to finance its expenditure in an efficient manner. It also allocates resources efficiently and has visible rules in place for signaling its transparency. Efficiency in public service provision allows companies to flourish.

The common underlying factor also implies that the various dimensions of fiscal policy cannot be strictly separated from one another. Quality public services generate trust towards the institutional framework, and contribute to general compliance with rules and paying taxes. These conditions create a favorable business environment where long-term planning is feasible for agents. The resulting high rate of investment can foster high levels of employment, which maintains a broad tax base. Together with general tax compliance, this ensures public finance sustainability with moderate tax rates, which preserve the profitability of labor and investment. The outcome is high rate of growth, which in turn reinforces the trust in the system. Figure 3.1. below illustrates the described virtuous cycle between trust and growth.

Figure 3.1. Virtuous cycle between trust and growth

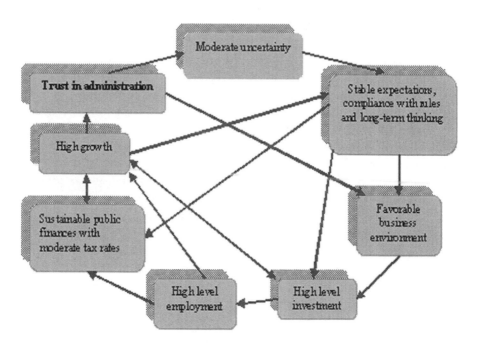

In the case of a corrupt and incompetent public administration, an opposite dynamic prevails. As discussed in the previous chapter, in such an environment there is no inner moral obligation to comply with the rules as the administration itself is constantly seen as breaking them. Not complying with the rules often becomes a form of resistance against the system and people assume that everyone else is doing the same. Under these circumstances uncertainty persists and tax compliance is low. This creates an unfavorable environment for business and thus investments materialize somewhere else. This in turn hurts employment prospects implying not only a narrow tax base but also a strong public pressure for social benefits.

Under such circumstances tax rates have to be high in order to ensure revenue financing expenditures.

In a low-growth, low-employment economy, political factors also contribute to the worsening of the situation. Since their long-term promises are not believed, politicians are able to raise support before elections only through promises for short-term material benefits. This problem can be particularly acute in new democracies, where the electorate has yet to learn that such spending comes at a cost in the long run.[12]

The above tendencies add up into a vicious cycle where low trust, high budgetary imbalances, and low growth reinforce one another. This is illustrated by Figure 3.2.

Figure 3.2. Vicious cycle between lack of trust and low growth

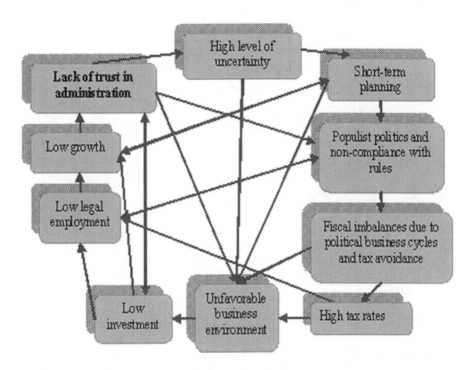

---

[12] The difference between old and new democracies in terms of election spending has been shown by Brender and Drazen (2005), who found that election cycles are mostly a characteristic of developing countries. Their finding supports the concept of fiscal illusion, which means that voters overvalue current benefits while discounting future taxes (Buchanan and Wagner 1977).

While the cycles described are self-reinforcing, it does not imply that change is impossible. Various external shocks can challenge the virtuous cycle, while a crisis might force a change in the case of a vicious cycle. Consequently when discussing the quality of public finances, it is also important to consider the question of change.

3.3.2. The difficulties of reform

Both trusted and distrusted administrations might face challenges, which require change in the status quo. As discussed in the previous chapter, in an open-ended world, technological change or other external influences require the constant revision of the institutional framework. Change in financing conditions might also necessitate adjustments even in situations, which could be considered sustainable before.

A major advantage of public trust is to serve as "a reserve of support that enables a system to weather the many storms when outputs cannot be balanced off against inputs of demands" (Easton 1965, 273). This implies that when potentially difficult changes have to be made, the government is able to implement first-best measures, even if they might be painful for the population in the short-term. In such a scenario, the perception of the public about the competence and integrity of the government makes the demands for sacrifice acceptable.

The problem of implementing real change in a low-trust environment comes from the lack of credibility in the promises of the government. If the electorate has no trust in the administration, promises about long-run benefits at the cost of short-run sacrifices are simply not credible. The main reason for this is that perceptions about both integrity and competence are crucially affected by the memory of previous outcomes: if citizens had experienced that governments were concerned only with their own short-term interests rather than the public good, it is unlikely that they presume different motives during the next campaign for change. Similarly, if they had seen that previous reforms resulted in very different outcomes than promised by the policymakers, it is unlikely that they will believe in similar promises by later governments. This implies that in a low-trust environment, where citizens are disillusioned from the political process, it is very difficult to make credible promises and overcome the resistance to structural reforms.

Resistance against structural change might emerge from a variety of sources depending on whether the individual ultimately would gain or lose from the reforms. Those, who permanently lose from the changes should be compensated from the gains to society—however, this promise is not credible from an untrustworthy administration. For those, who stand to gain from the changes, the uncertainty of the future and the unreliability of the promises of the government maintain their resistance to change. These problems are summarized in Table 3.1.

Table 3.1. Structural reforms: sources of resistance, solutions and the role of credibility

SOURCE OF RESISTANCE	SOLUTION	ROLE OF CREDIBILITY
Permanent losers from market forces	Compensation from societal gains	Uncertainty over whether promised compensation will be forthcoming
Short-term losses but long-term gains with short-term preferences	Policies facilitating adaptation to the new environment	Uncertainty over long-term gains
Uncertainty over reform outcomes	Provision of information	Unreliability of information

Source: Győrffy (2009b): 151

The result of the above problems is that it is more likely that instead of fostering genuine change, policymakers engage in a form of fire fighting and find some quick fix solution for the most urgent matters without addressing the source of problems. These steps might be successful in the short-term, but within a given period their insufficiency or the unintended consequences of solutions are likely to lead to the reemergence of the problems.

3.3.3. Implications for fiscal consolidation

The above theoretical discussion on the difficulties of reforms can be illustrated by examining the problem of fiscal consolidations. This is an issue that democracies have to face regularly. The pressure to stabilize can emerge from a variety of sources including pressures from financial markets, demography, or an obligation from supranational institutions such as the EU. When designing the consolidation package, the government has several choices to decide upon. On the revenue side it can increase taxes in a distortionary or non-distortionary manner, while on the expenditure side it can reduce spending—deciding between productive and non-productive expenditures. An important element of successful and lasting consolidation is to institutionalize the commitment of responsibility to fiscal rules and at the same time improve the efficiency of future decision making. At the same time, the most successful method to consolidate is to improve the performance of the economy through increasing the efficiency of public services.

Based on the theoretical discussion on reforms it can be expected that in a low-trust environment the method of consolidation is likely to be suboptimal—the primary motive in the decision over consolidation methods is likely to be short-term political rather than long-term economic. Short-term political perspective is likely to opt for raising taxes rather than cutting revenues—especially cash transfers, which are most visible for the public. If the government is forced to cut expenditures, public investments are more likely to be targeted than social benefits.

At the same time it has been shown that the success of fiscal consolidation is strongly affected by the composition of adjustment.[13] Addressing the experiences of Denmark and Ireland, Giavazzi and Pagano (1990) were the first to indicate that contrary to traditional Keynesian views, fiscal consolidation is not necessarily accompanied by a recession, as the decline in aggregate demand might be countered by positive expectations concerning the future prospects of the economy. Alesina and Perotti (1995) pointed out that in achieving non-Keynesian effects, the composition of adjustment is critical—while successful consolidations are based on the reduction of government wage bill and social transfers, unsuccessful consolidations are primarily oriented towards raising taxes. Alesina, Perotti, and Tavares (1998) explained this finding by arguing that under the former type of adjustment, increasing investment and decreasing labor costs improve growth prospects, and thus offset the negative effects on growth due to a fall in demand. These results are also supported by Ardagna (2004), who shows that these factors play a significant role in the success of adjustments even after controlling for differences in growth rate, expansionary monetary policy, or the devaluation of the currency.

The above literature provides three major reasons why an expenditure-based consolidation can prove more successful than a revenue-based consolidation:

1. Cutting expenditures, which are politically difficult, sends a signal about the commitment of the government to address the imbal-

---

[13] In the following I will provide only a brief review of the literature on successful fiscal adjustments. For a broader overview see Benczes (2008).

ances, which increases the credibility of the adjustment. Increased credibility leads to lower interest rates, which improves the fiscal balance in itself. In the case of increasing revenues, there is no such effect because an inefficient state cannot prevent the reemergence of imbalances even with more resources to redistribute.

2. Lower expenditures lead to expectations about lower future taxes, which increase profit opportunities and thus have a positive effect on investment. Raising taxes have the opposite effect.

3. Restraints on government wages make it possible to restrain wages in the private sector, which increases cost-based competitiveness. Decreasing social transfers have a similar effect as it raises the incentives for taking employment. In contrast, when raising taxes, lower net incomes might trigger demands for gross wages or a decrease in the motivation for taking employment.

Besides the effects of composition, presence or absence of trust also has an implication for the commitment of sustaining responsibility. In a low-trust environment, given the political costs of stabilization, once external pressure eases, an effort to compensate the electorate for the austerity is likely to follow. This can take the form of extra spending or tax cuts—both are likely to lead to the reemergence of imbalances. In such an environment, commitment to fiscal rules either does not exist or remains formal.

3.3.4. Implications for adjustment within the EMU

While in the institutional framework of the EMU the rules concern only fiscal policy outcomes, for the satisfactory performance of the arrangement, progress with structural economic reforms are also necessary. The major reason was partly discussed at the beginning of the chapter—with the loss of independent monetary policy alternative adjustment mechanisms are necessary in the case of asymmetric shocks.

In his path-breaking article, Mundell (1961) emphasized the role of labor mobility in the adjustment process.[14] McKinnon (1963) considered openness to trade as most important to have a fixed exchange rate and avoid price fluctuations—he advised the use of fiscal policy to handle external imbalances. Kenen (1969) emphasized the degree of diversifica-

---

[14] In the following selective overview by the conditions for OCA I will primarily rely on the survey of Horvath (2003).

tion in the economy as a major criterion of OCA—in a well-diversified economy one sector might be affected by an asymmetric shock, but another might prosper—thus the overall terms-of-trade does not change and there is no need for exchange rate adjustment. Later theories argued that mobility can be substituted by wage and price flexibility, while American economists pointed to the need for large fiscal transfers to act as shock absorbers (Eichengreen 1991).

Based on the various conditions of OCA, the main conclusion from the theory is a considerable skepticism towards the EMU project: although the EC is composed of diversified economies and there is substantial trade integration, labor mobility and fiscal transfers are considerably smaller than in the United States.

Later developments in the theory however allowed a more optimistic conclusion and suggested that the criteria do not matter since fulfilling them might be endogenous to the creation of the currency union: if economic actors recognize the opportunities and constraints presented by the new arrangement they will adjust their behavior. This would be a manifestation of the Lucas critique —changes in the institutional conditions lead to changes in behavior (Spahn 2001, 170). Frenkel and Rose (1996) argue that having a common currency promotes trade, which in turn leads to the synchronization of business cycles and thus asymmetric shocks become less likely. According to Corsetti and Pesenti (2002), deeper trade integration is not even necessary if rational, forward-looking agents set prices according to the common monetary policy. From this perspective it could be expected that following entry into the EMU there will be a strong pressure on countries to improve the mechanisms of adjustment and thus eventually the criteria of OCA would be fulfilled.

Once we consider the difficulties of structural change in a low-trust environment, we can see that the endogenous theory of OCA is more likely to work in a high-trust environment than in a low-trust environment. The unpopular reforms of increasing labor market flexibility either through easing employment protection regulations or cutting back social transfers are more likely to be accepted in a high-trust environment, where people can be convinced of the long-term positive effects of these measures on employment prospects, while losers can count on some form of compensation. In a low-trust regime large-scale resistance is likely to accompany such measures and thus muddling through and postponing reforms is the most likely outcome. The main implication is that losing independent monetary policy can be expected to be particularly costly for low-trust countries.

3.4. Prospects after the euro—hypotheses

In the previous section I have shown how the prevalent time horizon in society is reflected in economic policy decisions and how it is expected to influence performance within the euro-zone. While in a high-trust country virtuous cycles of long-term orientation in policy and good performance are expected, in a low-trust regime the short-term orientation in policy and poor performance reinforce one another. Having the same external framework for these two types of countries enhances their divergence.

The presence or absence of trust is naturally not limited to countries that have introduced the euro. Those countries that opted out from the euro given concerns over sovereignty or have not joined because of failing to fulfill the Maastricht criteria represent a useful comparison to euro-area member states. Including them into the analysis results in four groups, about which the following hypotheses can be formed based on the discussion from the previous section.

1. *High-trust regimes in the euro-zone*: countries in this group are expected to benefit the most from monetary integration. They are likely to be committed to the sound money paradigm and if a need for consolidation emerges they are likely to implement measures, which ensure the sustainability of public finances. Their ability to maintain financial discipline and implement structural change makes them competitive, allows alternative adjustment mechanisms to work, and thus enables them to enjoy the benefits of greater competition from a larger market.

2. *High-trust regimes outside the euro-zone*: countries in this group are primarily those that value their sovereignty more than EU integration. Given their high quality institutions, they do not need the credibility provided by the common currency. At the same time compared to international reserve currencies such as the dollar or the euro, ensuring exchange rate stability requires even greater discipline than within the euro-zone, where there is a possibility for freeriding.

3. *Low-trust regimes in the euro-zone*: for these countries the credibility provided by the euro was probably worth more than the sacrifices needed for the consolidation of public finances. At the same time they are most likely to have chosen a method of consolidation that is politically the least costly and likely to be unsustainable. The difficulties of structural reforms also imply that in the highly com-

petitive environment of the single market and the euro they are going to suffer from competitiveness problems, which results in low
growth and thus increases dissatisfaction. This in turn reinforces the
difficulties for change and the vicious cycle becomes deeply entrenched. A window of opportunity for change might be presented
by a large external shock such as a crisis, but even then getting out
of the vicious cycle is far from certain unless measures succeed in
lengthening the time horizon in society.

4. *Low-trust regimes outside the euro-zone*: in such regimes, the euro
   might not be popular enough for making the sacrifices required by
   the convergence criteria. Without the euro, weak institutions produce regular imbalances and macroeconomic volatility. Such effects can be fought through implementing a hard peg,[15] which however makes it difficult for countries to address external imbalances
   and thus problems of competitiveness are likely to emerge. For
   those countries that do not turn towards the hard peg, the volatility
   of exchange rate might make the euro attractive and thus policymakers might have some incentive to fulfill the criteria.

* * *

The major objective of this chapter was to develop hypotheses about how
the time horizon that prevails in individual planning, depending on the
level of institutional trust, affects decision making over economic policy.
The establishment of the EMU is a particularly suitable case for examining this issue because it represents the same external framework for a
divergent group of countries and thus makes differences in policy particularly visible.

In order to assess the role of trust in economic policies associated with
the euro, a distinction was made between unique and recurrent decisions,
which helps to understand the difference between the act of self-
commitment to an institutional framework and the subsequent decisions
over the costs and benefits of respecting that commitment. While the former decision is the outcome of a complex, elite-led bargaining process
involving considerable uncertainty, the latter decisions have to be made
regularly within a relatively well-known domestic setting, with the agenda

---

[15] Empirical studies have shown that for developing countries with weak institutions a
fixed exchange rate providing policy credibility delivers the lowest level of inflation as
well as the highest rate of growth (Rogoff et al. 2003).

of maintaining electoral support. In such situations, policymakers cannot remain impervious to societal pressures and the presence or absence of trust plays a key role in the shaping of economic policy.

The chapter has shown that once we recognize the implications of trust for economic policy, we can see the inherent tensions in the EMU arrangement. While high-trust countries are able to implement long-term oriented policies and flourish in the highly competitive environment brought about by the single market and the euro, for low-trust countries such an environment exacerbates the consequences of their weaknesses. In the following chapters I will provide an empirical examination of these hypotheses.

CHAPTER 4

Fiscal Developments
in the EU-15, 1992–2007

In the previous chapter, several hypotheses have been formulated regarding the economic policies of different countries following the introduction of the euro. Fiscal policy has received a particular emphasis—although decision making remained in national hands, supranational rules strongly constrain governmental discretion. As fiscal policy lies at the heart of domestic politics, it was hypothesized that high-trust countries are more likely to be able to respect EMU fiscal rules than low-trust regimes, where politicians cannot remain impervious to societal pressures towards short-term decision making.

The major objective of this chapter is to provide empirical support for the above hypotheses based on the experiences of the old EU member states (EU-15) between 1992 and 2007. This period covers both the convergence period to the EMU as well as a decade afterwards, when large divergence could be observed in spite of the unchanging external framework. The presence of three non-EMU countries represents an important control group for assessing the role of the external framework in the adjustments. Such setting provides almost laboratory conditions to assess whether the prevailing tendencies are in line with the proposed hypotheses.

The nearly two-decade period that will be analyzed saw a series of fiscal consolidations which took place for different reasons and came in different compositions. In the EU-15, the Maastricht criteria was not the only source of external pressure for consolidation—the losses suffered during the 1992–1993 EMS crisis necessitated stabilization measures even in those countries that did not plan to introduce the euro. At the same time the success of consolidation differed substantially and the main objective of this chapter is to underline the role of trust in this divergence. The central argument is that the role of institutional trust is critical in whether or not an internal commitment to responsibility emerges besides the direct external pressures for fiscal stabilization. Such a commitment influences the method of consolidation and thus prospects for success.

The detailed examination of the composition of fiscal adjustment in the EU-15 provides empirical evidence on the outcome of the hypothesized interactions between institutional trust and economic policymaking. However, in order to better understand the processes behind these outcomes, in the second part of the chapter two case studies—Sweden and Portugal—will be presented, which best demonstrate the proposed mechanisms at work. Their cases exemplify the evolution of virtuous and vicious cycles between trust, fiscal balance, and growth.

In the following, I will start the analysis with a brief overview of the EMS crisis, which was a difficult start for the convergence period and had important influence on fiscal consolidation in most member states. Then I will briefly review the overall trends in consolidation prior to the 2008–2010 financial crisis, through examining compliance with the Stability and Growth Pact (SGP). Afterwards I will make a typology based on the motivation for fiscal consolidation and identify four different groups of countries regarding fiscal consolidation. The following section will assess how trust mattered in their differences and how it affected the composition of adjustment. The sixth section will contain the comparative analysis of Sweden and Portugal, which illustrate how these differences emerge. The final section will summarize the findings.

4.1. The EMS crisis—the start of the convergence period

The convergence period in the EU took place immediately following the crisis of the European Monetary System (EMS), which had important implications for fiscal policy in almost all member states. A brief overview of the crisis helps to understand better the initial conditions of the convergence period.

As in the case of most crises, several factors contributed to the events:[1]

- Following the establishment of the single market in 1986, capital controls were gradually removed in the EU. This led to strong credit growth in several member states with inflationary consequences and an overvaluation of the exchange rates.

---

[1] While a thorough analysis of the crisis is beyond the scope of this chapter, in the following brief sketch of the EMS crisis I will rely on Eichengreen (2000) as well as Buiter, Corsetti, and Pesenti (1998).

- Overvaluation and the ensuing competitiveness problems were particularly serious in the new members of the EMS—UK, Spain, and Portugal.
- Competitiveness considerations were further worsened by the collapse of the dollar vis-à-vis the Mark.
- At the same time, the collapse of the Soviet system followed by serious trade disintegration contributed to lower global demand, which was especially harmful for those countries with overvalued currencies.
- The unification of Germany led to a contradiction between internal and external stability as the inflationary pressures due to the transfers to the East required higher interest rates, while to help other members of the EMS fighting with recession would have necessitated low rates.

The crisis started in September 1991, in Finland, which was hit hardest by the collapse of the Soviet markets. In order to restore competitiveness, the country was forced to devalue its currency and leave the EMS. In July 1992 as the Maastricht Treaty was rejected by the Danish voters and the future of the common currency came into doubt, speculative pressures intensified for countries with overvalued currencies and high rates of unemployment. As Germany was unwilling to lower interest rates and help others managing the recession, the EMS started to disintegrate as Sweden, UK, Italy, Spain, Portugal, and Norway eventually devalued and left the system. Even in countries that could maintain the band with the Mark (France, Belgium, and Denmark), interest rates had to be risen further, thus exacerbating the recession. The crisis was eventually solved in 1993 with the widening of the ERM band to ±15 percent.

The losses of the crisis varied according to countries (Table 4.1). While Finland and Sweden were hit most seriously where output losses were over 4 percent of the GDP, most EU member states also registered negative growth rates in 1993. As a result of the crisis, unemployment also surged everywhere with the exceptions of Austria and Luxembourg.

For the future, the crisis provided three important lessons. First, it strengthened the perception that there is a need for a strong common currency to protect against the uncertainty of market sentiments. Second, it underlined the theoretical argument that a fixed exchange rate cannot be maintained with differences in inflation rates and thus the crisis provided a strong justification for the Maastricht criteria. Third, similarly to earlier experiences with monetary cooperation, the crisis highlighted the importance of having an independent monetary authority, which makes its deci-

Table 4.1. Growth, unemployment and fiscal balance in the EU-15 (1991–1994)

Country	Growth				Unemployment rate				Net lending (GDP %)			
	1991	1992	1993	1994	1991	1992	1993	1994	1991	1992	1993	1994
Austria	3.4	1.3	0.5	2.4	3.4	3.4	4.0	3.8	-3.0	-2.0	-4.2	-5.0
Belgium	2.0	1.6	-1.5	3.0	6.6	7.3	8.9	10.0	-6.2	-6.9	-7.2	-4.8
Denmark	1.4	1.3	0.8	5.6	8.4	9.2	10.1	8.2	-2.2	-2.4	-2.8	-2.6
Finland	-6.3	-3.3	-1.1	2.2	6.6	11.7	16.4	16.6	-1.5	-5.7	-7.9	-6.0
France	1.0	1.5	-0.9	2.1	9.5	10.4	11.7	12.3	-2.0	-3.9	-5.6	-5.6
Germany	5.0	2.2	-1.1	2.3	5.6	6.6	7.9	8.4	-3.2	-2.8	-3.5	-2.6
Greece	3.1	0.7	-1.6	2.0	7.0	7.9	8.6	8.9	-11.5	-12.8	-13.8	-10.0
Ireland	1.9	3.3	2.6	5.8	14.8	15.4	15.6	14.3	-2.3	-2.4	-2.3	-1.6
Italy	1.4	0.8	-0.9	2.2	8.6	8.8	10.3	11.2	-10.0	-9.5	-9.4	-9.1
Luxembourg	6.1	4.5	8.7	4.2	1.7	2.1	2.7	3.2	1.9	0.8	1.7	2.8
Netherlands	2.3	2.0	0.8	3.2	5.8	5.6	6.6	7.1	-2.9	-3.9	-3.2	-3.8
Portugal	2.3	2.5	-1.1	2.2	4.0	4.2	5.7	7.0	-6.0	-2.9	-6.1	-6.0
Spain	2.3	0.7	-1.2	2.3	16.4	18.5	22.8	24.1	-4.5	-4.1	-7.0	-6.4
Sweden	-1.1	-1.4	-2.2	4.1	3.1	5.6	9.1	9.4	-1.1	--7.8	-11.9	-9.9
UK	-1.5	0.1	2.3	4.4	8.8	10.1	10.4	9.6	-2.3	-6.1	-7.8	-6.7
EU-14*	1.7	1.2	-0.4	2.8	8.2	9.2	10.7	11.1	-4.2	-5.1	-6.1	-5.4

* Excluding Luxembourg

Source: European Commission (2000): 254-255, 268-269, 434-435

sions based on the interests of the community rather than on the basis of internal considerations of a single country.

Overall the crisis strengthened the case for the euro and made the economic reasons behind the specific institutional arrangements evident to all. It also made the fulfillment of convergence criteria more difficult— stabilizing the large-scale fiscal imbalances, which followed the crisis (Table 4.1), was critical for the fulfillment of other Maastricht criteria as well: for reducing public debt in a sustainable manner, deficit reduction is essential; long-term interest rates strongly depend on the credibility of sustainable fiscal policy, while restraining public spending is an important way to bring down inflation. As recognized in the Stability and Growth Pact, the above considerations apply not only to the convergence period but they are especially important in the success of the common currency during its operation. To what extent these lessons were taken seriously in general is the subject of the following section.

4.2. The working of the EMU fiscal rules

At the beginning, the fiscal rules of the euro-zone appeared to be working. In the 1990s fiscal consolidations were much more successful than before (Larch and Turrini 2008, 9). By 1997, eleven member states fulfilled the Maastricht criteria, while Greece followed by 1999. Between 1998 and 2000 the improvement appeared to be lasting, and in a number of cases the outcomes were even better than the plans in the stability programs. However, as it later became evident, the performance was due to the exceptional growth rates rather than to an increased commitment to fiscal restraint. Instead of saving for a downturn, during the years of economic boom a number of countries started new fiscal programs or implemented tax cuts (Fatas et al. 2003). With the slowdown of the world economy these problems came to the fore.

By 2002, it became evident that Germany and Portugal will be unable to keep their deficits below the 3 percent threshold.[2] However, in spite of recommendations from the Commission, the Economic and Financial Council (Ecofin) failed to issue an early warning to the two countries. Meanwhile the French budgetary situation also deteriorated, but the warning was issued with a year delay similarly to Germany and Portugal. Still,

---

[2] The source for the following chronological overview is European Commission (2008), 135.

excessive deficit remained in France and Germany that should have led to a fine according to the SGP. However, in November 2003 the fine was voted down by the Ecofin. In the debate, the small member states (Austria and the Netherlands) were unable to fight the big countries, which voted against levying the fine. The decision was invalidated by the European Court of Justice in 2004, but this did not lead to a fine either. The Stability and Growth Pact apparently collapsed.

Given the harsh criticisms of the Pact,[3] in 2005 the rules were modified. Under the new rules greater emphasis was placed on fiscal sustainability, country-specific circumstances, as well as on prevention. However, the most important element of the revision was the lack of change in the most critical aspect—enforcement. It is thus unsurprising that critiques saw the reform as the end of the SGP (Beetsma and Debrun 2007) as well as the enhanced possibility for discretionary decisions (Csaba 2007). In contrast to these assessments, Buti (2006) argued that while there is indeed greater opportunity for avoiding the restrictions, peer pressure for respecting the rules might increase as only the most irresponsible countries are going to break the new rules. Still, the changes confirmed the thesis of Schucknecht (2004), who claimed that the SGP should be interpreted as a soft law, which is built primarily on voluntary compliance.

Lack of enforcement and voluntary compliance raises the question about whether there has been any benefit from the fiscal rules of the EU. While the positive contribution of the convergence period to fiscal responsibility is generally recognized, following the introduction of the euro the disciplinary effect of rules has been often questioned. While earlier analysis emphasized the differences between large and small member states (Von Hagen 2003, Buti and Pench 2004, Chang 2006), later studies argue that after accession rules have been generally ineffective (Hughes-Hallett and Lewis 2008, Kocenda, Kutan, and Yigit 2008). At the same time both types of approaches can be criticized—while the former theories do not explain the emergence of deficits in the first place, the aggregate statistical analyses of the latter hide the important cross-national differences in complying with the rules. Furthermore in both types of analysis fiscal responsibility is interpreted as a result of EU pressures, which is not necessarily the case.

Based on the above, it is useful to examine the sources of commitment to fiscal responsibility and separate this effect from the anchor role of the EU.

---

[3] On the critiques of the SGP see Fischer, Jonung, and Larch (2007).

4.3. Motives for change: internal commitment vs. external anchor

In the previous chapter it was argued that when faced with an external shock, lasting adjustment can be expected only in those countries where public trust in the system is high. In low-trust countries, only technical adjustments are likely, which are bound to erode once the external pressure eases. In order to assess the motivation for change and their relation to trust, I will follow a two-step strategy. First, I try to separate the role of external factors from internal commitment to responsibility and create a typology based on these two dimensions. After classifying the EU-15 members within this framework, I will examine whether the level of institutional trust and the differences in the composition of fiscal consolidation in the four groups are in line with the predictions of the theory. This exercise will also help in selecting the two most different cases, which will be analyzed to show the process through which presence or absence of trust leads to virtuous or vicious cycles of trust, fiscal balance and growth.

Table 4.2. The motive for fiscal change: internal commitment vs. external anchor

		EMU effect	
		Yes	**No**
Change in internal commitment to responsibility	**Yes**	**1.** Belgium Spain	**2.** Finland Netherlands Ireland Sweden Denmark
	No	**3.** Greece Italy Portugal	**4.** Austria France Luxembourg Germany Great Britain

When differentiating between external and internal motives for consolidation in the EU-15, a distinction has to be made between commitment to fiscal adjustment in order to fulfill the Maastricht criteria and introduce the common currency versus commitment to fiscal responsibility due to the recognition of the harmful effects of fiscal imbalances. In the first case fiscal adjustment is only a means to an end, while in the second case it is an end in itself. It is hypothesized that if fiscal adjustment is only a means to an end, the least costly solution will be implemented, and once the end is reached, the means can be disbursed with.

Based on the dimensions of external anchor and internal commitment, four groups of countries can be identified—Table 4.2 shows the classification of the 15 countries. In the following I will introduce the four groups and provide a qualitative explanation for this ordering based primarily on the field research by Hallerberg (2004).

Group 1.
In Belgium and Spain the Maastricht criteria played an important role in creating a commitment to reduce budgetary imbalances at both the federal and regional levels. During the convergence process this commitment was institutionalized and internal rules were established to maintain fiscal responsibility. Following the introduction of the euro, fiscal balance was maintained and neither country broke the SGP rules up to the subprime crisis (Figure 4.1). In these two countries the external anchor and internal commitment together resulted in substantial improvement in fiscal balance.

Belgium was strongly affected by the oil crisis in the 1970s and governments were unable to consolidate the budget up to the 1990s—between 1978 and 1993 fiscal deficit was never below 6 percent, while the public debt reached 134 percent of the GDP by 1993.[4] The major reason for the imbalances was the fight between the Flemish and the Walloon regions, which always proved more important than balancing the budget. This situation changed with the Maastricht Treaty as all political actors were convinced that Belgium has to introduce the euro in the first round (Hallerberg 2004, 131–134). During the preparation period the High Council of Finance played a key role, which was composed of representatives of the central bank, the Central Planning Bureau, and the regions. The main task of this body was to ensure that all regions contribute to fiscal adjustment and to monitor the fulfillment of agreements (European Commission 2006b, 154).

Following the collapse of the dictatorship, Spain embarked on the process of developing a Western-type welfare state, which involved the increase of state redistribution from 20.7 percent in 1970 to 40.4 percent by 1985 (Balmaseda, Sebastian, and Tello 2002, 202). Since revenues did

---

[4] In the discussion about the four groups all data is from the European Commission (2010) unless otherwise noted.

not keep pace with the increased expenditures, fiscal deficits became regular, and public debt increased from 14.7 to 41.7 percent. As it was discussed earlier, the ERM crisis further contributed to the imbalances, thus the Maastricht criteria served as an important external anchor for the necessary consolidation. At the same time, fulfilling the Maastricht criteria was only the first step in consolidation for Spain—the budget act of 2003 prescribed balanced budget for the regions and public enterprises (IMF 2005a).

Figure 4.1. Fiscal deficit in Belgium and Spain 1995–2007 (% of GDP)

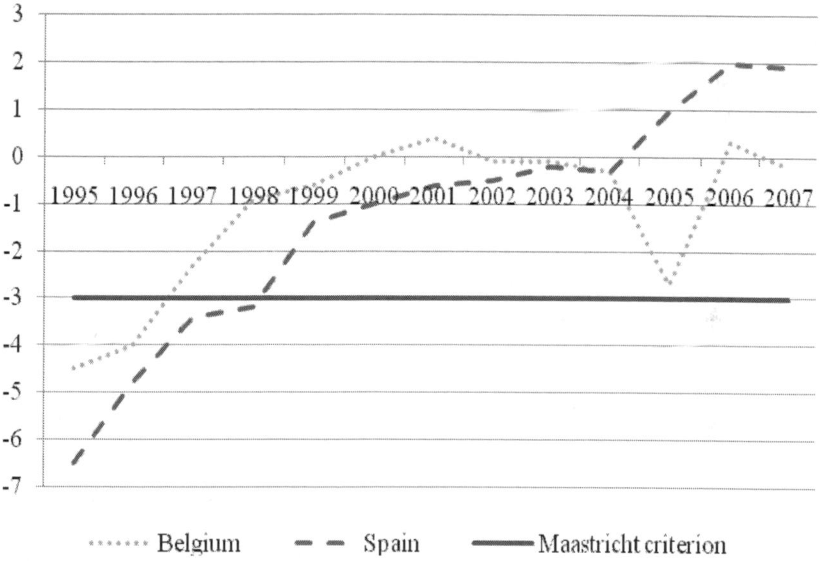

.... Belgium   – – Spain   ——— Maastricht criterion

Source: European Commission (2010): 180-181

Group 2.

The main characteristics of the countries in Group 2 (Finland, Netherlands, Ireland, Sweden, and Denmark) is that they implemented lasting fiscal consolidation based on learning from earlier policy mistakes and independently of the pressures from the Maastricht Treaty. These countries were not motivated by the Maastricht criteria and they did not need the SGP to maintain responsibility either. In these countries, voters require responsible public finances and fiscal surplus is the norm—out of the five countries only the Netherlands broke the 3 percent threshold of the SGP once in 2003 (Figure 4.2).

In Denmark the minority governments of the 1970s often had to buy interest groups in order to be able to govern. Large deficits led to growing public debt, which reached 80 percent of the GDP by 1983. The downgrades from international rating agencies induced the conservative government to embark on a program of radical expenditure cuts. This program however did not receive majority in the parliament thus the prime minister asked the consent of voters at a new election. After receiving a mandate to implement his program, he turned within 3 years a 7 percent deficit into a 3.2 percent surplus (Hallerberg 2004, 172–174). While in the early 1990s the deficits returned and increased over 3 percent, this period proved to be temporary and from the mid-1990s surpluses became the norm. Considering that the country did not want to introduce the euro, it seems evident that internal commitment to responsibility was the main driver of consolidation.

Compared to other European countries, in the 1970s and 1980s Finland conducted responsible fiscal policy, which was indicated by its very low debt level at less than 15 percent of the GDP up to 1991. However, the EMS crisis exposed the vulnerability of the budget system—within three years the public debt rose to 57 percent of the GDP. Fiscal consolidation was a shared priority of the entire society, and the parties that campaigned on the promise of harsh expenditure cuts won the 1995 elections. By 1997 there was a fiscal surplus, which was rewarded by another victory for the ruling parties. In this process, EMU accession played a secondary role—first, its rules were considered too lenient, second, policymakers wanted to avoid blaming the EU for unpopular decisions (Hallerberg 2004, 143–145).

In the Netherlands, as a result of overspending in the 1970s, public debt reached 70 percent of the GDP by 1986, while state redistribution increased from 43 percent in 1970 to close to 70 percent during this period. These processes brought about a commitment to fiscal responsibility. From 1982, fiscal consolidation was the most important theme of election campaigns and all parties promised the reduction of state expenditures. The efforts by five consecutive governments stopped the growth of debt, which started to decrease only after the implementation of reforms from 1993 (Schick 2004, 89). While the improvement coincides with the Maastricht process, the recognition and handling of the problems clearly started earlier.

Starting in the 1970s, public debt in Ireland increased to over 100 percent of the GDP by 1985, which was not only ineffective to mitigate the effects of the oil crisis, but in itself became the cause of decreasing employment and stagnant growth (Boltho 2000). By the mid-1980s, the inevitability of fiscal adjustment became clear, and in order to bring it about representatives of the state, the trade unions, and the employer association signed a comprehensive social partnership in 1987, which prepared for the rebuilding of the economy. The success of its measures is shown that while fiscal deficit averaged 11 percent in the early 1980s, since 1989 until the subprime crisis it did not reach 3 percent. Similarly to the previous cases, in Ireland recognition of the problems with fiscal imbalances came earlier than the Maastricht process, which played a negligible role in consolidation.

Figure 4.2. Fiscal deficit in Finland, Netherlands, Ireland, Sweden, Denmark 1995-2007 (% of GDP)

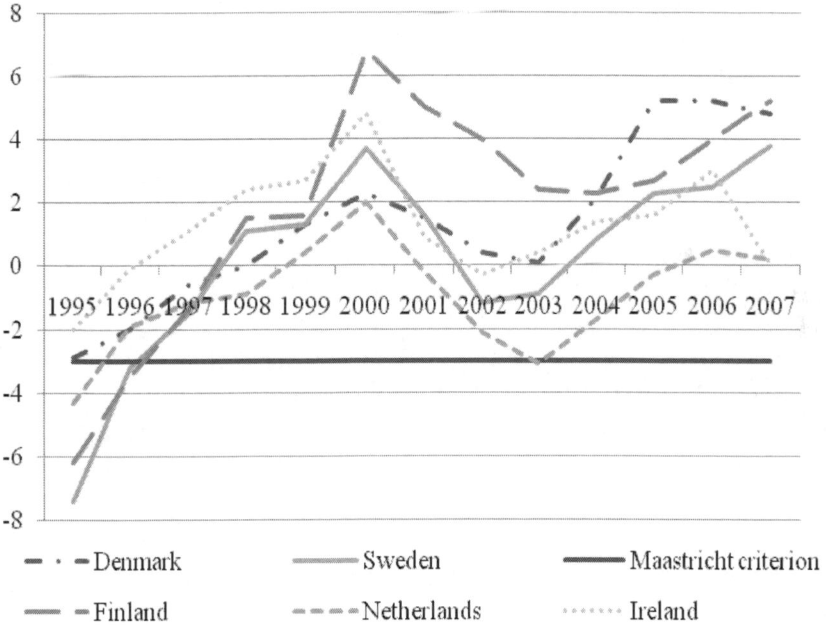

Source: European Commission (2010): 180-181

In the 1970s budgetary imbalances became characteristics in Sweden and public debt rose over 60 percent of the GDP. As it was shown earlier, the EMS crisis further exposed the vulnerability of the budget to the economic cycle as in 1993 the deficit was 11.2 percent, while the debt surpassed 70 percent of the GDP. Due to the crisis, both the government and the opposition committed themselves to stabilization and structural reforms. As a result, by the second part of the 1990s fiscal surplus became the norm. Similarly to Denmark, Sweden does not want to introduce the common currency, which makes it evident that the Maastricht process played almost no role in the consolidation.

Group 3.
The countries of Group 3 (Greece, Italy, and Portugal) share the heritage of fiscal imbalances and macroeconomic volatility. Given these traditions and their accordingly weak currency, the stability represented by the euro enjoyed considerable popularity in these societies. The attitude of the public towards the common currency gave the accession criteria an important anchor function in the fiscal consolidations of the 1990s. Here, however, fiscal consolidation was only a means to an end, thus once the external pressure eased, imbalances reemerged (Figure 4.3).

In Greece following the fall of dictatorship in the 1970s, the accommodation of various interest group demands led to the abandonment of strict fiscal policy that characterized the authoritarian regime (Kazakos 1994). During the late 1980s, fiscal deficits fluctuated around 10 percent of the GDP. This process culminated in the explosion of public debt, which grew from 17.7 to 98.3 percent of GDP between 1970 and 1993. High public debt was accompanied by stagflation and a weak currency, which made the introduction of the common currency highly popular for the majority of the population. Pressure on the political class increased further as the country was left out from the first round of the euro. Greece achieved the Maastricht deficit criterion by 1999 via strengthening the position of the finance minister and stricter tax administration—however in retrospect it is clear that creative accounting also played an important role (Hallerberg 2004, 110–112). Following the introduction of the euro, imbalances reemerged and with the subprime crisis it became clear that Greece never had a deficit below 3 percent in the past three decades.

Overspending also has a strong tradition in Italy. Fiscal deficit was over 6 percent even before the first oil crisis and it grew to 12 percent during the period of stagflation of the 1970s. Throughout the 1980s the deficit reached 10 percent of the GDP without exception. As a consequence public debt rose to 121.8 percent of the GDP by 1994, which implied debt service costs amounting to 12 percent of the GDP (Hallerberg 2004, 165). Introducing the euro with such a background seemed next to impossible—however, similar to Greece, the electorate was strongly in favor of the common currency, and it became the leading campaign promise in the 1996 election. The county eventually qualified for the euro, but after the pressure was gone, breaking the rules of the SGP was a regular event.

Figure 4.3. Fiscal deficit in Greece, Italy, Portugal 1995–2007 (% of GDP)

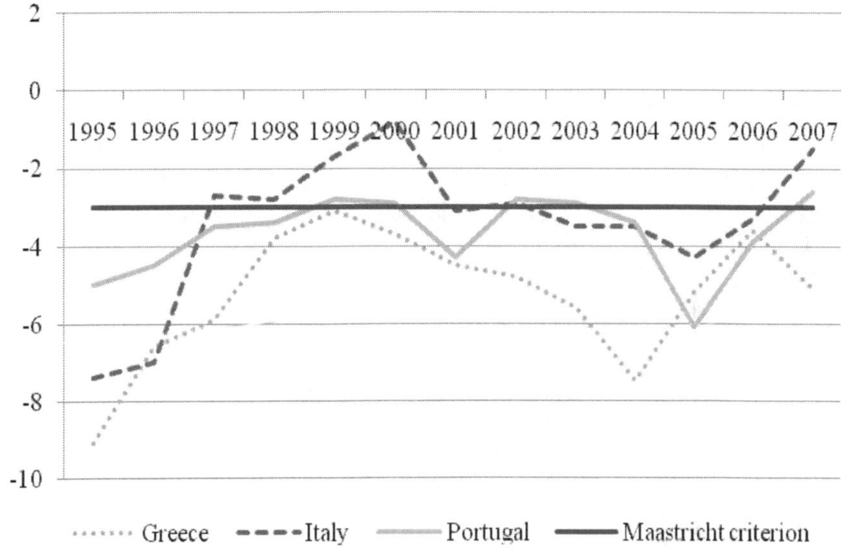

Source: European Commission (2010): 180–181

Similarly to the other two Mediterranean countries, overspending has a long tradition in Portugal. Following the fall of the dictatorship, state re-distribution increased from 29 to 40 percent of the GDP in an effort to build a modern welfare state. As revenues did not increase with the growth of expenditures, fiscal deficits were generally over 5 percent and the public debt grew from 14.5 percent to 58.3 percent between 1973 and 1985. The recession of the 1990s further worsened the problem, and in addressing the imbalances the Maastricht process proved critical. Similarly to the other two countries, the society was strongly in favor of intro-ducing the euro, and by the end of the qualification period the criteria were fulfilled—primarily through one-off measures (Hallerberg 2004, 210–211). However as in the other two countries once the external pres-sure was gone, imbalances returned, and Portugal was the first to break the SGP in 2002.

Group 4.

In the countries of Group 4 (Austria, France, Luxembourg, Germany, and UK), fiscal policy barely changed following the Maastricht Treaty. Unlike countries in the other three groups, these countries showed remarkable degree of responsibility in the 1970s and 1980s—the electorate required responsible public finances and it punished irresponsible spending. Given these internal pressures for balance, the rules of EMU were considerably less influential, especially in the three large countries: without France or Germany there would have been no euro, while the UK did not want to introduce the common currency in the first place. The rules proved to be particularly ineffective when France and Germany broke them and instead of the fines envisioned by the rules, there was a revision of the fiscal framework. At the same time it is also important to note that breaking the rules did not imply a skyrocketing deficit as in the Mediterranean countries—the worst balance during the 1998–2007 period was recorded by France in 2003 at 4.1 percent. By 2006, both France and Germany complied with the 3 percent threshold (Figure 4.4). These developments suggest that countries with a long tradition of responsibility are unwilling to accept external pressure from states who for decades have been known for their profligacy.

Figure 4.4. Fiscal deficit in Austria, France, Germany, Luxembourg, UK 1995–2007 (% of GDP)

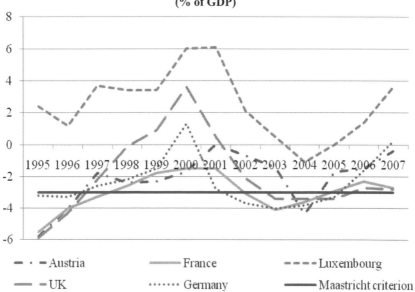

Source: European Commission (2010): 180–181

In Austria the tradition of neo-corporatism and a culture of stability very similar to Germany guaranteed a stable macroeconomic environment, including low inflation and stable exchange rates until the 1980s. However, the large rate of redistribution over 50 percent of the GDP eventually became a hindrance for growth. The low rates of growth in the first part of the 1980s showed the importance of rethinking the role of the state, and in the second part of the 1980s there was considerable fiscal adjustment and tax reform. The measures were implemented in a consensual manner as they were generally seen as inevitable for maintaining the informal exchange union with Germany (Hochreiter and Tavlas 2004, 6). There was a loosening of fiscal stance during the recession caused by the EMS crisis, but through the establishment of a grand coalition the country was able to fulfill the Maastricht requirements (Hallerberg 2004, 216). The EMU process thus played some role in decreasing the deficit below 3 percent by 1997, but unlike countries in Group 1, there was no need for a serious break with the past, as large imbalances did not characterize the country. In line with the culture of stability, fiscal responsibility remained even after the introduction of the euro and the country did not breach the requirements of the SGP—at the same time, its performance cannot be compared to that of countries in Group 1 and 2 where large surpluses could be observed.

Up to 1991 France had no problem with its fiscal performance as the deficit almost never reached 3 percent. However, due to the EMS crisis and some political struggles, fiscal balance became a problem exactly when the Maastricht criteria had to be fulfilled. Introducing the euro however was never an issue for debate, and thus from 1996 strong measures were implemented to comply with the criteria (Hallerberg 2004, 108). Following the introduction of the euro however, the country did not feel the SGP rules were binding and it regularly broke the 3 percent threshold (Clift 2006). As one of the major criticizers of the SGP, France played a key role both in weakening enforcement as well as in the loosening the rules in 2005 (Chang 2006). Following the reform however, a consolidation took place and the deficit was reduced below 3 percent by 2005.

In 1996, Luxembourg was the only EU member state that fulfilled all the Maastricht criteria. The country is characterized by a strong stability culture, which is most evident from the public debt, which has remained below 10 percent of GDP since the 1980s. Here there was no need either for a learning process or an external anchor in order to keep public finances in balance. Before and after the introduction of the euro, fiscal surplus has been the norm.

While in the United Kingdom the tradition of stability is not as strong as in Luxembourg, fiscal deficit did not increase over 5 percent even during the years of the oil crisis. The Conservative government headed by Margaret Thatcher from 1979 made further efforts to balance the budget primarily through decreasing expenditures. While this did not increase their popularity, Thatcher was reelected in 1983 in spite of the restrictive measures. The budgetary situation deteriorated during the EMS crisis (Table 1), but once the crisis passed, the figures improved. As the UK has an opt out from the common currency, it seems evident that the commitment to responsibility has internal origins—similarly to the other countries in the group, the electorate expects responsible fiscal policy from its leaders and punishes the government if it behaves irresponsibly (Hallerberg 2004, 84). At the same time a firm commitment to surplus had not emerged and the country narrowly breached the 3 percent threshold a few times. The probable reason is that public debt showed a declining trend during the 1970s and 1980s, and thus there was no need for overly strict policies up to the subprime crisis.

From the 1950s, Germany was the model of stability in Europe and the leader of the EMS system. While in most other countries, the 1970s and 80s was a time of overspending, in Germany the deficit remained below 3 percent for most of the period. This situation changed considerably with reunification as intergovernmental transfers reached over 5 percent.[5] The recession in 1993 further deteriorated the budgetary position and by 1996 it was questionable as to whether the country could fulfill the Maastricht criteria. Between 1992 and 1998, public debt grew from 42 percent to over 60 percent. Since a common currency was unimaginable without Germany, the government made serious efforts from 1996 to achieve the criteria. However, the primary drive for consolidation has been the electorate, which punishes irresponsible macroeconomic policy similarly to the UK (Hallerberg 2004, 102). This is also responsible for the fact that while the slow growth from 2001 led to a regular breach of the SGP, from 2005 governments made serious efforts to balance the budget and comply with the reformed rules.

The overview on the motivations for fiscal consolidation shows that the Maastricht convergence process was neither necessary nor sufficient condition for fiscal adjustment. It played an important role only in 5 countries, while in the other 10 countries domestic factors were decisive in the adjustment. From the overview it is also evident that lasing consolidation

---

[5] For a detailed analysis of the nature of these transfers see Sinn (2003).

was achieved primarily in those countries where a strong internal commitment rather than external pressure was the driving force of consolidation. In the next part I will show the mechanism through which this relationship prevails.

4.4. Institutional quality in the EU-15

Based on the theory above it can be expected that countries characterized by high levels of trust will not need external pressure to consolidate their public finances in a lasting manner. As discussed in the introduction, measuring institutional trust is a highly difficult and contested issue. For the purposes of this analysis the World Governance Indicators are used.

Figure 4.5. Quality of governance in the EU-15 (1996)

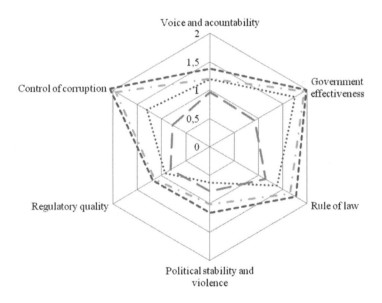

··· Group 1. (ESP, BE)   ▬ ▬ ▬ Group 2. (DEN, FIN, IRE, NL, SWE)

▬ Group 3. (EL, IT, POR)   ▬ · ▬ Group 4. (AT, FR, GER, LUX, UK)

Source: World Governance Indicators data base: http://info.worldbank.org/governance/wgi/index.asp

The various dimensions of good governance in the four groups of countries are shown on Figure 4.5. The data is from 1996, which is the date of the first survey and which lies closest to the start of the convergence period. In the figure, the various dimensions are connected and the larger the area covered the higher the quality of governance. We can see that at first approximation the data fits the proposed hypothesis rather well: those countries that consolidated due to internal commitments to responsibility (Groups 2 and 4) have much higher quality of governance than those that needed external pressure to stabilize their public finances (Groups 1 and 3). Indeed we can also observe that the ranking, which can be proposed on the basis of fiscal performance, is the same as the ranking on the basis of good governance: Group 2 > Group 4 > Group 1 > Group 3. The difference in rankings is particularly pronounced for the control of corruption and the government effectiveness indicators. These two can be viewed as the major elements of institutional trust—integrity and competence of the administration.

In the following section I will show how the particular method of consolidation serves as the causal link between institutional trust and the success of consolidation.

4.5. Approaches to fiscal consolidation

As mentioned in the previous section, the main reason for differentiating between internal and external forces in adjustment is to uncover the motivations behind the different choices of adjustment, which in turn critically affect both the sustainability of consolidation as well as growth performance.

In the sustainability of consolidation, the composition of adjustment has a critical role. As discussed in detail in the previous chapter, given their effects on expectations and employment, expenditure cuts are more likely to be lasting than consolidations, which focus on raising revenues.

Due to the political costs of decreasing expenditures, it might be hypothesized that those countries that only aim at fulfilling the Maastricht criteria are likely to choose the less politically costly tax raises. While from the perspective of sustainability and growth these are inferior to an expenditure-based adjustment, they might be sufficient to achieve the objective of EMU accession. Structural reforms and expenditure-based adjustment are most likely in those countries where there is an internal commitment to lasting fiscal responsibility. Analyzing this hypothesis is particularly interesting following the introduction of the euro, since the external pressure from the SGP is considerably weaker than the Maastricht convergence criteria.

Figure 4.6. Change in primary expenditures* in the EU-15 1992–2007 (% of GDP)

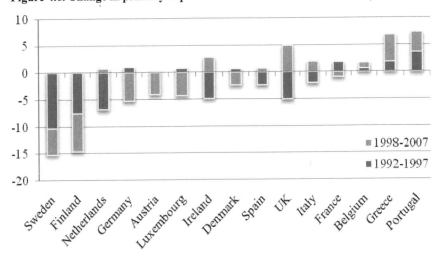

* Primary expenditures: total expenditures–debt service costs.
Note: Data for Sweden is available from 1993, while for Spain from 1995.
Data: European Commission (2010): 160–161, 178–179

Figure 4.6 provides some support for the above hypothesis. It shows the development in primary expenditures between 1992 and 2007 with a break in 1997—the end of the qualification period for the euro. Looking at primary expenditures instead of total expenditures is useful because this indicator does not include the change in debt service costs, which significantly decreased during this period for all countries due to positive expectations of the common currency. When examining political commitment to consolidation, however, it is more useful to analyze costs, which are under the direct control of politicians. As we can see in Figure 4.6, between 1992 and 1997 primary expenditures decreased in 8 out of the 15 countries. With the exception of Spain and Italy, these countries are cases of internal commitment where consolidation was independent of the EMU process. In two out of the three countries of Group 3 (Greece and Portugal) expenditures rose even during this period, while following the introduction of the euro, all countries in this group raised primary expenditures. This implies a lack of commitment to resist spending pressures especially after the external pressure passed. Indeed, cuts in expenditures following the accession to the euro-zone took place only in Group 2 and 4, where internal commitment to balance characterizes fiscal policy.

Figure 4.7. Social benefits other than social transfers in kind in the EU-15 1992-2007 (% of GDP)

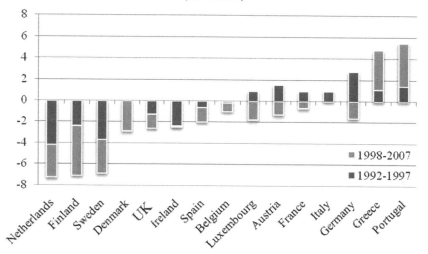

Note: Data for Sweden is available from 1993, while for Spain from 1995.
Data: European Commission (2010): 156-157

Figure 4.8. Change in total revenue in the EU-15 1992–2007 (% of GDP)

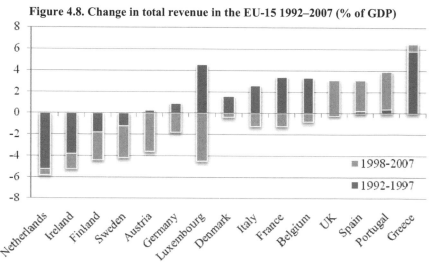

Note: Data for Sweden is available from 1993, while for Spain from 1995.
Data: European Commission (2010): 172–173

While the detailed examination of the composition of expenditures is beyond the scope of this chapter, in order to illustrate the importance of political economy considerations it is useful to examine the most politically sensitive items: monetary transfer to households. These include social security benefits in cash such as retirement pensions, disability pensions and maternity support. In these areas savings are possible only through structural reforms, so changes here can be considered as an important indicator on the willingness to reforms. In Figure 4.7, it can be seen that in line with the hypothesis, countries in Group 2 implemented the largest cuts as the five countries can be found in the first six positions. Although transfers decreased in countries of Group 1 as well, the reduction is considerably less than in Group 2. In accordance with the theory, in Group 3 these expenditures actually increased, which is particularly significant in the case of Portugal. In three countries of Group 4 (Austria, Luxembourg, and France) change in these expenditures is insignificant, while Germany and Great Britain implemented cuts following the convergence period, which signals the dominance of internal factors in the process.

As discussed above, in countries where expenditure cuts cannot be implemented, consolidation takes place on the revenue side. As it can be seen from Figure 4.8, in the five countries where the EMU process was decisive in the consolidation, revenue increases were implemented with the exception of Portugal during the period 1992–1997. It is also an important lesson from the figure that significant tax cuts were possible only in those countries in Groups 2 and 4, which significantly decreased their expenditure as well (Sweden, Ireland, Netherlands, Finland, Austria, Germany, and Denmark).

Figure 4.9 summarizes the sources of consolidation and ranks countries according to the improvement in fiscal balance between 1992 and 2007. The best performance was recorded by Sweden and Finland, which were most hit by the EMS crisis—and also had high levels of initial state redistribution. Countries in Groups 1 and 3 recorded considerable improvement as well—however, from the figure it is evident that with the exception of Spain, the source of this improvement on the expenditure side was primarily the sharp decline in debt service costs, which reflects the convergence in interest rates due to positive expectations of the common currency. This fact supports not only the hypothesis on the importance of motive behind consolidations, but also underlines the rationality of introducing the euro in these countries. Finally, in line with the hypothesis, change in balance in Group 4 was minimal—they faced very little change in their debt service, while the change in expenditure was generally followed by a decrease on the revenue side.

Figure 4.9. Sources of fiscal consolidation in the EU-15 1992–2007 (% of GDP)

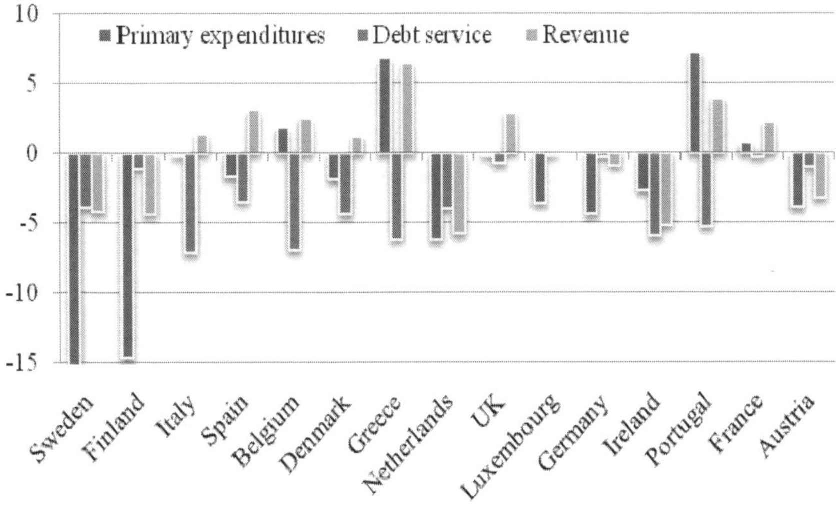

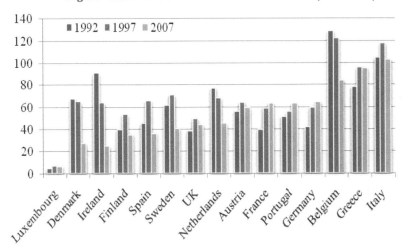

Data: European Commission (2010): see Figures 6 and 8.

Figure 4.10. Public debt in the EU-15 1992–2007 (% of GDP)

Data: European Commission (2010): 184–185

The difference between the various consolidation strategies can be observed in the evolution of public debt. Looking at Figures 4.9 and 4.10 together suggests that the public debt could decrease substantially primarily in those countries (Denmark, Ireland, Finland, Spain, Sweden, and Netherlands) where the decline in interest expenditures was accompanied by cuts or at least a lack of increase in primary expenditures. At the same time in Group 3 the high debt level barely changed—in Portugal it even increased. In Group 4, little change could be observed in the level of debt, which supports the claim that there was little change in the attitude towards fiscal balance either from internal origins or in relation to the EMU.

Table 4.3. Average change in selected indicators by country groups 1992–2007
(% of GDP)

	GROUP 1	GROUP 2	GROUP 3	GROUP 4
Primary expenditures	0.05	-8.16	4.6	-2.28
Social transfers other than in kind	-1.5	-5.34	3.77	-0.38
Total revenues	2.8	-3.68	3.93	0.18
Debt service	-5.25	-3.88	-6.23	-0.52
Debt	-27.1	-33.04	9.2	11.66

Note: Data for Sweden is available from 1993; data for Spain is available from 1995.
Source: European Commission (2010): 156–157, 160–161, 172–173, 178–179, 184–185

Table 4.3 summarizes the consolidation strategies by groups. Overall it can be concluded that the three countries in Group 3 which consolidated their public finances solely out of an intention to introduce the euro gained most on interest rate expenditures, while increasing revenues was the second major source of adjustment. In contrast, countries in Group 2 considerably decreased their primary expenditures, while the savings on interest expenditures were used to decrease revenue. The two countries in Group 1 fall in between—there was considerable savings on interest expenditure and a decline in primary expenditures, which were accompanied by an increase in revenues as well. Improvement in fiscal balance thus came from three sources—it is unsurprising that both countries could significantly reduce their debt level. Finally, countries in Group 4 show slight changes in most indicators in line with the qualitative assessment—however this translated even before the subprime crisis into a steady increase of public debt.

In this section I provided an overview of the reasons behind the different fiscal performances in the four groups, which was discussed in the previous part. In the following, I will underline the importance of internal commitment and discuss the internal sources of a difference in commitment though the contrasting cases of Sweden and Portugal, which are representatives of the two most different groups—and represent the two poles in the change in primary expenditures. Their cases also serve as illustrations about the consequences for economic growth for different paths of adjustment.

4.6. Virtuous and vicious cycles at work: Sweden vs. Portugal

Sweden and Portugal are the two most different cases from the perspective of fiscal consolidation, and given the different level of public trust in their institutional framework, they can be considered as illustrative examples for the theory from the previous chapter. The comparison of their experiences is particularly interesting once we consider that on the basis of its lower level of development, Portugal could be expected to grow faster and show convergence with Sweden.

In the following I will discuss the different level of public trust in the institutional framework then give a short summary of their economic performance in the past two decades. Finally, through comparing their experiences I will address the question how the level of trust affected fiscal policymaking.

4.6.1. Institutional conditions

As discussed in the previous chapter a key factor in the establishment of virtuous and vicious cycles of growth is the presence of public trust in the system, which is critical in whether institutions are able to reduce uncertainty of the environment or contribute to it. In Chapter 2 we have also seen that there is no mono-causal explanation of institutional trust; several factors contribute to its presence or absence. While in the previous section I relied on the World Governance Indicators to approximate trust given their potential for comparison, in the case studies it is possible to provide a broader picture of the institutional environment. In the following, I will concentrate on four factors which have a clear impact on institutional trust, and which provide support for the cliché that Sweden can be considered a high-trust society, while Portugal is a low-trust country.

Historical background: The current Swedish system has its origins in the 1930s when in response to the depression of the 1920s the Social-Democratic government aimed to build a regime, which can combine full employment and income security. At the heart of the solution was an economy working at close to boom levels through maintaining macroeconomic stability and competitiveness (Lundberg 1985). In order to fulfill the egalitarian aspirations of the population, a universal welfare state was built and financed through high taxes on income and wealth. While the model seemed to fall into crises by the 1970s, essential features of the welfare state, including universal provision of health care and education as well as generous income replacement for the inactive population, remained intact. Having the tradition of a welfare state greatly increases public trust in the system (Rothstein 1998).[6]

Portugal was a conservative dictatorship between 1933 and 1974 with a motto of "Deus, Pátria e Familia" emphasizing social order and economic growth. While the regime reached several of its objectives, including high rates of growth, it fell after the loss of its colonial empire, as a military coup took place in 1974. In the following two years a turbulent period saw political purges and nationalizations. Eventually neither extreme prevailed, and the country began the path toward European integration. However, some of the legacies survive—Cuhna, Clegg, and Arménio (2008, 4) emphasize the "culture of fear" as a result of decades of the secret service spying on people, while others point to the neglect of education—the over 30 percent illiteracy rate in the 1970s was barely erased by 2000s (Magone 2004, 87). Neither factor is conducive to public trust in the system.

Public administration: Sweden has a tradition of independent offices and small core ministries with a depoliticized civil service, ensuring efficient provision of public services. According to Blondal (2001, 43), "the separation of policy and operational functions into ministries and agencies has been a hallmark of Swedish Government organization for over 200 years." In contrast, Portugal has a highly centralized system with poorly educated bureaucrats (Magone 2004, 114–115), where administrative posts are generally rewards for supporters of parties—as parties lack strong roots in society, state resources are critical in their fight for power (Jalali and Lisi 2009). These differences translate into different administrative cultures. According to Cuhna, Clegg, and Arménio (2008, 23), "more than 4000 articles regulate the Portuguese state administrative

---

[6] It should be also noted however, that the line of causality is far from evident: as Bergh and Bjorskov (2011) claim, high level of trust is conducive to large redistribution.

workforce. In Sweden, 42 articles serve the same purpose. The Portuguese rules are presented in two thick volumes with more than 1500 pages each; in Sweden the 42 articles appear in 4 A5 pages."

Corruption: In line with the public administration traditions, Sweden regularly ranks among the least corrupt countries in the world, while Portugal is generally below 30th in recent surveys according to Transparency International.[7]

Inequality and poverty: As a result of the generous welfare state, inequality in Sweden, as measured by the Gini coefficient,[8] is the second lowest among advanced economies at 0.234, while Portugal has one of the most unequal societies in the OECD with a score of 0.385. The result comes from a sharp educational divide in Portugal, which was discussed above. The same factors are responsible for poverty rates—measured as 50 percent of the median income, Sweden's poverty rate has fluctuated around 4 percent since the 1970s, while in Portugal this ratio is 14 percent (OECD 2009).

Although the above factors are necessarily selective, they can help establish the proposition that the Swedish environment is considerably more conducive to trust than the Portuguese. In the following I will discuss economic developments in the past two decades then analyze how social conditions affected these processes.

4.6.2. Fiscal policy and growth following the EMS crisis

As for most countries in the EU-15, the EMS crisis represented an external shock for both Sweden and Portugal, implying the possibility for change in fiscal policy. While the shock for Sweden was considerably more serious than for Portugal (Table 4.1), the responses to the crisis still illustrate the important differences in the quality of economic policymaking in a high- and in a low-trust country.

Sweden
The EMS crisis hit Sweden particularly hard due to a credit boom that developed following the deregulation of the financial sector in the 1980s.[9] The expansion of credit led to an asset boom, rising inflation

---

[7] For the findings of annual surveys see the website of the organization: http://www.transparency.org.

[8] The Gini coefficient is a measure of the inequality of a distribution, a value of 0 expressing total equality and a value of 1 maximal inequality.

[9] The following overview of Swedish economic policy following the crisis draws considerably on my earlier works: Győrffy (2007) and Győrffy (2008).

implying an overvalued currency, and a loss of competitiveness.[10] These problems could be fought neither by income policy, given the collapse of centralized wage bargaining in the 1990s (Swank 2001, 136), nor by devaluation since Sweden joined the EMS in 1987. This situation made Sweden vulnerable to external shocks.

When the international economy entered into a recession in 1990, the declining competitiveness of Swedish products meant a sharp decline of export revenue and consequently employment. This triggered speculations about a forthcoming devaluation, which was initially resisted by the Riksbank through a sharp rise in interest rates. This only deepened the crisis as savings increased and consumption collapsed. The situation was exacerbated by an ill-timed withdrawal of housing subsidies, which led to the collapse of asset prices followed by collapse in demand, which strongly affected the banking sector. The overall result was the worst economic crisis since the 1930s as GDP fell by 6 percent between 1991 and 1993, unemployment rose to 9 percent, and the deficit approached 12 percent of GDP in 1993 (Table 4.1).

The first step to resolve the crisis was allowing the krona to float on November 1992. The resulting sharp devaluation halted the crisis and improved the competitiveness of the economy. The next step was the rescue of the banking system. For this purpose the government implemented a three-pillar strategy: it guaranteed all liabilities of all banks; established an independent institution to administer the guarantees and took over the bad loans (Svensson, Mabuchi, and Kamiwaka 2006, 48). The strategy was successful: in comparison to other countries, the costs of rescue were considerably smaller and recovery faster (Drees and Pazarbasioglu 1998, 35).

The halting of the financial crisis marked the start of economic reforms, which aimed at stabilizing public finances in a lasting manner. At the time of the EMS crisis, Swedish economists saw the disincentives associated with the welfare state as the major source of the crisis. In his comprehensive assessment of the Swedish welfare state, Lindbeck (1997, 1295–1300) points to three major channels that undermined competitiveness of the economy. First, squeezing profits and high taxation gave little incentive to private savings, which greatly hindered the development of small- and medium-size enterprises. This contributed to a highly concentrated market structure, where entry of new firms was limited, resulting in low levels of competition. Second, the declining wage differentials during

---

[10] In the following brief overview of the Swedish crisis I will rely on Drees and Pazarbasioglu (1998), and Cerra and Saxena (2005).

the 1970s reduced the economic incentives to acquire skills, contributing to the declining enrollment into higher education. Third, given the large income replacement ratios, moral hazard problems were clearly present in the case of sick benefits, unemployment insurance, and early retirement. Together with high tax rates the generous transfer system meant a serious disincentive to work.

Following the crisis, there was no dismantling of the welfare state, and tax rates remained among the highest in the world (IMF 2001, 5). At the same time, a gradual move toward lower taxes and lower spending started, which were shown in the previous section. In response to the EMS crisis, cuts in spending came primarily from the reduction of the income re-placement ratio, the introduction of waiting days for sickness and unem-ployment benefits, as well as short-term measures such as the freezing child benefit allowances and pensions. Besides expenditure cuts there were also important structural reforms in order to ensure long-term sus-tainability. The most important was the 1998 pension reform, which aimed at improving the link between benefits and contributions through introducing notional personal accounts including individually managed investment accounts. Through changing the calculation of benefits, the new arrangement strongly contributed to financial sustainability.[11] A simi-larly important reform was the complete redesign of the institutions regu-lating budgetary decision making.

The main problems of the old system were the bottom-up approach dur-ing the planning and adoption phases, a relative neglect of transparency, as well as inadequate attention to long-term developments, which allowed the dominance of interest groups during the budgetary decision-making proc-ess.[12] The solution to these problems was a combination of numerical and procedural rules, which strengthened the decision-making framework during all phases. To facilitate continued debt reduction, the government commit-ted itself to a budget surplus amounting to 2 percent of the GDP over the cycle. This rule was complemented by ceilings for the individual budgetary items including all central government expenditures, local government grants, as well as pensions for the next three years. Compliance with the objectives of this legally binding multi-year fiscal framework was to be strictly monitored. In the planning and adoption phases, a strong top-down framework was implemented, implying that the aggregates of the budget are decided first and detailed appropriations afterwards. This method gives

---

[11] For a detailed overview of the Swedish pension system see IMF (1998), 58–61.
[12] The following overview relies on Molander (2000).

a strong position to the Ministry of Finance, which is responsible for aggregate spending. The transparency of the budget also improved considerably making informed decision making easier.

The overall outcome was even better than the ambitious targets envisaged in the original program. The improvement in government finances during the period between 1994 and 1998 was 11 percentage points of the GDP—1.5 percentage points higher than planned—which was mainly due to the lower-than-expected interest payments. This showed the overall credibility of the adjustment: believing the government's resolve to cut deficits, investors assigned lower and lower risk premium for Swedish debt, which in turn improved performance further and reinforced positive expectations. The achievements of the package proved to be sustainable: in spite of its large level of redistribution Sweden has a regular surplus in its budget and succeeded in cutting its debt considerably (Figures 4.2 and 4.10). The country is among the most competitive economies in the world[13] while it was able to preserve the universality of its welfare provisions. As can be seen on Figure 4.11, with the exception of 2001 Sweden considerably surpassed EU-15 averages between 1998 and 2007. Its performance contrasts strongly with that of Portugal during this period.

Figure 4.11. Growth rates in Portugal, Sweden and the EU-15 1995–2007

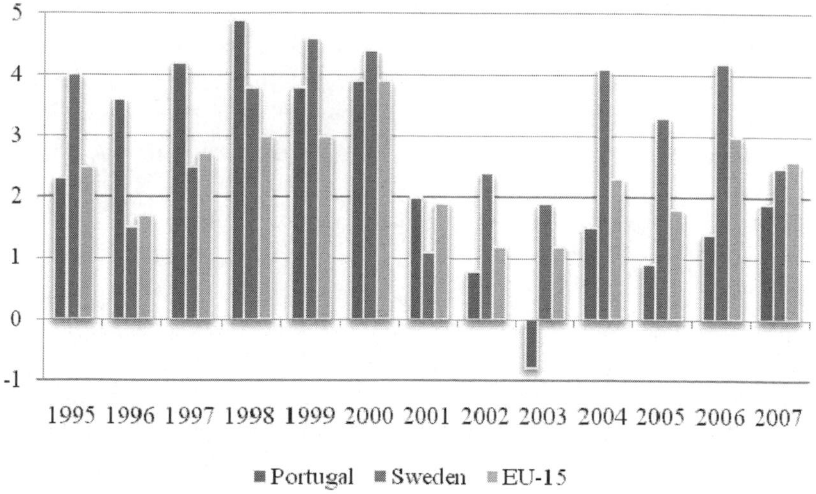

■ Portugal   ■ Sweden   ■ EU-15

Data: European Commission (2010): 48-49

---

[13] See the annual surveys of the World Economic Forum at http://www.weforum.org.

Portugal

Portugal joined the European Union in 1986 and started on a path of dynamic growth—between 1986 and 1991 it registered growth rates over 4 percent, well above the EU average. In 1989, the country abandoned its crawling peg policy and joined the EMS. However, similarly to Sweden, the booming economy resulted in very low unemployment, which put an upward pressure on wages particularly in the public sector. This led to the real appreciation of the currency and the subsequent loss of competitiveness (Macedo 2003, 173). As the EMS crisis developed, and Spain devalued the peso, Portugal was also forced to devalue in November 1992 by 6 percent. This was followed by two more devaluations: 6.5 percent in March 1993 and 3.5 percent in May 1995 (Constancio 2005, 208).

The devaluations of the escudo did not lead to a loss of credibility as the government was firmly committed to introducing the common currency. Capital inflow into Portugal surged, especially after capital controls were finally removed in line with the EU single market directives (Macedo 2003, 180). Increased policy credibility had two effects. First, as discussed in the previous part, given the sharp decrease in interest expenditures, there was little incentive to implement structural reforms. Second, the inflow of capital led to a growing indebtedness of companies and households, which took advantage of the sharp fall in interest rates (Constancio 2005, 208). The two developments together were responsible for the fact that following the introduction of the euro the period of high growth ended, and after a mild recession, growth rate was around 1 percent in the past decade (Figure 4.11). As a result, real convergence in Portugal did not materialize and the country has been stagnating at around 78 percent of the EU average.

By 2000, the presence of a credit boom became evident. A large part of the resources went into the real estate sector and financed consumption (IMF 2000b, 25–27). First it generated considerable growth and a reduction in unemployment, which went from 7.2 percent in 1996 to 4 percent in 2000 (European Commission 2010, 34). The reduction in unemployment went with the above-productivity increase of wages, which led to reduced competitiveness. This was reflected in the worsening current account, which averaged 7.4 percent between 1996 and 2000 then 8.6 percent between 2001 and 2005 (European Commission 2010, 198).

Reduction of competitiveness became particularly serious when following the breaking of the technology bubble and the 2001 terrorist attacks a recession took place in the world economy resulting in a reduction in demand for Portuguese exports. The fall in export demand was not compensated by domestic demand for two reasons: first, the indebtedness of households could not be increased further; second, as fiscal deficit breached the SGP limit, Portugal was forced to implement fiscal consolidation during the recession. The result of the recession was low growth for a decade. While growth accelerated somewhat in 2006 and 2007, it did not reach 2 percent, and as the analysis of the IMF (2007b, 5) shows, the reason for this acceleration was not due to structural changes but rather to an acceleration of demand in Portugal's main export partners. The subprime crisis stopped even this process and Portugal fell into recession in 2009. As servicing of its high level of debt became increasingly difficult given the fragility of international markets, the country was eventually forced to ask for a bailout package.

The quality of fiscal policy had a strong role in the lack of capacity to adjust. Its role was especially important as devaluation was not available to restore competitiveness as in the early 1990s. Under these conditions adaptation can occur in two ways: cutting wages or increasing productivity. Fiscal policy affects both channels.

In the euro-zone, given low inflation, cutting wages needs to involve a reduction in nominal wages, which faces particularly strong opposition on the part of employees. As Blanchard (2007, 7–8) emphasizes, these considerations are especially important in Portugal, where besides strict employment protection laws, regulations also exist against unjustified wage cuts. While this concerns regulatory policy, fiscal policy also plays a role in wage rigidity. The most important channel is the rise of public sector wages, which started after the revolution in the 1970s and slowed only after 2000.[14] This is particularly problematic given the low quality public administration in Portugal. As mentioned earlier, employment in the public sector is driven primarily by the objective to reward party supporters (Magone 2004, 110). As a consequence administrative reforms are resisted, while most civil servants have low qualifications, with the majority having secondary education or lower (Magone 2004, 118). While poor quality public administration is a serious problem in itself, the relatively high wages in the public sector are also problematic from the perspective of wage cuts, as the private and public sector share the same labor pool.

Fiscal policy contributes even more to the difficulties in raising productivity. In Portugal, productivity has been steadily declining since the

---

[14] Compensation of employees in the public sector rose from 9.2 percent of the GDP in 1977 to 14.7 percent by 2002, which was then the highest in the euro-zone (European Commission 2010, 152).

1990s—by 2004 it was only 55% of the average in the euro-zone. The direct reason for this performance is the slowness of structural change in the economy—in comparison to Ireland but also to several Central East European countries (CEEC) advanced sectors using ICT have a small share in the economy, while the traditional industries including textiles and shoes have declined mostly in connection with competition from Asia (Barry, Crespo, and Fontura 2004). The deeper reasons for this problem lie in poor physical and human capital. While in this aspect there are other reasons than fiscal policy, according to IMF (2006) about two thirds of the lag could be affected by public policy measures.

The major part of the problem is the lack of capital investment, which is affected by almost all dimensions of fiscal policy quality. The most important issue is naturally the problem of uncertainty and the possibility for economic calculation. As it has been shown, fiscal deficit in Portugal is persistent and implies a steadily increasing debt stock. Even if the tax burden is not extraordinary, the weak performance in the dimensions of simplicity and stability contribute to low investments (IMF 2007b, 17). However the poor productivity performance has deeper causes.

One of the most important determinants of investments, especially in the high-tech sectors, is the quality of human capital, which is a function of the quality of education and by investments into R&D. Portugal performs worse than the advanced OECD countries in both aspects and worse than CEE countries—the latter is particularly damaging as spending levels are about the same (Barry, Crespo, and Fontura 2004). In the EU-15 Portugal is the only country to spend less than 1% of its GDP on R&D, while only Greece performs worse in the PISA tests (IMF 2006, 20). These factors illustrate the importance of the structure and efficiency of public spending.

However as Blanchard (2007, 14–15) argues, the solution for the problem of low productivity probably does not lie in increasing R&D spending. First, he emphasizes that easing employment protection laws would make possible the adaptation to seasonality, for example in tourism. Second, he points to the large share of the informal economy as the most important reason for low productivity. The problem with the informal economy is that it hinders the working of the market forces and allows low-productivity firms to survive. This in turn makes it difficult for companies working legally to increase their market share, and thus firm sizes are far from optimal, which is particularly problematic in the construction sector for example. A further problem with tax avoidance is that it makes labor cheaper than investment, which is a further factor in low productivity.

As it was discussed in the previous chapters, tax avoidance and the subsequent share of the informal economy is strongly related to the quality of public finances and trust—overregulation and the accompanying corruption both weaken the incentive to obey the rules and thus strengthen the informal economy. The poor quality public services are also expensive, as shown by high governmental wages, which in turn necessitate high taxation relative to service quality, a further factor in low investments.

Overall, the Portuguese economy illustrates the costs of avoiding structural reforms. While the lack of change in the early 1990s prevented neither accession to the euro-zone, nor a temporary upsurge of growth based on the capital inflows due to the credibility boost, after the credit boom ended, the problems clearly came to the fore. The country entered onto a path where low growth makes it difficult both to keep the budget in balance as well as earn the trust of the public on the implementation of structural reforms.[15] In the following section, through comparing the experiences of Sweden and Portugal, I will examine the role of trust more closely in their different performances.

4.6.3. The political economy of fiscal reforms

In order to see how trust affects fiscal reforms, it is useful to consider the effect of external factors, including the role of crisis in the reforms as well as the effect of the EMU. These considerations also help to understand why countries with an internal commitment to fiscal balance fared considerably better than those that relied solely on an external anchor.

Global factors: Both Sweden and Portugal experienced the EMS crisis as well as faced the decline of external demand after 2001. The option of devaluation was open to both countries in 1992. However, while for Sweden devaluation was only a first step to deeper changes in public finances, Portugal did not take advantage of the opportunity provided by the crisis and the Maastricht convergence process. The consequences were shown after 2000—while Sweden was also affected by the global downturn, it returned to a high-growth path by 2003, while Portugal was trapped on a low-growth path. Although at this time Portugal as a euro-zone member did not have the opportunity to devalue, while Sweden had its own currency, this could have given Portugal a strong incentive for structural change,

---

[15] This is also the conclusion on the difficulties of reforms by Macedo (2003), the former Portuguese Minister of Finance.

which did not take place. This supports the argument that an external crisis represents only an opportunity for change rather than a necessity.[16]

EMU: While Sweden ended up not introducing the euro, at the time of the EMS crisis the question was undecided, and the dominant opinion was to keep the option open (Hallerberg 2004, 167). However it still could not play an important role in the changes, because the skepticism towards the EU would have made such references counterproductive.[17] The EMU's lack of effect on fiscal reforms could also be observed in the campaign discourses prior to the referendum on the euro in 2003, when both the "Yes" and the "No" campaigns emphasized problems of the non-compliance with the SGP (Lindahl and Naurin 2005, 71–75). In contrast, for Portugal the accession to the euro-zone implied such a boost for credibility that—as discussed earlier—the country had no need for fiscal consolidation and taking unpopular measures. As Macedo (2003, 184) puts it, "Portugal has become a victim of the euro hold-up." The experiences of the two countries allow a conclusion about the effect of the EMU similar to the role of crisis—its influence strongly depends on internal factors. While in the case of Sweden it was irrelevant, for Portugal it actually led to the postponement of necessary changes.

Internal factors: As shown above, the influence of international pressures strongly depend on domestic factors. In this aspect the institutional conditions that were discussed earlier are critical.

In Sweden the institutional conditions are supportive to a tradition of consensus, which allows decision making with a long-term view of the common good. As the crisis erupted, the center-right government invited the Social Democratic opposition to agree on the necessary expenditure cuts. The Social Democrats accepted these cuts under the condition that the major features of the welfare state would remain intact (Kato and Rothstein 2006, 85). They also played a role in the resolution of the banking crisis and participated in the governmental board responsible for the rescue operation (Svensson, Mabuchi, and Kamikawa 2006, 49).

The tradition of consensus also allowed experts to play a significant role in designing the reform measures and implementing international best

---

[16] This finding relates to the argument by Rodrik (1996, 27), who pointed out that crisis-based explanations of reforms are problematic as they are both tautological and non-falsifiable: if the economy in crisis is not reformed, then the explanation that the crisis has not been severe enough is rather unsatisfying (27).

[17] The skepticism towards the EU can be followed in the Eurobarometer surveys, which show that less than 40 percent of the population thinks EU accession as a good thing. See: http://ec.europa.eu/public_opinion/index_en.htm.

practices. The first paper, which established a relationship between the strength of budgetary rules and fiscal outcomes, was published in 1992 by Jürgen Von Hagen. The same year, Per Molander, head of the research department in the Swedish Ministry of Finance, undertook an examination of the Swedish budgetary framework based on the research of Von Hagen. His report showed that Sweden's budget framework ranked between Greece and Italy, which were the weakest in the European Union. This finding was very important in ensuring support for modifying the fiscal framework (Hallerberg 2004, 160–167).

The eventual success of the reforms made them self-reinforcing—as growth rates were high and satisfaction with the system increased[18] there was no need to win elections through short-term populist promises, which could have eroded the fiscal balance.[19] Thus a virtuous cycle could be observed between trust, fiscal reforms, and growth.

The situation was very different in Portugal. As it has been discussed, the EMU contributed to the missed opportunities for reforms. Internal factors were critical in this outcome. According to Magone (2004, 110), "all reform attempts tended to end in failure due to the vicious cycle of neopatrimonial behavior inherent in politics and public administration." This allowed the dominance of vested interests in fiscal policymaking, which was particularly evident in the case of tax reforms aimed at broadening the tax base (Macedo 2003, 186–191). The resistance to change can be also observed in budgetary procedures—in contrast to Sweden, and most other EU countries, budgetary procedures weakened between 1994 and 2003 (Fabrizio and Moody 2009, 46).

The low rate of growth eventually led to public disillusionment, and satisfaction with the system steadily decreased between 1990 and 2001.[20] As discussed in the previous chapter, in such an environment elections can be won by short-term material benefits, which give rise to political business cycles. This hypothesis is supported by empirical analyses: looking at employment in municipalities, Coelho, Veiga, and Veiga (2006) find

---

[18] According to Eurobarometer surveys between 1995 and 2004 the share of population which is either 'very satisfied' or 'fairy satisfied' with the regime increased from 54 percent to 74 percent. See: http://ec.europa.eu/public_opinion/index_en.htm.

[19] Since the reforms, elections took place in 1998, 2002, and 2006. While there was a worsening of fiscal balance in 2002 during the economic downturn, in 1998 and 2006 the improvement in fiscal balance was uninterrupted (see Figure 3).

[20] According to Eurobarometer surveys, between 1990 and 2001 the share of population which is either 'very satisfied' or 'fairy satisfied' with the regime decreased from 71 percent to 37 percent.

strong evidence in favor. Similar results are obtained by Veiga and Pinho (2007) through examining intergovernmental grants. In sum, Portugal is a good illustration of the case of a vicious cycle between distrust, fiscal imbalances, and low growth.

* * *

The major objective of this chapter was to present the first part of the empirical analysis on the presence of virtuous and vicious cycles between trust, fiscal policy, and growth. Through focusing on the experiences with the European fiscal framework in the EU-15, a typology has been developed to emphasize the difference between external and internal factors in fiscal reforms. It was found that while external pressures might lead to fiscal consolidation, without an internal commitment to responsibility these changes are likely to remain temporary. The reason for this is that the less painful methods of adjustment are also less sustainable. It was also shown that in line with the hypotheses, internal commitment was formed in countries with high quality institutions. The polar cases of Sweden and Portugal provided an illustration about how the presence or absence of public trust in the institutional environment influences commitment to responsibility and the choice of adjustment method. Their experiences offer support for the theory of virtuous and vicious cycles of development.

The case of Portugal illustrates how the postponement of reforms leads to low growth and results in public dissatisfaction from the system, which in turn makes reforms even more difficult. Once such a vicious cycle develops, the question of how to break it is naturally raised. In providing an answer, the experiences of the post-communist EU member states (CEE-10) are particularly illustrative, as distrust is a lasting heritage of the previous regime. The success of some of these countries to introduce the common currency can offer important lessons about breaking a vicious cycle. This will be the subject of the next chapter.

CHAPTER 5

The Maastricht Process
in the CEE-10

Post-communist Europe is an excellent place to study the effects of distrust on economic policymaking. In this part of the world decades of communism and a painful transition process bred considerable disillusionment from the political system. Still, following the transition the region achieved considerable results in terms of convergence, which implies that the consequences of distrust on economic policy can be mitigated under certain conditions. The major objective of this chapter is to unveil these conditions and look at how a vicious cycle of low trust, populist economic policies, and low growth can be avoided or if present, how a country can break out of it.

In order to answer the above question, this chapter looks into the experiences of the 10 new post-communist member states of the EU (CEE-10). Similarly to the previous chapter, first the role of external factors, primarily the accession to the EMU, will be examined. Noting the divergent influence it has had on domestic economic policies, the contrasting experiences of Hungary and Slovakia will be analyzed more in depth in order to discover the domestic factors that condition the influence of external forces. The major argument of the chapter is that breaking out from a vicious cycle is far from being assured even within the EU, and the combination of several domestic factors are necessary for external forces to have a positive influence. In this process, human agency—most importantly the beliefs of reformers as well as their relationship within the elite—have a critical role.

The chapter proceeds as follows. In the next section, the sources of distrust in the region will be examined, including the legacy of the communist regime and the transition. Then I will discuss the external forces that facilitated convergence in the region in spite of these legacies. In the third section, I will classify the countries in the region into three groups based on their exchange rate arrangement, then provide a brief overview of their performance with regard to EMU accession. A deeper examination of the influence of distrust on their economic policy will follow. Finally, I will turn to the cases of Hungary and Slovakia and provide an answer to the original question of the chapter.

5.1. An environment of distrust

In the Central European region, decades of communism and disillusionment from the transition resulted in an environment characterized by widespread distrust of the state. The two major factors, which contributed to this outcome, are the lack of respect for the rule of law and the paternalistic concept of the state.

5.1.1. Paternalism and rule of law under communism

In a general sense paternalism means that the state places restrictions on a person's choice for her own good (Buckley 2005, 134). While some degree of paternalism can be found in almost every society with the recognition of bounded rationality, in the communist regime this philosophy played a critical role in all areas of life. The system of central planning was an extreme manifestation of state paternalism, since it is based on the assumption that the leadership not only knows the kind and quantity of products needed by the country but also knows the best method to produce them.

The main beneficiaries of central planning in the economy were the weak sectors and companies that received subsidies channeled from better performers. This incentive was enhanced by a strong preference for stability, which protected the managers of weak companies from removal (Antal 1985, 96–99). On the other hand, those companies that overperformed could expect increased norms during the next planning cycle, which led to a strong incentive to restrain their performance (Kornai 1980, 53). This arrangement meant strong disincentives to improve productivity, while efforts were concentrated on maximizing benefits from the state. According to Kornai (1980, 567), this incentive structure resulted in a widespread attitude of "passivity, complaints over difficulties, begging for the help of the state instead of coping with trouble on one's own initiative."

The reliance on the state was naturally not restricted to companies. Citizens were assured that in return for their compliance, the state will take care of them. This implied guarantees about employment and housing as well as universal access to health care and education. For the population, it could seem that these benefits were free as personal income tax was either non-existent or very low, consumer tax was not explicit during transactions, and social insurance fees were paid by the companies. The main reason was that the state had plenty of other means at its disposal to collect revenues—instead of taxing wages it could restrain the growth of nominal wages or reduce real wages through higher retail prices (Bönker 2006a, 37). This arrangement resulted in a substantial degree of fiscal illusion, which means that the relationship between taxes and state provisions remained unclear in public thinking.

The generous promises of the system coexisted with limited resources, however, and as a consequence the fight for state benefits was an inherent aspect of socialism. In this fight, lack of rules and discretionary decisions were dominant.

At the level of companies, plan targets were always negotiated between planners and the executors of the plans (Kornai 1980, 53–54). Bargaining between the two parties was necessary as the needs were known only at the lower levels, while the resource constraints only at the top (Antal 1985, 115). During the bargaining process the final plan depended heavily on personal relationships, the ingenuity of the negotiator, mutual favors, and corruption.

At the level of households the rule of law was weakened by the growth of the informal economy. The leaders of the system attempted to reduce the social stress due to shortages and the resulting low level of consumption through allowing private deals very often involving the use of state resources. The state authorities were willing to overlook these dealings and show leniency although it was unpredictable when they changed their mind and applied the law to its fullest extent (Kornai 1992, 451–452). While the second economy indeed improved the standards of living, it also led to a lasting heritage of shared disregard for rules by both citizens and authorities.

The absence of rules-based behavior was however most prominent at the elite level. Being exempt from rules was one of the fringe benefits of belonging to the nomenclature. In Kornai's words "the bureaucracy is not subordinated to the legal system. The line of effect is precisely the opposite direction. The formal system of law is subordinate to the current endeavors of the bureaucracy" (1992, 47). This was a clear double standard, which strongly influenced the socialization of post-communist elites.

Overall the heritage of socialism stood in sharp contrast with the concept of rule of law. Decisions were not made through transparent and unambiguous principles, there was no equality before the law, and there was no independent body to enforce the rules. The major role was played not by rules but by personal relationships and the position within the hierarchy. In this context the alienation of the citizens from the rules was natural, which meant that circumventing the laws was a passive and accepted form of resisting the regime.

5.1.2. The heritage of transition

Following the collapse of communism, it was unrealistic to expect that the behavioral legacy of socialism would quickly disappear. As people spent their whole lives relying on the state for protection, it was unlikely that following the transition they would immediately adopt a self-reliant attitude. Similarly, as companies and citizens alike were habitually circumventing the rules, any expectation that they suddenly start respecting the law was rather naïve. However, during the transition even expectations about a slow improvement proved to be illusionary.

At the time of transition everyone expected that once inefficient structures are dismantled, there would be an immediate improvement in the standard of living (Csaba 1995). Most citizens equated democracy and capitalism with the standard of life in Western countries. In Kornai's words "most people are prepared to accept the ideas and values of the Western world, and, in fact, positively want to have democracy, civil liberties, market economy, competition and the security of private property. But concurrently, they expect the new regime to redeem in the shortest possible time all the unfulfilled promises made by the old" (1993, 431–432). These expectations proved to be illusionary early in the transition. GDP during the transformational recession fell by 20 percent and unemployment soared. This went hand in hand with an increase in inequality, which was particularly difficult to accept in a society in which the idea of equality was strongly emphasized. Furthermore, many of the difficulties did not disappear even with the transformational recession—inequality, unemployment, and crime remained high even with the return of growth.

The above processes naturally led to disappointment and disillusionment with the regime. The increased uncertainty also placed the old regime into a new light, when a basic standard of living was quasi-guaranteed. The nostalgia towards the old regime can be observed on Figure 5.1. It shows that while during the transformational recession it was understandable to prefer the security of the old regime, these attitudes did not disappear with the return of growth and the surpassing of former GDP levels. In six out of the 10 post-communist EU member states the majority of the people thought, even in 2004, that materially they were better off during the former regime. This is rather surprising as in these countries a number of consumer goods became available, which was unimaginable before.[1]

Figure 5.1. Views on the old regime in the CEE-10*

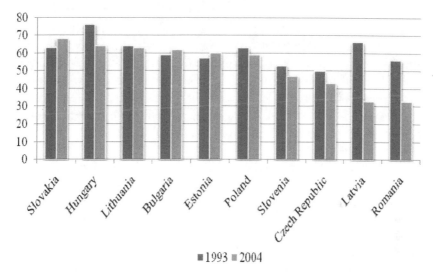

■1993 ■2004

* % of population agreeing with the statement that life was better under communism.
Data: Rose (2006): 39

Increased uncertainty and inequality following the transition implied that the expectation about state support did not decline following the transition. Based on survey results from Hungary, Molnár and Kapitány (2007, 221) show that the more one fears for her job, the more she supports increased state redistribution. However, besides the objective uncertainties of a market system, subjective factors—such as perceptions about inequality—also play a role in expectations of the state. According to Tóth (2003), in Hungary inequality increased between 1987 and 1992 then largely stagnated. At the same time, the proportion of those who thought inequality is too high increased constantly, and by the end of the 1990s it reached 90 percent. The

---

[1] EBRD (2007, 6–7) considers cell phones, personal computer, and credit opportunities among these goods.

subjective perception of inequality has a strong effect on expectations about state involvement (Förster and D'Ércole 2005).

In the corporate sector, while state subsidies decreased, there was strong lobbying for hidden forms of support. These include soft regulations on competition, tax allowances, or market protection. The foreign companies entering these markets did not change these practices but rather lobbied for such benefits themselves (Voszka 2003, 21).

Companies' search for state support was one of the factors that contributed to the slowness of establishing the rule of law and the perception of widespread corruption in the new regime. Shady privatization deals and an overly favorable regulatory environment for the new owners point to strong ties between business and political interests. According to EBRD (2007, 25), in the Central European region only 10 percent of the population thinks that there is less corruption than in the previous regime. These perceptions create a self-reinforcing cycle since if the people feel that they can receive some service only through corruption, they will turn to such practices themselves.

The problem of over-regulation strongly relates to corruption. Since corruption is unpopular, in order to increase their popularity politicians introduce rules which aim to counter this problem. However, the complexity of these rules in itself can be the hotbed of corruption—based on a sample of 69 countries, Friedman et al. (2000) find that companies go underground not primarily for evading high tax rates but for evading bureaucratic costs. Corruption and over-regulation hits small and medium-size enterprises particularly hard since they cannot negotiate with the government for allowance—thus they are forced to break the rules for survival (Csaba 1998b, McIntyre and Dallago 2003).

Besides perceptions of widespread corruption and the need for survival, the circumvention of rules in the post-communist region also has a moral dimension. Transition is widely perceived as unjust and it is believed that its main beneficiaries were members of the old nomenclature. The real or perceived injustice maintains the alienation from the law, which characterized the socialist system. This negative myth of rules is very different from the situation when the system of rules is surrounded by a positive myth, which maintains that in disputed cases the rules make just decisions possible and breaking them implies not only punishment but social exclusion as well (Kurkchiyan 2003, 29).

Overall, due to the dual heritage of socialism and transition, a basic feature of Central Europe is the prevalence of distrust. According to the theory proposed in Chapter 3, in such an environment long-term orientation in economic policymaking is particularly difficult, as political promises are not believed. From the theory, tax avoidance, political business cycles, and the postponement of structural change are to be expected. At the same time a steady path of economic convergence could be observed in all countries prior to the subprime crisis, which can be seen on Figure 5.2. In this performance external factors played a critical role.

Figure 5.2. Convergence in the CEE-10
(GDP per capita in Purchasing Power Standards)

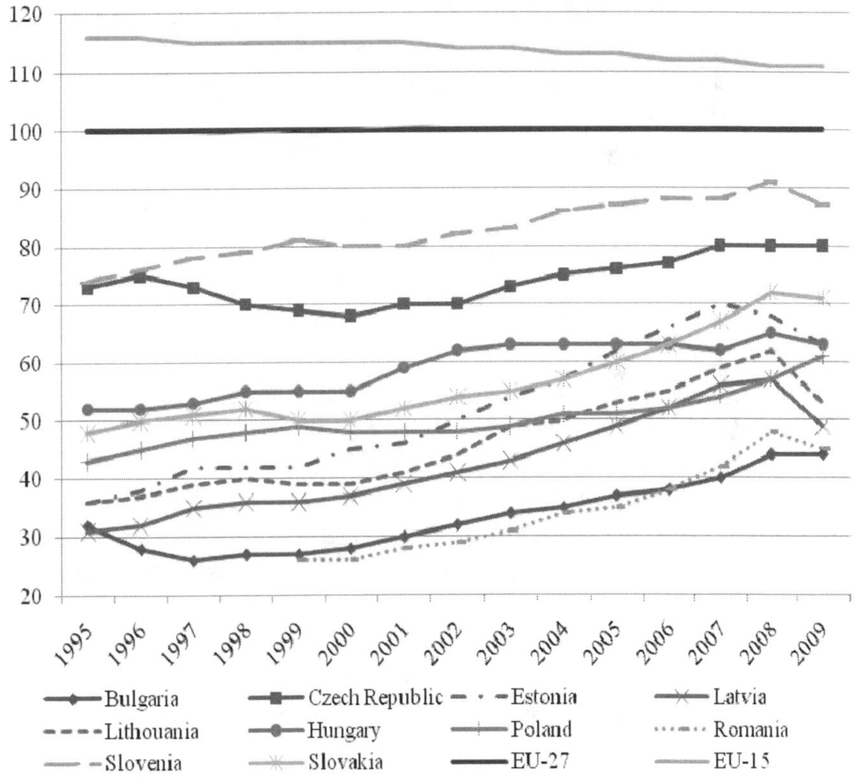

Source: Eurostat structural indicators database

5.2. The role of external constraints in an environment of distrust

Post-communist transition did not take place in a vacuum, and in retrospect, external factors proved to be critical in establishing functioning market economies and avoiding a number of policy mistakes, which could be expected from the low level of trust and weak institutional environment. The two major external forces are international financial market pressures and the accession process to the European Union.

5.2.1. International financial markets

Given the threat of a currency crisis, financial markets might represent considerable pressure for financial discipline and restrain governments in buying support through short-term spending. Irresponsible public finances can trigger a crisis in two ways: in the case of a fixed exchange rate, persistent deficits lead to the exhaustion of reserves—however, before that, speculators are likely to attack the peg in order to benefit from the reserves.[2] Second, if persistent deficits lead to a high level of debt then investors lose confidence in the ability of government to service this debt and will leave the country.[3] This leads to a sharp devaluation both in the case of fixed and floating exchange rates.

The fear of a currency crisis in many cases is sufficient for the elite to establish consensus on the importance of fiscal responsibility since crises are accompanied by severe economic recessions and social stress. The threat of crisis is particularly effective in fostering consensus if politicians are aware of the risks and have seen the consequences. Naturally, this greatly varies across countries.

However, in spite of the above considerations, the disciplining effect of markets is rather unreliable—while it works during times of distress, in times of liquidity markets are often unconcerned about the true level of risk.[4] Furthermore while they might ask for higher interest rates from less disciplined countries, this might be a small price for politicians to pay—as very often it is the next government that has to pay.

The above implies that markets in themselves do not enforce discipline—under- and overreaction to fundamentals is a regular occurrence. In

---

[2] This is the logic of the first-generation crisis models proposed first by Krugman (1979).

[3] The unsustainable level of debt does not mean an objective threshold but rather depends on the perception of investors and greatly varies among countries. For an elaboration of the concept and determinants of debt intolerance, which shows the level of debt investors are willing to tolerate, see Reinhart and Rogoff (2009), 21–33.

[4] This has become particularly clear during the subprime crisis. Darvas (2009, 9) shows that prior to the crisis there was almost no relationship between the pricing of risk and foreign liabilities. This changed during the crisis, and the foreign liabilities became a good predictor of CDS prices. A similar mispricing of risks became evident in the old EU member states as well.

times of liquidity, markets often foster lack of discipline and contribute to financial laxity through providing easy access to credit. This has happened not only prior to the current crisis, but also in the 1970s when lenders stood in line to offer loans to Latin American governments believing that sovereign countries cannot default (Lámfalussy 2000).

Overall, while international financial markets can contribute to financial discipline their contribution is rather uneven and strongly depends on international credit conditions. During the transition in Central Europe another external factor, the accession process to the European Union, played the critical role in protecting from the possible consequences of a disillusioned electorate.

5.2.2. The EU as an anchor

The accession to the European Union provided the CEE-10 countries with a clear set of tasks as declared in the Copenhagen criteria, which require the "stability of institutions guaranteeing democracy, the rule of law, human rights, respect for and protection of minorities, the existence of a functioning market economy as well as the capacity to cope with competitive pressure and market forces within the Union."[5] Aiming at these goals facilitated consensus in institution building in these societies, as this proved to be extremely challenging in countries that lacked the EU as an anchor (Csaba 2007, 117). The process of implementing the aquis communautaire provided these countries with clear guidelines in building a Western-type market economy and legal system.[6] As a result of the EU driven transition process, the countries of Central Europe stepped on the path of export-driven growth and attracted substantial FDI, which in turn helped to upgrade their economic structure.[7] The case studies in the second part of this chapter will provide illustration about how these processes worked in practice in the cases of Hungary and Slovakia.

---

[5] Presidency Conclusions, Copenhagen European Council 1993, available: http://www. europarl.europa.eu/enlargement/ec/pdf/cop_en.pdf.

[6] The decisive impact of the EU on transition is widely accepted and there is a large literature on the issue both in economics and political science. See for example Havrylishin (2006), Aslund (2007), and Csaba (2007). For a broad overview of the political science literature see Jacoby (2006).

[7] The papers in Winiecki (2009) ed. provide a thorough overview of data and mechanisms in this process.

5.2.3. The Maastricht process as an anchor

While the accession process to the EU had a decisive influence on managing the transition, following accession this anchor is largely gone. Partly this reflects the fact that the threat of being left out is not there anymore. It is equally important that further reforms should not be shaped on the basis of current arrangement in core EU member states as they are themselves in need of reforming the quality and efficiency of their public sector in order to remain competitive at the global level (Csaba 2007, 170–176).

Still, in the implementation of major structural reforms, the fulfillment of the Maastricht criteria and the introduction of the euro could in theory play an important anchor function. According to the Copenhagen criteria "membership [of EU] presupposes the candidate's ability to take on the obligations of membership including adherence to the aims of political, economic, and monetary union."[8] This implies that after joining the EU, the next step of integration is the introduction of the common currency, which is an obligation from the accession treaty in the new member states.

Although the subprime crisis has greatly changed the calculations about the costs and benefits of the euro, prior to the crisis, it was widely believed that the obligation to introduce the euro also lies in the interest of candidate countries—similarly to the Southern states of the EU-15, gaining credibility is an important policy objective for these states. Furthermore based on the traditional OCA criteria reviewed in Chapter 3, these countries are not in a worse position and sometimes fare even better than current member states of the euro-area (Darvas and Szapáry 2008, 36). This implies that the possibility of asymmetric shocks is low, while the potential gains from sound money can bring substantial economic benefits for these countries.[9]

However, future gains from the euro should be weighed against the possible loss of popularity, which go with the fulfillment of the Maastricht criteria. As it was shown in the previous chapter, given the large popularity of the euro in the Southern member states the public accepted the needed measures and tax increases. The situation is very different in the CEE-10 countries. In Figure 5.3, public opinion from 2006 is presented from the 10 countries which joined the EU in 2004. As it can be seen from the figure, there is a great diversity regarding preferences for the euro—a

---

[8] See footnote 5.

[9] At the time even unilateral introduction of the euro was suggested as beneficial, even though it would not have given access to the reserves of the ECB nor a voice in the setting of the euro-area interest rate. For an overview of the debate on unilateral euroization see Wojcik and Backé (2004).

strong majority can be found only in Slovenia and to a certain extent in Slovakia. Regarding the timing of accession the option "as soon as possible" is the least favored alternative in seven of the ten countries.[10]

Figure 5.3. Preferences regarding the introduction of the euro (2006)

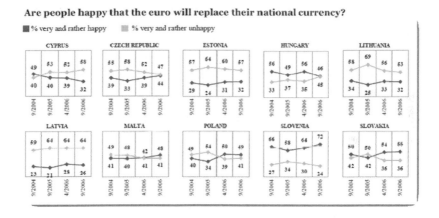

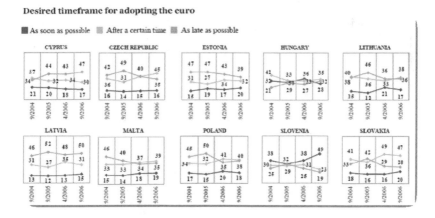

Source: Eurobarometer (2006): 37, 39

Given the moderate level of popularity of the euro and the short-term sacrifices needed for its introduction it can be hypothesized that the introduction of the common currency is far less conducive to establishing consensus over

---

[10] Eurobarometer surveys started measuring attitudes towards the euro in Bulgaria and Romania only since 2007. According to the latest results, public opinion is evenly split in Bulgaria, while the euro is strongly favored in Romania. See Eurobarometer (2009), 31.

policy objectives than it was the case with joining the EU. However, given the long-term interests of the countries in the region, it is possible to form a second hypothesis that the introduction of the common currency will be more likely in an environment of trust, where long-term planning is possible.[11] These hypotheses will be examined in the next section.

5.3. Institutional quality and exchange rate choice

Among the CEE-10 countries, three groups can be distinguished based on their exchange rate arrangements. Three countries have introduced the euro, three have hard pegs and four have a floating exchange rate. The different experiences among and within the three groups can help us to understand better the links between institutional trust and the introduction of the euro. Similarly to the previous chapter I will take the short cut of using the world governance indicators as a proxy for institutional quality and trust. I will use data from 2004, the year of accession for eight out of the ten countries under examination. While all such choices are necessarily somewhat arbitrary, this year can be taken as a starting point for preparing for the euro as accession had been achieved. At the same time, given the general shortcomings of aggregate indicators as discussed in the previous chapter, I will offer a more nuanced view of trust in the case studies.

Group 1. EMU countries
Among the new post-communist member states of the EU three countries have already introduced the euro: Slovenia in 2007, Slovakia is 2009 and Estonia in 2011. As we can see from Figure 5.4, governance indicators in Slovenia and Estonia are considerably higher than the regional average, which gives support to the hypothesis that the euro can be expected in an environment characterized by trust. Slovakia is the somewhat surprising third member of this group, as its institutional quality is barely above the regional average. While all three countries were newly established following the collapse of communism, they represent three different approaches to the common currency. These paths also reveal important differences in the way institutional trust can matter in economic policy.

---

[11] Since I examine the Maastricht process prior to the subprime crisis, it is legitimate to build on the then prevailing assumption about the clear desirability of the common currency even if it has been questioned since the crisis.

Figure 5.4. Quality of governance in Estonia, Slovakia, and Slovenia (2004)

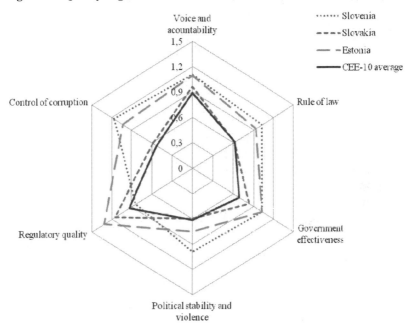

Source: World Governance Indicators data base: http://info.worldbank.org/governance/wgi/index.asp

Slovenia was the first among CEE countries to introduce the common currency. In a number of aspects it can be considered a special case, since it is the only neocorporatist country in the region. Slovenia was the export center of the old Yugoslavia and had extensive experience with firm-level self-management, which meant a uniquely favorable start for transition. After gaining independence in 1991, the country embarked on a gradualist path of transition characterized by consensual decision making between the government, the central bank, employer and employee associations (Bohle and Greskovits 2007). Macroeconomic stability was widely perceived as necessary for successful economic policy, thus following the accession to the EU there was a widespread consensus about the desirability of introducing the euro. Sharing this objective was conducive to moderating demands either from the budget or wages, which made the fulfillment of the Maastricht criteria relatively smooth, and the country could introduce the euro in accordance with the plans. Overall, in Slovenia a shared common ground made long-term oriented cooperation possible among different interest groups in society.

Slovakia is perhaps the greatest surprise in the region as it managed the transition from being a quasi pariah in the region to a model country within a decade. After being the laggard among the Visegrad countries and almost excluded from the first round of eastern enlargement during the rule of Vladimír Mečiar, a change in government in 1998 meant stepping on the path of reform and achieving first accession to the EU, as well as the introduction of the euro in 2009. Playing successfully on the problem of national identity, major reforms could be implemented without strong opposition (Greskovits 2008, 285). These reforms were largely sustained even after the fall of the Dzurinda government, and the country remained one of the major success stories in the region.

The accession of Estonia to the euro-zone was approved in July 2010. While this places the country into the leading group of the region, its path to the euro-zone is almost the opposite of Slovakia's. Since the early 1990s, Estonia was considered as a pacesetter of economic reforms and the introduction of the euro was expected to take place around 2007 (Feldmann 2006). It introduced a currency board regime in 1992, and it was the first country in the region to introduce unilateral free trade and a flat tax (Feldmann 2008, 245). As shown by Figure 4, it also has the highest governance quality in the region. The source of reform zeal lies in the four decades under Soviet rule—following independence, the nation was united in the goal of distancing itself from this past (Bohle and Greskovits 2007). The introduction of a currency board necessitated an adherence to stability culture, which is enshrined in a constitutional balanced budget provision and shown by the fact that in the past decade the budget was mostly in surplus (Figure 5.5). However, the very measures which signaled the success of this model, including fast capital liberalization, minimal state involvement in the economy, and a strong currency, eventually became responsible for the delay of the euro—the large capital inflows led to the overheating of the economy and the state did not have measures to sterilize these flows (Feldmann 2008, 257). According to Csaba (2009a, 106–107), fiscal brakes, including tax increases, could have been used to fight overheating, and the neglect of these measures can be attributed to the ruling free market ideology, which he considers as a form of economic populism. Feldman (2008, 257) explains this neglect by differentiating between the policy of sound money and the policy of austerity—while the public accepted the former, it refused the latter. Indeed, it is somewhat paradoxical that the subprime crisis became the factor that helped EMU accession through cooling down the economy.

Figure 5.5. Fiscal balance in Estonia, Slovakia, and Slovenia 1995-2007 (% of GDP)

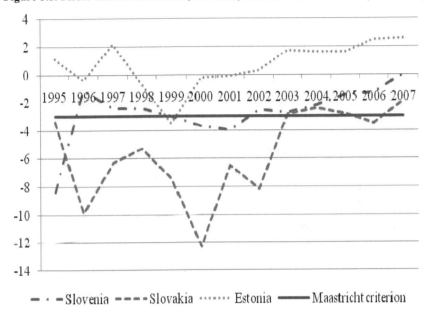

Data: European Commission (2010): 180-181

The different cases of Slovenia, Slovakia, and Estonia indicate that there are many paths to the EMU. Their experience however is far from being supportive of a strong EMU role in domestic economic policy. As we can see from Figure 5.5, real change in fiscal balance can be observed only in Slovakia, while Slovenia and Estonia adhered to a stability culture well before EU membership. Given their quality of governance, their cases support the importance of institutional trust for long term oriented economic policy. The surprising case is Slovakia, which will be examined more in depth as a case study.

Group 2. Countries with fixed exchange rate

Bulgaria, Latvia, and Lithuania peg their currencies to the euro—Bulgaria and Lithuania have a currency board arrangement, while Latvia has a narrow band of ±1 percent. As we can see from Figure 5.6, these three countries have a weak institutional framework and score around or below the regional average particularly in terms of corruption. Implementing a hard peg was for them a short cut to gain credibility and access to the international financial markets. With such an exchange rate arrangement, these countries gave up independent monetary policy,[12] while there are also strong restraints on fiscal policy, since having deficits calls the sufficiency of reserves into question. At a basic level given the inherent disciplining effect of such an arrangement, the introduction of the euro should not cause problems for these countries in theory. However, the examples of these countries indicate that maintaining a fixed exchange does not necessarily ease euro accession and financial imbalances manifest themselves in other economic indicators.

Figure 5.6. Quality of governance in Bulgaria, Latvia and Lithuania (2004)

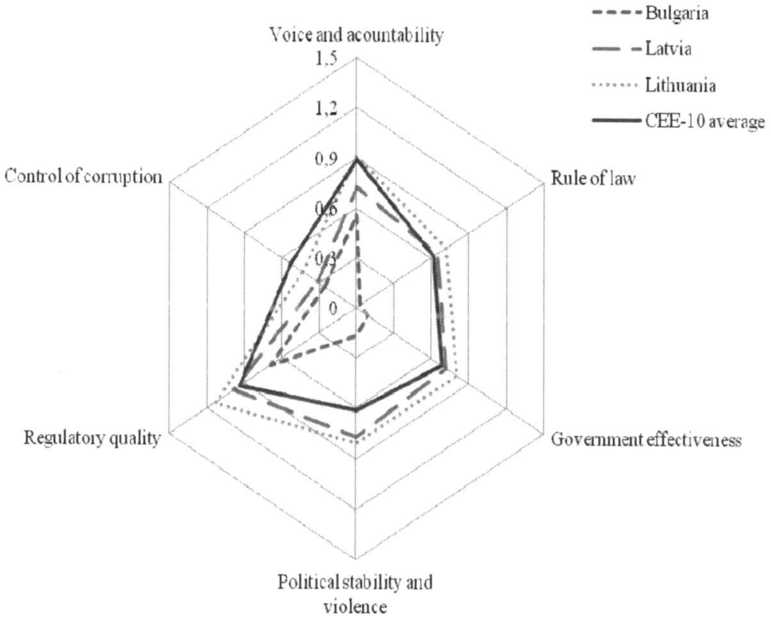

Source: World Governance Indicators data base: http://info.worldbank.org/governance/wgi/index.asp

Latvia shows strong similarities to Estonia in aiming to distance itself from the Soviet legacy through radical reforms. It introduced a de facto

---

[12] The main task of monetary policy in such an arrangement is to maintain full convertibility of the currency at a fixed exchange rate. This is done by having sufficient reserves to convert all money in circulation (notes and coins) into the reserve currency. The monetary authority cannot thus act as a lender of last resort for banks in trouble nor can it set its own interest rate.

currency board in 1994, which also implied a strong domestic commitment to macroeconomic stability. While there is no balanced budget
clause in the constitution, as in Estonia, deficits have been generally low
(Figure 5.7). Latvia was also the first country in the region to implement
radical welfare reforms. These reforms affected most the country's Russian population (close to 20 percent of total population) as Russian industries were hardest hit by transformational recession. Their ability to pro-
test however was debilitated by not having citizenship (Bohle 2010, 5). At
the same time the effects of the transition were not limited to the Russian
population and low social benefits increased dissatisfaction among the
electorate.[13] Latvia managed the challenges arising from dissatisfaction
through anchoring its policies in the EU accession process, opening its
market to foreign banks, and ensuring widespread access to credit. The
latter policy was indeed popular, but eventually led to a large-scale housing boom, the highest inflation among the Baltic states (20.3 percent in
2007),[14] and an enormous current account deficit (22.5 percent in 2006
and 2007).

Lithuania followed a similar road to Estonia and Latvia, introducing a
currency board regime in 1994.[15] Similarly to Latvia, there is no balanced
budget provision though deficits have been low (Figure 5.7). Still, among
the Baltic states, commitment to the stability culture is the weakest in
Lithuania, and the country announced in 1997 that it would end its currency board regime. However, during the turbulence caused by the Russian crisis in the following year, it decided to maintain the hard peg
(Feldmann 2008, 246). In March 2006, the country submitted a request for
convergence assessment, which was turned down given concerns about
the sustainability of low inflation. In retrospect this was a correct assessment—while at the time of submitting the application the country ex-
ceeded the target only by 0.1 percentage point (2.7 percent versus the
reference rate of 2.6 percent), the same year inflation jumped to over 4
percent then over 6 percent the following year. As in the other two Baltic
countries the problem was clearly overheating. The crisis from 2008
cooled down the economy and the high rates of inflation were followed by
deflation (-2.3 percent in 2009) but the fiscal costs of the crisis implied a

---

[13] This will be discussed further in the next section.

[14] In the rest of the chapter, unless otherwise noted, I will refer to data from European
Commission (2010).

[15] Originally the litas was pegged to the US dollar, but in 2002 the euro replaced the dollar
peg.

sharp worsening of the fiscal balance and an over 8 percent deficit for 2009 and 2010.

Figure 5.7. Fiscal balance in Bulgaria, Latvia, and Lithuania 1995–2007 (% of GDP)

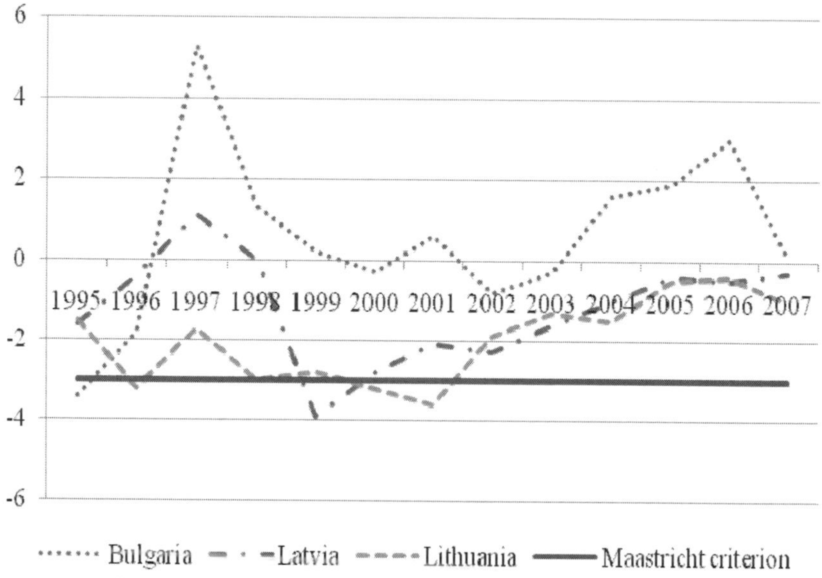

Data: European Commission (2010): 181.

Bulgaria introduced a hard peg following a banking and currency crisis in 1996–1997, which developed given the slowness of structural reforms during the early phase of transition. This implied the survival of soft budget constraint and rent-seeking from the Socialist system. The result was not only severe public finance imbalances financed by the central bank through printing money or borrowing, but also the increase of non-performing loans in the largely state-owned banking system (Gulde 1999, 3–4). In 1996, 15 banks had to be closed. This led to the withdrawal of deposits and their exchange into foreign currency triggering the collapse of the exchange rate and a surge in interest rate payments. GDP fell by nearly 10 percent in 1996. In order to stabilize the economy, in March 1997, a currency board was introduced and the central bank was forbidden to finance government deficits (Dimitrov 2006, 154). The regime helped Bulgaria step onto a steady growth path (Figure 5.2), which has ensured its continued public support. This in turn translates into a commitment of politicians towards respecting the importance of fiscal discipline, which is signaled in the steady surplus of the budget since 1997. As the debt level is also below 20 percent of the GDP (from 105.1 percent in 1997), the main problem in front of EMU accession was overheating and inflation similar to the Baltic states.

Overall in the three countries with a currency board arrangement, inflation posed the major difficulty with regards to the Maastricht criteria. As shown by Figure 5.7, fiscal discipline was maintained and in all three countries fiscal deficits have mostly remained below 3 percent of the GDP. The commitment to responsibility comes from the currency board arrangement, which was implemented for purely domestic reasons well before accession to the EMU could be considered. Furthermore, given the success of the arrangement up to the subprime crisis, the population of these countries had not been very enthusiastic about replacing their currency with the euro—in all three countries the majority of the people were unhappy about the prospect (Figure 5.3). Essentially, up to the subprime crisis the currency board could provide a strong anchor and credibility for these countries' economic policies. However, the experiences of the group also indicate the limits of this arrangement—while public finances are roughly in balance, financial imbalances are still present, showing up in high levels of inflation, which has made the introduction of the euro difficult. In the next section I will return to this issue and attempt to relate it to the problem of trust.

Group 3. Countries with a floating exchange rate
Countries in the last group are far from introducing the euro. This is rather surprising as three out of the four countries are the former leaders of the transition process—the Czech Republic, Hungary, and Poland. As indicated by Figure 5.8, in 2004 the quality of governance in Hungary and the Czech Republic was comparable to the level in Group 1. In this third group, Romania appears as the outlier given its weak institutions comparable only to Bulgaria. The experiences of this diverse group indicate the lack of determinacy in the EMU accession process.

The Czech Republic initially appeared as a prime candidate to introduce the euro. At the time of EU accession, only the deficit criterion was somewhat above the target, while the other criteria were met. At the same time, following accession, the performance was worsening and excessive deficits persisted (Figure 5.9). According to Bönker (2006b) this was due to three major reasons: 1. the weak alignment of the economy with the euro area and the resulting possibility of asymmetric shocks, which make the loss of independent monetary policy costly; 2. lack of enthusiasm let

alone consensus within the elite regarding the benefits of EMU accession;
3. weak reform capacity of the successive governments, which made the
structural reforms necessary for the fulfillment of the Maastricht criteria
difficult. Furthermore, given low interest rates and stable exchange rates,
it is unsurprising that the Czechs feel no rush into the euro-zone. In this
case having strong domestic institutions have translated into international
credibility.

**Figure 5.8. Quality of governance in the Czech Republic, Hungary, Poland and
Romania (2004)**

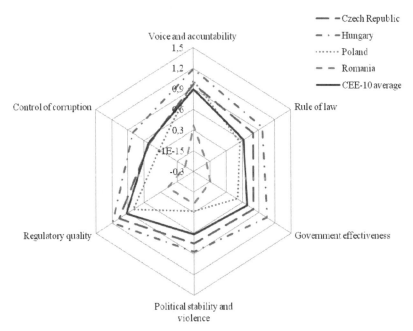

Source: World Governance Indicators data base: http://info.worldbank.org/governance/
wgi/index.asp

Hungary was among the most ambitious countries that aimed at introducing the euro as soon as possible after accession to the EU. Its apparently strong institutions also would have predicted the reality of this objective. However, following a fiercely fought election campaign on the
basis of irresponsible welfare promises in 2002, budget deficits soared,
leading to high inflation, ballooning public debt, and high interest rates.
These developments meant that none of the Maastricht criteria was fulfilled in the following years. None of the countries in the region have registered such a downturn in performance during the first decade of the new

millennium, which makes the country a good case for comparison with the positive surprise Slovakia.

Similarly to the two countries above, Poland could not introduce the euro after EU accession because of large fiscal deficits, which are primarily due to the high level of social spending and structural rigidities in the budget (Zubek 2008, 294). Since the elite is sharply divided on EMU accession, public finance reforms have proved very difficult. While the Social democratic government between 2001 and 2004 made attempts to consolidate the budget and introduce the euro fast, the following Kaczińsky cabinet openly declared that it does not seek EMU entry (Zubek 2008, 302). Although the moderate government of Donald Tusk has since 2007 slightly altered this position, considering that Poland was the only country in the EU to grow during the subprime crisis—partly due to the sharp devaluation of its currency—it is unlikely that it will rush into the EMU following the crisis.[16]

Figure 5.9. Fiscal balance in the Czech Republic, Hungary, Poland, and Romania 1995–2007 (% of GDP)

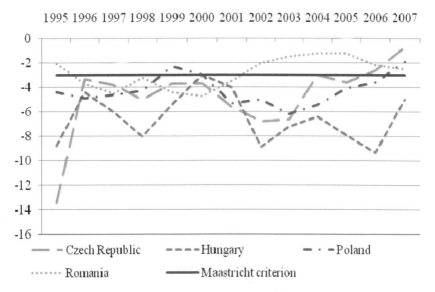

Data: European Commission (2010): 181.

---

[16] Postponement of accession can also be expected on the basis of public opinion—in contrast to the pre-crisis period, currently the majority of the Polish population thinks that the introduction of the euro would have a negative impact on the national economy (Eurobarometer, 2012, 67).

Romania is an outlier in this group—while the other three countries were the pacesetters of transition, Romania was the permanent laggard. The country implemented the tasks of transition such as privatization and hardening the budget constraint a decade after others in the region (Papadimitriu 2006). It was admitted into the EU only in 2007 with Bulgaria, but unlike the latter country it did not face a debt crisis to force the adoption of harsh measures like a currency board. While the lack of reform shows up only in institutional quality (Figure 5.8), and budget deficits appear better than in the other three Visegrad countries, once the subprime crisis hit the region, the country had to turn to the IMF. The problems, which will be discussed in depth in the following section, are very similar to those of Group 2 and include a credit-boom, overheating, inflation rate over 10 percent, and a current account deficit above 10 percent of GDP between 2006 and 2008. Once access to foreign capital dried up during the subprime crisis, financing these imbalances became very difficult and the country had to turn to the IMF for a bail-out.

While the experiences of this group are very different from those of Group 2, a common thread is the absence of a strong influence of the EMU on domestic economic policy. In the three Visegrad countries, domestic welfare arrangements have remained largely intact even when it implied a postponement of EMU accession. In fact if EMU had any influence, it was the credibility it provided for these countries and the resulting easy access to credit on the global financial markets, which will be discussed in the next section. However, up to the subprime crisis this policy did not seem to have negative repercussions, since only Hungary experienced a downturn in the convergence process (Figure 5.2). These considerations suggest that in normal times a relatively developed institutional framework (Figure 5.8) allows an independent currency without excess volatility.[17] The exception in the group is Romania, which has even weaker institutional structures than Bulgaria—here however there was no debt crisis given the lack of debt at the beginning of transition and thus financial markets did not play the same disciplining role as in Bulgaria.

Summarizing the experiences from the three groups, we can conclude that the decisive influence of the EMU could be observed only in the case of Slovakia, which introduced the euro without the prior existence of a stability culture that existed in the other two successful cases. This is in

---

[17] This falls in line with the theory proposed by Rogoff et al. (2003) that developing countries should choose hard pegs to earn credibility, while with development the gains from flexibility increase.

line with the findings from the previous chapter, which showed that in the large majority of the old EU member states, the EMU had very limited influence on domestic economic policies. This implies that the EMU project cannot replace the anchor role played by the EU during the early phase of the transition. One of the reasons is that the ECB is not very encouraging with possible new entrants—Poland was advised against early entry, while Lithuania was not accepted due to mildly surpassing of the inflation criteria (Zubek 2006, 300 and Feldmann 2008, 248). Domestic policy entrepreneurs thus did not receive external backing in their quest, which make domestic conditions decisive in outcomes.

The findings also point to the limited explanatory power of institutional quality regarding the decision over the introduction of the euro. While the cases of Slovenia and Estonia, which have the highest level of governance in the region, support the theory over the importance of trust for such a long-term oriented decision, accession by Slovakia and non-accession by Hungary and the Czech Republic show that other factors are also at work in this unique decision.

From the perspective of the theory the most important implication of the limited influence of the EMU is that unlike in the case of EU accession, there is no force that counteracts the effects of low trust on economic policy after enlargement. In the following section I will discuss how the expected short-term orientation is manifested in economic policy.

5.4. The impact of distrust on economic policy in the CEE-10

In the old EU member states, the quality of institutions correlates well with fiscal developments as shown in the previous chapter. However, as we could see above, in most CEE-10 countries fiscal imbalances did not pose a major problem. This is particularly true for countries in Group 2, which have weak institutions but were able to maintain fiscal responsibility. In their cases, the main reason for not being able to introduce the euro was overheating due to the inflow of foreign funds. Given such clues, in the following I attempt to reveal the influence of low trust on economic policy by examining not only fiscal but also credit developments between 2002 and 2007. 2002 is the date of closing the negotiations with the 8 CEE countries, all of which joined in 2004, while 2007 can be considered the last year before the subprime crisis. During this favorable period external disciplining forces were very weak—as shown in the previous section, the EMU conditions did not exert a strong influence on domestic policy, while the global financial markets were characterized by abundant liquidity. This has provided ample opportunity for domestic leanings to manifest themselves. In the following I will first consider fiscal developments, then turn to credit developments, and finally consider the consequences of these policies.

5.4.1. Fiscal policy in the CEE-10, 2002–2007

As it could be seen from the previous section, in most countries of the region, fiscal policy did not indicate pressures for populist spending. For countries in Group 1 and 2, the fulfillment of the Maastricht criteria and constraint represented by the currency board led to strong incentives for fiscal responsibility. However, as we could see in the previous chapter, fiscal discipline could be reached in several ways and not all are sustainable or conducive to growth. In the previous chapter, I emphasized the importance of examining social benefits other than transfers in kind as indicative of a country's commitment to responsibility. For the old EU member states, this indicator turned out to perform rather well in predicting the sustainability of adjustment.

Figure 5.10 shows social benefits other than in kind for the CEE-10 countries. From the figure it is clear that in most countries in the region, dissatisfaction with the regime did not translate into high welfare expenditures. In 8 out of the 10 countries these expenditures decreased, and a rise can be observed only in two countries of Group 3, the Czech Republic and Hungary. Even more importantly, in the majority of the countries, the Baltic states and in Romania in particular, these expenditures were already well below the EU-15 average of 15.9 percent in 2002.

A commitment to responsibility can be observed in Figure 5.11 as well, which summarizes the sources of fiscal consolidation, ranking countries from left to right by the improvement they made. It is noteworthy that during this period the fiscal balance improved in all countries of the region although the sources of this improvement differ. Cuts in primary expenditure, which exclude interest payments, were present in 8 out of the 10 countries, while an increase could be observed in two countries of Group 3, Romania and Hungary. These cuts were mostly accompanied by an increase in revenue—only two countries of Group 1, Slovenia and Slovakia, could translate large expenditure cuts into tax cuts. From the figure it is also noteworthy that unlike the highly indebted countries in the EMU, in the CEE-10 countries' consolidation could not rely on savings on interest payments due to the low initial level of debt—with a 2.2 percent saving Slovakia registered the largest gains, but this is far from the gains in excess of 5 percent made by Italy, Greece, or Belgium during the convergence period and afterwards. This also explains why revenue increase was a necessity almost everywhere—especially in the Baltic states or Romania where initial expenditure was very low and thus large cuts could not be expected.

Figure 5.10. Social benefits other than social transfers in kind in the CEE-10 2002–2007 (% of GDP)

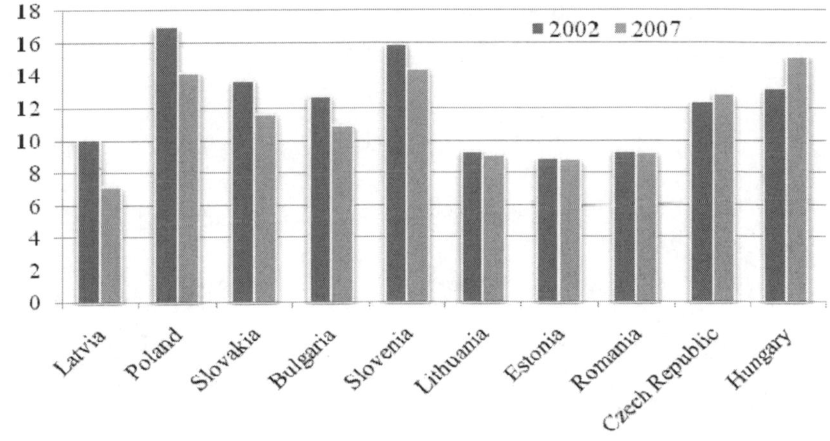

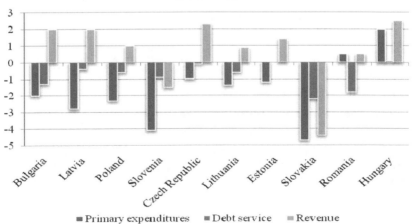

Data: European Commission (2010): 156–157.

Figure 5.11. Sources of fiscal consolidation in CEE-10 2002–2007 (% of GDP)

Data: European Commission (2010): 160–161, 166–167, 172–173

In order to summarize fiscal developments in the region, it is helpful to observe the evolution of public debt. Figure 5.12 shows that in most countries the low level of public debt decreased even further during this period, and in 8 out of 10 countries public debt is below 30 percent of the GDP. An increase could be observed only in three countries of Group 3, which supports the analysis in the previous section about the delays of fiscal consolidation in these countries.

Figure 5.12. Public debt in the CEE-10 2002–2007 (% of GDP)

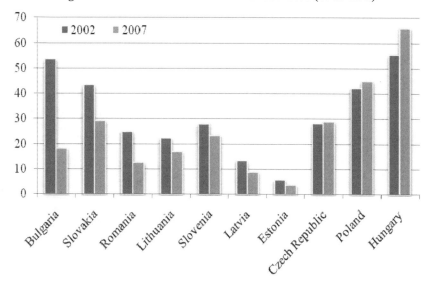

Data: European Commission (2010): 184–185

5.4.2. Credit developments in the CEE-10, 2002–2008

On the basis of fiscal policy it might appear that disillusionment among the population was not managed through welfare benefits in most countries in the region. However, state provisions do not constitute the sole possibility for increasing consumption—the availability of cheap credit might serve the same purpose. This solution is nothing new, since Ludwig von Mises (1949, 794–798) more than half a century ago warned about credit expansions, which are almost always encouraged by state authorities given the popularity they gain from the ensuing economic boom. Naturally, from a short-term oriented political economy perspective, it is only a second-best solution to public debt—credit eventually have to be

repaid by the borrowers, while public debt is financed by future generations. However, once there are strong constraints on the indebtedness of
the state such as in the case of a currency board, increasing credit might
help to appease the electorate for stringent public policies.

If we look at Figure 5.13 we can see the large credit expansion that
took place in these countries between 2002 and 2008.[18] From the picture it
appears that the largest increase in indebtedness took place in countries
with a hard peg, which had the most disciplined fiscal policy.

Figure 5.13. Credit to private sector in the CEE-10 2002–2008 (% of GDP)

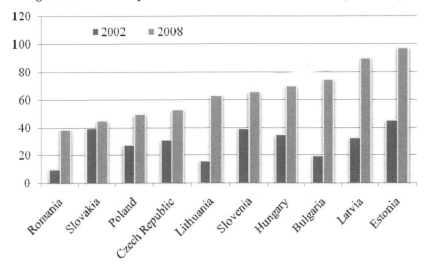

Data: World Bank Data Catalog
Available: http://data.worldbank.org/indicator/FS.AST.PRVT.GD.ZS

A simple correlation between public debt and private debt on Figure
5.14 provides some evidence about the presence of a substitution effect.
However, the relationship is rather weak given two outliers: Romania and
Hungary. Credit growth in Romania was much smaller than it could be
expected based on its low public debt, while in Hungary both public and
private debt soared during the period under examination. In the previous
section both cases have been already recognized as outliers: Romania did
not introduce a currency board which could have been expected based on

---

[18] For details on the main features and sources of credit boom see Arcalean et al. (2007) as
well as Darvas and Szapáry (2008), 37–42.

its weak institutions, while Hungary could not introduce the euro in spite of its relatively high quality institutions and commitment to do so.

Figure 5.14. Public and private debt in the CEE-10 in 2007/2008

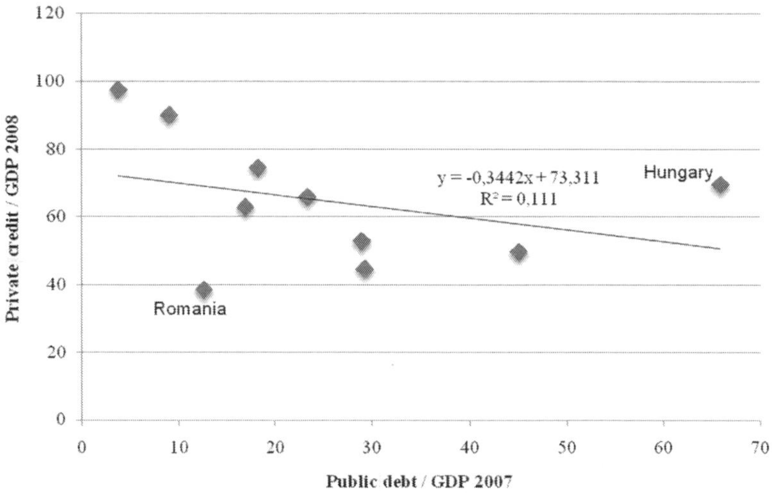

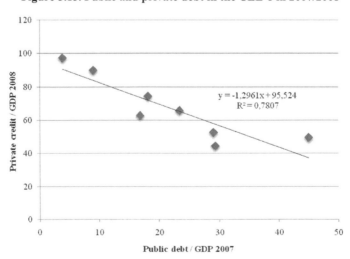

Source: see Figure 5.12 and 5.13.

Figure 5.15. Public and private debt in the CEE-8 in 2007/2008

Source: see Figure 5.12 and 5.13.

In the case of Romania weak institutions and lack of a currency board providing credibility constrained access to the international financial markets thus placed limits on becoming indebted. Still, in anticipation of its EU accession there was a lending boom but given the very low base and a late start, the expansion could not reach the proportions it did in other countries of the region.[19] The Hungarian case is the reverse—as a former leader of the transition, the country had access to international financial markets, and both the public and private sector made use of this opportunity. As it will be shown in the next section the case is an extreme illustration of the theory on trust and economic policy. In the regional context, however, the total lack of restraint makes it an outlier.

Removing the two outliers from the sample yields a very strong correlation between public and private debt as shown by Figure 5.15. This provides some evidence on the hypothesis about the substitutability of welfare spending and credit.

The hypothesis that access to cheap private credit can substitute excessive welfare spending is also supported by the findings of Hilbers, Ötker-Robe, and Pazarbasioglu (2007), who provide a thorough overview on the policy responses to rapid credit growth in the post-communist region, and conclude that they were inadequate with a few exceptions such as Poland. In the case of Latvia, which shows the largest reduction in welfare spending and the largest increase in private credit, Bohle (2010, 8–9) suggests clear political motives in encouraging private indebtedness. Based on the assessment of Darvas and Kostyleva (2011, 29), the country also had the weakest financial regulation framework in the region, and between 2003 and 2007 it became even weaker.

Besides the weak regulatory response to credit growth, lack of an adequate policy reaction is also evident from the steady worsening of the current account in the most indebted countries as shown by Figure 5.16. The large current account imbalances, especially in Group 2 countries, indicate weakening competitiveness due to the overheating caused by the credit boom. A sharp increase in domestic demand due to the availability of credit translated into strong inflationary pressures, growth in unit labor costs, and a sharp rise in housing prices (Darvas and Szapáry 2008, 43–44). Lack of recourse to devaluation meant that for restoring competitiveness, a painful internal adjustment would have been necessary. However, this was postponed until the subprime crisis made such changes unavoidable since the financing of these deficits became impossible from the markets.

---

[19] For a detailed overview of Romanian credit developments see Hudecz (2012), 372–380.

Institutional Trust and Economic Policy

Figure 5.16. Current account balances in the CEE-10 2002–2007

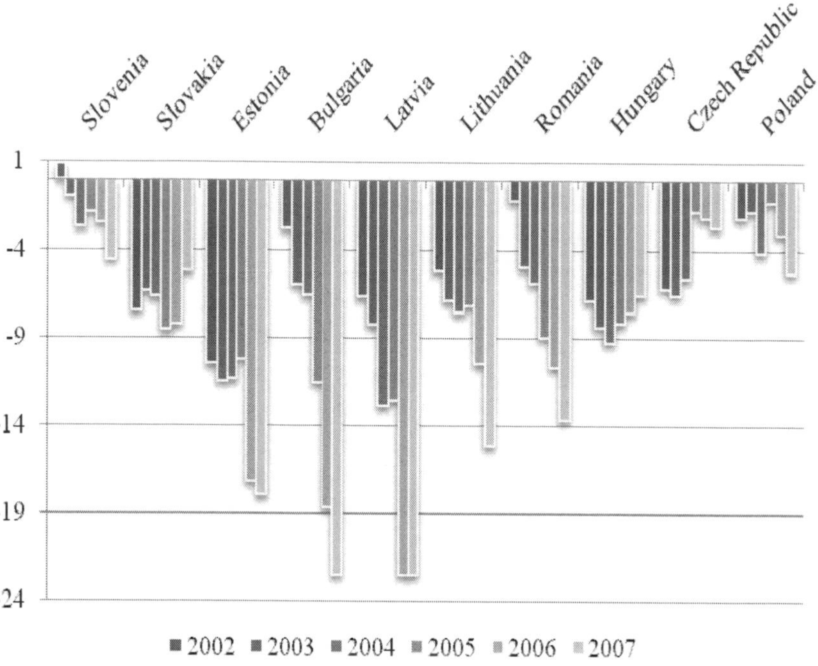

Data: European Commission (2010): 116-117

The vulnerability due to large indebtedness and large current account imbalances was further enhanced by the fact that in most countries, loans were denominated in foreign currency. With the exception of the Czech Republic and Poland, over 50 percent of the loans were foreign-currency denominated, while in Estonia and Latvia this proportion was over 90 percent (ECB 2010, 27). Although this can be partly explained by negative real interest rates due to inflation in hard peg countries and interest rate differentials in Hungary and Romania, Brown, Kirschenmann, and Ondega (2010) also call attention to supply-side factors—lenders preferred foreign currency lending given the fact that in this way exchange rate risks are born by borrowers rather than the banks.[20] This is the well-known "original sin" as countries with weak institutions cannot

---

[20] For further empirical evidence on the determinants of foreign currency lending in Central and Eastern Europe see Rosenberg and Tirpák (2008) as well as Zettelmayer, Nagy, and Jeffrey (2010).

raise loans in their own currency, which makes them vulnerable to capital flow reversal.[21]

5.4.3 Assessment

The experiences of the CEE-10 countries indicate that there is no easy solution to counter the consequences of a weak institutional environment and low level of trust in the system. This can be best illustrated by the experiences of currency board countries—while this arrangement provided substantial credibility for an otherwise very weak institutional system, as well as served as an anchor for fiscal discipline, it led to severe unintended consequences, which culminated in the output collapse following the subprime crisis.

In contrast, countries with better governance quality did not need a shortcut to credibility and could manage a floating exchange rate even if they did not introduce the euro. The experiences of the Czech Republic and Poland show that moderate policies can be relatively successful even without major structural changes.

From the overview of the CEE-10 experiences it is also clear that the prospect of accession to the EMU and the related increase in credibility for these countries had the unintended consequences of softening financial discipline rather than strengthening it. With the availability of credit, long-term structural and institutional changes in the economy could be postponed.[22] Even if a country avoided a deep crisis, low growth and a halt in the process of convergence can be foreseen.

Overall, the EMU proved to be insufficient as an anchor for policy change and avoiding the consequences of low levels of trust for most countries of the region. However, there has been an exception to this trend—as mentioned above, Slovakia seems like an outlier in a number of dimensions. Understanding how it became a pacesetter from a laggard can be very illustrative to answer the question how to break a vicious cycle between low trust and low growth. The lessons from its experience can be underlined by the presentation of the contrasting case of Hungary, which went in an opposite direction going from a leader to a laggard.

---

[21] For an extensive overview of this problem see the edited volume by Eichengreen and Hausmann (2005).

[22] According to Csaba (2009, 88) minimal state involvement in the economy and the resulting overheating are a new variety of macroeconomic populism, which stands in contrast to the old type of populism, which concentrated on fiscal overspending.

5.5. Reforms without trust: Hungary vs. Slovakia[23]

On a number of dimensions Hungary and Slovakia share important similarities that make them particularly suitable for comparison. They are neighboring countries and share a long common history. They are also small open economies and since 2004 members of the European Union. Both have declared their intention to introduce the euro as soon as possible—even though only Slovakia eventually fulfilled this objective. The main dissimilarity between them is that Slovakia became an independent state only in 1992. This difference however should not be the whole explanation for the more successful reforms in Slovakia, since as the contradictory experiences of the Baltic states and the Western Balkans show, new-found statehood can be a reason both for implementing and for postponing reforms. The history of economic reforms in Slovakia also reflects this duality, which in itself needs explanation.

5.5.1. Roots of distrust

From the perspective of the theoretical framework of this book, the most important similarity of these two countries is the low level of public trust in the state, which would predict poor economic policy in both countries and makes it puzzling why their performances differ. While a thorough overview on the roots of this distrust would require a separate analysis, four major reasons can be mentioned for the persistent lack of trust in the two countries.[24]

Material losses, due to the transformational recession, are a shared experience of the two countries. The loss of output between 1989 and 1993 amounted to 18 percent in Hungary and 25 percent in Slovakia (UN ECE 2003, 112). The consequences were decreasing consumption and rising unemployment. Real total consumption expenditure reached its pre-transition levels only in 2000 in Hungary and 2002 in Slovakia (UN ECE 2003, 113). In Hungary, by 1996 employment decreased to 69.8 percent of 1989 levels, while Slovakia did better on this indicator, reaching the bottom at 84 percent in 1994. However, better employment performance came with an extremely high unemployment rate: by 1999 unemployment reached 19.2 percent, while it fluctuated around 10 percent in Hungary (UN ECE 2003, 115–117). Rising inequality accompanied these proc-

---

[23] A previous version of this part was published as Györffy (2009b).

[24] In this section I rely substantially on Kornai (2006), 227–237.

esses: over the transition the Gini-index rose by 19 percent in Hungary and 38 percent in Slovakia (Kornai 2006, 229).

Figure 5.17. Trust in public institutions in Hungary (2006)

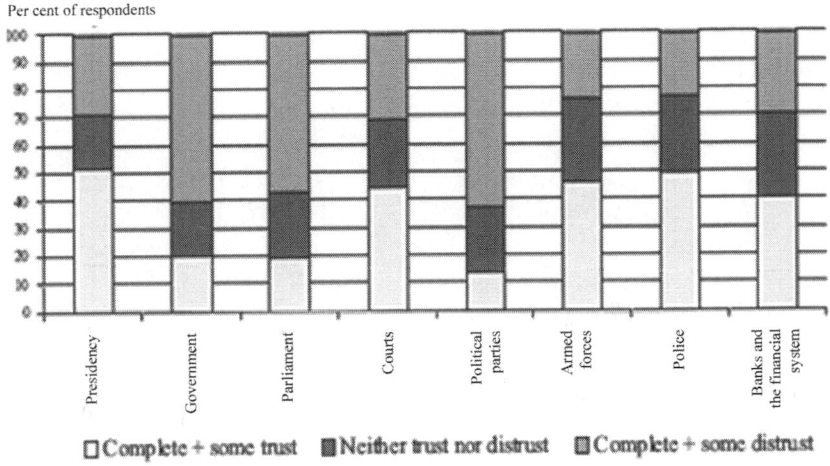

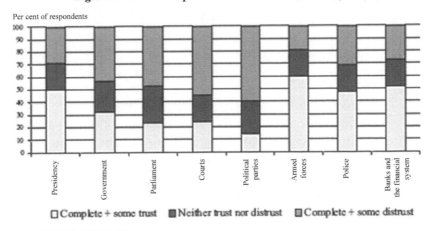

Source: EBRD (2007): 51

Figure 5.18. Trust in public institutions in Slovakia (2006)

Per cent of respondents

☐ Complete + some trust ▓ Neither trust nor distrust ☐ Complete + some distrust

Source: EBRD (2007): 75

Subjective feelings of injustice aggravated the objective losses. The old elite were generally perceived to have fared much better during the transition than the population at large. Incumbents dominated or were perceived to dominate privatization, which led to the cementing of their position in the new regime. In Slovakia, the dominance of the old managerial class during privatization is a historical fact (Appel and Gould 2000), while in Hungary it is only partially true but still remains a widespread perception (Laki and Szalai 2006).

Unrealistic expectations of the new system can similarly contribute to the general disillusionment. Transformation was originally perceived as a way to close the gap in living standards with the advanced West. As this did not materialize, disappointment was coded into the system. In spite of the considerable increase in living standards as measured by the availability of various consumer goods (EBRD 2007, 6), nostalgia for the previous regime has remained widespread. The strong attachment to the old regime both in Slovakia and Hungary can be seen from Figure 5.1.

Failures of the new system are also a source of justified disillusionment. Endemic corruption, policy and institutional failures contribute to a sense of skepticism regarding the new system. Over 70 percent in Hungary and 60 percent in Slovakia believe that there is more corruption in the new system than in the old regime (EBRD 2007, 51 and 75).

Figures 5.17 and 5.18 show a strong general distrust towards the new regime and especially towards the representative institutions such as parliament and political parties. The next two sections examine how the theoretical considerations about the difficulties of reforms in a low-trust environment prevailed in Hungary and Slovakia.

5.5.2. Vicious cycles in Hungary

Elite consensus over transition

During the early phase of transition lack of trust did not seem to influence policy. In the 1990s Hungary was among the leaders of post-communist transition—it signed an association agreement with the EU already in 1991 and was the first country to submit its membership application in 1994. These reflected considerable advantages over other transformation countries. First, market reforms had already started as early as 1968, and in spite of periodic reversals they continued up until the transition. As a result of the reforms undertaken by the last socialist government, by the time of regime change 90 percent of the prices had been already liberalized and thus there was no need for stabilization.[25] Second, there was a

---

[25] The last socialist government from 1988 pursued a radical liberalization policy: 1. it abolished import restrictions without compensation for domestic producers; 2. liberal-

widespread consensus among the major political actors over the main tasks of transformation—the establishment of democracy and a market economy that would eventually lead the country into the European Union. Furthermore, the idea that for a small-open economy, export-led growth is the way to sustainable development was also widely shared, and this proved to be very important in two major areas: privatization to foreign investors and the hardening of budget constraints.

Privatization in Hungary started already in the 1980s when spontaneous privatization by management was encouraged. After the regime change, the second round of privatization's major objective was to generate revenue for the state and additional capital for enterprises, which practically meant the sale of enterprises to foreign investors. This stands in sharp contrast with the experiences of most other transition countries where various public distribution schemes had been tried before selling to foreigners. In Hungary, the obligation of inherited debt, which was 73 percent of the GDP in 1989, made foreign sale politically feasible and thus paradoxically helped the country toward the path of export-led growth (Mihályi 2001).

Besides the creation of real owners, the hardening of budget constraints was also seen as essential for the functioning of a market economy. The measures to reach this objective amounted to a microeconomic shock therapy for the economy (Csaba 1998, 1382). In January 1992, four major laws were introduced, all of which aimed at hardening the budget constraints for all actors in the economy and end the situation of circular indebtedness in the economy.[26]

The foreign-dominated privatization and the hardening of the budget constraints in the economy were very successful in bringing about the fast adjustment of domestic production. Hungary was the major beneficiary from foreign direct investment among the transition countries until 1995 (UN ECE 2003, 127). It was second only to Poland in recovering its industrial output to reach its pre-transition level by 1998 (UN ECE 2003, 114).[27] At the same time, the radical measures also had their costs. During

---

ized all prices except energy as well as abolished exchange rate controls; and 3. encouraged privatization with a preference for sale to the highest bidder (Csaba 1998a, 1381).

[26] The law on the central bank prohibited the monetary financing of the budget deficit. The law on financial institutions introduced the prudential, safety, transparency, and disclosure requirements of the Basel Convention. The law on accounting required companies to comply with international accounting standards. Finally, the bankruptcy law introduced an automatic trigger, which obliged debtors under criminal law to initiate bankruptcy procedures if they were in default for than 90 days.

[27] No other transition country could achieve this before 2000.

the early-1990s over 30,000 companies went through some form of bankruptcy procedures (Ábel and Szakadát 1997, 640) which had far-reaching consequences. As discussed in the previous section, during this period, employment dropped by 30 percent, unemployment rose to over 12 percent and the loss in GDP was close to 20 percent. The wave of bankruptcies affected the banking sector as well, and the share of non-performing loans reached 32 percent of total company loans by 1993 (Ábel and Szakadát 1997, 643).

Disillusionment, crisis and the breakdown of consensus

The transformational recession resulted in fast disillusionment with the transition and soon led to the collapse of the elite consensus. The loss of employment opportunities and rising popular dissatisfaction placed increasing demands on the welfare system of the country. In response to these pressures, the government considerably eased the regulations regarding disability pensions, early retirement, and maternity benefits[28] thus sowing the seeds for the later problems of the economy. The pressure to consolidate the banking system further contributed to eroding the earlier commitment of lowering state redistribution. By 1994, consolidated expenditures reached 60.8 percent of the GDP, up from 55.8 percent in 1991 (László 2001, 846). The upcoming elections were not favorable for fiscal restraint either and gave a further reason for the government to postpone fiscal consolidation. The massive overspending however did not save the government: the Hungarian Democratic Forum still suffered a devastating defeat at the elections, which were won by the Hungarian Socialist Party.

While a large fiscal deficit (see Figure 5.9) and the accompanying current account deficit due to foreign financing required immediate actions, the government postponed harsh measures in order to prepare for the municipal elections that were held in October that year. The problems were addressed only in March 1995 after financial crisis hit Mexico, and it was feared that Hungary would be the next to fall. The surprise package implemented by the new minister of finance, Lajos Bokros, relied on monetary, fiscal, and income policy to stabilize the economy. The main elements were a one-off devaluation, the introduction of a crawling peg exchange rate, the levying of an 8 percent import surcharge and nominal wage freeze in the public sector. Structural reforms played only a marginal role and instead there was an across-the-board type cut reducing

---

[28] For an overview about the systemic logic of this process see Szalai (2007), 104–129.

primary expenditures from 51.9 to 41.6 percent of GDP. After the package, the process of privatization, which was stopped before the elections, was resumed in order to generate revenue to cover the debt burden. Similarly to the earlier years, the privileging of foreign strategic investors for the sale of banks and other large enterprises was an explicit governmental policy.

The package achieved its main objective and Hungary avoided a financial crisis without entering into a recession or suffering further employment losses. The devaluation of the exchange rate and the nominal wage freeze greatly improved the competitiveness of the economy and kept the country on an export-led path of growth—the value of merchandise exports doubled between 1995 and 1999 (UN ECE 2003, 121). As a result, by 1997 growth resumed and Hungary maintained its reputation as one of the leaders of the transition signaled by the highly positive evaluations from international institutions from the EBRD to the European Commission.

The above results however came at a serious social and political cost. Inflation jumped to 28 percent, eroding real wages, which fell by a total of 18 percent in 1995 and 1996. The reduction of entitlements, such as introducing needs-based family allowances or tuition fees in higher education, aimed to signal the importance of individual responsibility in the new regime but their main result was the triggering of a serious resistance to the package. The opposition denied that such harsh measures were necessary and Bokros soon became the least popular figure in the country. After the crisis was over he was forced to resign from his post in 1996. While a three-pillar pension system was introduced by his successor in 1997, no further major reforms took place for a decade after his leave.

The shock administered by the Bokros package had long-lasting influence on Hungarian economic policymaking. First, the country avoided a financial crisis and thus Hungarian policymakers never learned the dangers of irresponsibility in the age of capital mobility. Instead, the unpopularity of the package and the loss of the following elections in 1998 made them extremely reluctant to introduce fiscal restrictions. Promising material benefits to buy support became the norm for all parties before subsequent elections. Second, as the opposition took advantage of the difficult situation of the government and exploited the resistance to the measures, the consensual policymaking characterizing the early phase of transition turned into open hostility among the major factions. These developments eventually eroded the results of the package even though until 2000 the new center-right government successfully maintained fiscal discipline.

The emergence of vicious cycles

Following the turn of the Millennium, the consequences of low trust became manifest in Hungarian policy-making. While the early consensus
regarding economic transformation broke down already in the 1990s, the
closure of EU accession negotiations in 2002 meant that an important external anchor also disappeared. Budgetary cycles accompanying elections
became the dominant feature of the Hungarian economy. As can be seen
from Figure 6, while peaks in the deficit could be observed during elections
in the 1990s, vote-buying was not the primary concern in the period between elections, which is shown by the measures described in the previous
section as well as by the early success of transformation. The period after
2000 can be characterized by permanent election campaigning and the lack
of any major reform, even in midterm governments. The dominance of political factors in budgetary decision making is well documented by Ohnsorge-Szabó and Romhányi (2007, 265), who show that in the absence of
politically motivated spending[29] since 2000, public debt would have been
36.9 percent of the GDP in 2006 instead of the 66 percent.

On the surface the persistence of electoral considerations after 2000 is
due to two factors: the large number of elections and referenda in this
period[30] and the intensifying antagonism between the major political parties after the close outcome of the 2002 elections that brought back to
power the Hungarian Socialist Party. However, if we look deeper, three
factors could be identified, which contributed to the dominance of election
cycles in economic policymaking:

- In a low-trust environment support can be bought only through short-
  term material benefits and thus regardless of the ideological leaning of
  the parties, overspending is the norm rather than the exception.[31] This
  phenomenon also implies that the public is unaware of the consequences of irresponsible fiscal policy, and fiscal illusion[32] is rampant.

---

[29] Among others these include subsidized credit for housing, increase in the public sector
wage bill, increase in pensions, and other social security benefits.

[30] These include municipal elections in the autumn of 2002, referendum on accession to
the European Union in May 2003, European parliamentary elections in May 2004, referendum on dual citizenship and hospital privatization in December 2004, followed by the
parliamentary elections in 2006.

[31] In the Hungarian context János Kis was the first to call attention to the relationship between
lack of policy-maker credibility and short-term economic decision-making (Kis, 2004, 301).

[32] This was manifested in a Gallup survey between the two rounds of parliamentary
elections in 2006, which showed that only 18 percent of the voters of the winning

- The institutional structure provides ample opportunity for the political class to manipulate the budget according to electoral considerations[33] as well as contributes to the fiscal illusion of the electorate.[34] Naturally, policymakers have no incentive to strengthen these institutions as that would only make vote-buying more difficult for them.
- During this period there was no external factor that would enforce discipline and the international financial markets provided ample financing to cover the imbalances.

The period between 2000 and 2008 in Hungary demonstrates the difficulties of structural reforms in a low-trust environment. The imbalances, which were due to populist electoral politics, were temporarily reduced in the midterm through suboptimal revenue-increasing measures that led to a worsening business environment. The increase in taxes and the administrative measures to fight the informal economy substantially increased administrative costs and created an unfavorable environment for investment.[35] Small and medium-size enterprises are particularly hard hit since they do not have the means to lobby individual exemptions from taxes or regulations (OECD 2008, 147). As this sector employs 69 percent of the labor force in Hungary, it is unsurprising that after Malta and Poland, Hungary had the third lowest employment rate in the European Union at 57.3 percent in 2007. Low employment in turn affects both growth and the fiscal balance. As labor is underutilized, growth prospects of the country decline. Low legal employment also means low contribution to the budget while at the same time entrenches demand for high welfare provisions. These provisions then have to be financed by high taxes on those who

---

party considered the high fiscal deficit (close to 10 percent that year) a serious economic problem.

[33] The major problems of the institutional framework concern the overly optimistic planning of the budget, the lack of restrictions during the adoption phase to increase spending, the discretion of the government to change the budget during the execution phase, as well as the lack of transparency. The extreme weakness of the Hungarian institutional framework for budgeting even in a Central European comparison has been noted by a number of observers. See Gleich (2003) or Kraan et al. (2007).

[34] The attempts in 2004 and 2005 to hide the budget deficit through creative accounting are examples of this relation. For these measures see Kraan et al. (2007, 12).

[35] The rankings of various international institutions reflect these developments. On the World Bank "ease of paying taxes" list Hungary ranks 127th out of the 178 countries just ahead of Vietnam (World Bank 2008, 47–49). Administrative costs in the economy reach 6.8 percent of the GDP, the highest in the European Union (European Commission 2006a, 3).

work, which provides considerable incentives for tax evasion and little incentive to work legally.[36] These developments undermined public trust in the state even further and thus created a vicious cycle between lack of trust and low growth.

The situation was further worsened by rapid credit growth (Figure 5.13), which took place mostly in foreign currency.[37] The major reason for foreign indebtedness was the large interest rate differential between loans in the domestic currency and in the euro. Given the weak credibility of Hungarian economic policy due to the above reasons, domestic interest rates remained steadily high—as a result, between 2004 and 2007 the difference between euro loans were cheaper by 6.5 percent for housing and 15.5 percent for consumption goods (Darvas and Szapáry 2008, 40). The high interest rate influenced foreign currency lending through the exchange rate channel as well—the forint remained strong and stable in relation to the euro, which contributed to the underestimation of exchange rate risk by borrowers. As the credit boom created the illusion of prosperity it is unsurprising that the sharp increase in foreign currency borrowing was not countered by effective policy measures.[38] The growing indebtedness in foreign currency made the country extremely vulnerable to any change in market sentiment and the volatility of the currency.

Hungary and the subprime crisis

Hungary was hit by the subprime crisis in an extremely weak state. The economy was characterized by large fiscal imbalances, high public and private debt, as well as a high share of foreign currency loans. The political situation was similarly fragile given the deep divisions within the elite and the extreme unpopularity of the Gyurcsány government, which even-

---

[36] For an extensive overview of the composition of stabilization efforts in Hungary between 2000 and 2007, see Szakolczai (2009). He documents both the increase in taxes as well as monetary welfare transfers.

[37] By 2008, the share of foreign currency lending approached 70 percent of total household loans. For a detailed overview on the buildup of these loans see Hudecz (2012), 381–386. I rely primarily on his assessment in the following discussion of the main causes of foreign currency lending in Hungary.

[38] The complete lack of response to the growth of foreign currency lending is unique in the CEE region as shown by Bethlendi (2011, 211). Based on interviews with the participants, the reluctance of the government to constrain the credit boom is documented by Szentkirályi (2011). This was especially important, since financial supervision in Hungary is separate from the independent central bank, and the supervisory body (PSZAF) is under the authority of the Ministry of Finance.

tually led to the collapse of the governing coalition and a minority government in April 2009 under a new prime minister, Gordon Bajnai.

Given the above circumstances it is unsurprising that following the collapse of Lehman Brothers in September 2008, the subsequent freeze of the global financial markets and the sharp devaluation of its currency, Hungary was the first EU country to turn to the IMF for help. As a consequence the country had to implement deep fiscal cuts[39] in the midst of the subprime crisis, deepening the collapse of output, which reached -6.3 percent in 2009. Following a decade of resistance by the political elite, in the context of the bailout package the parliament adopted strict fiscal rules constraining the growth of debt and established a fiscal council to provide independent assessment of budgetary policy and evaluate legislative proposals based on their budgetary impact.

Following stabilization however, a new government came to power with a different agenda led by Viktor Orbán. The mismanagement of the economy and the subsequent pain of adjustment during the financial crisis swept away the socialist government in the 2010 elections. The center-right Fidesz, in coalition with the Christian Democrats, received a two third majority in the Parliament on the bases of promises of an alternative economic policy, which involves no further restrictive measures but promotes growth instead. While they promised a radical turnaround, the short-termism of the earlier period only intensified as checks and balances in the institutional framework were removed.

The program of the new government relied on a mix of conservative and nationalistic elements. During its first year of office, the Orbán cabinet introduced the flat tax, substantially increased benefits to families with children, as well as a loosened labor market regulations and welfare benefits in order to encourage employment. While these measures copied the earlier Slovakian reform program,[40] they did not produce the same results

---

[39] The measures included "1. a nominal wage freeze and the elimination of the 13th monthly salary for all public sector employees; 2. the elimination of the 13th monthly pension for all early retirees and a cap on the 13th monthly pension to HUF 80,000 for other pensioners; 3. postponement or elimination of indexation of selected social benefits; and 4. across-the-board cuts in other spending allocations to ministries (0.5 percent of GDP). Within the capital expenditure envelope, priority will be given to investment projects cofinanced by EU structural funds. On the revenue side, the authorities have already announced that tax cuts previously envisaged for 2009 will be postponed until sufficient fiscal space has been created through expenditure restraint. Under the program, the authorities will also not make any changes in the tax code that could lead to a net revenue loss" IMF (2008), 10.

[40] This will be discussed in the next section.

given the parallel measures, which aimed to compensate for the loss of state revenues. Unlike in Slovakia, the reduction of taxes on labor was not matched by similar cuts in state expenditure. Instead the government de facto nationalized the second pillar of the pension system and special taxes were introduced for banks and multinational companies. The problem of foreign currency indebtedness was addressed through a long moratorium on evictions as well as the possibility to repay the foreign currency loans at an exchange rate well below the market rate.[41]

A common feature of the main measures was the method of implementation—they were mostly implemented in an ad hoc manner without consultations or impact studies. Impromptu decision making became a defining feature of policy (Csaba 2012, 303). The unconcealed desire of the government for increasing the discretion over policymaking was signaled by the systematic cut down on institutional checks and balances. Steps towards this objective included the nomination of party members to the posts of President and the head of the State Audit Office, as well as the elimination of the newly established Fiscal Council. The power of the Constitutional Court was also curbed following its resistance to retroactive laws. While the inclusion of a 50 percent debt rule in the new Constitution could seem like a step towards rules-based fiscal policy, in reality the government made sure that the rule applies only to future governments.[42]

The impromptu decision making and the weakening of institutional checks and balances greatly increased uncertainty for all actors. So although the government was able to reduce debt from 81.4 (2010) to 78.5 percent (2011) and maintain a deficit below 3 percent,[43] growth is expected to be sluggish around 1 percent—way below regional peers. Part of the reason for this is the lack of confidence from global and domestic investors, which is manifested in the country's downgrade into speculative category, a weakening exchange rate, an outflow of foreign capital, increasing risk premium, and growing difficulties in obtaining credit for both companies and households.[44]

Overall, Hungary can be considered as a primary example of how lack of institutional trust makes short-turn decision making a constant feature

---

[41] For a detailed overview of the efforts to fight foreign currency indebtedness see Hudecz (2012, 400–407).

[42] The Law on Financial Stability postponed the obligations under the debt rule to 2016.

[43] Data on Hungarian economic developments is from European Commission (2012, 49 and 210).

[44] For an extensive overview of these processes see NBH (2012).

regardless of who is in power. While lack of trust could be compensated by elite consensus and an external anchor during the early years of transition, following the disappearance of these factors distrust manifested itself in growing financial imbalances. As the global financial crisis made the continuation of such policies impossible, short-termism assumed a new form and manifested itself in the attacks against multinational companies and banks. The sad consequence is the continuation of a vicious cycle between distrust and economic performance.

The case places the example of Slovakia into a very favorable light, which was able to avoid a similar outcome. In the following, I will try to decipher the major causes of this performance and then analyze the reasons behind the unexpected differences between the two countries.

5.5.3. From isolation to star performer: reforms in Slovakia

Postponing transformation under Mečiar

Czechoslovakia entered the transition period without any of the reforms that took place in Hungary since 1968. This made shock therapy, simultaneous stabilization and liberalization necessary at the beginning of transition, which were implemented by Václav Klaus in January 1991. Given its different industrial structure, Slovakia was particularly hard hit by these measures—between 1990 and 1992 its GDP declined by 22 percent and employment fell by 13 percent. The respective figures in the Czech Republic were 13 percent and 9 percent (UN ECE 2003, 112 and 115). This lent increasing support to the vigorous opposition of Vladimír Mečiar, who argued that transition polices should be tailored to Slovakia's special conditions and cause minimal social disruption (Fisher, Gould, and Haughton 2007, 987).

Looking only at the aggregate numbers it would appear that Mečiar reached his goals. After a sharp initial downturn, GDP started to recover by 1994, while inflation was reduced below 10 percent by 1996 (Morvay 2000, 22). However, the favorable macroeconomic indicators hid serious microeconomic problems. Unlike in Hungary, privatization took place via voucher methods (1990–1992) and domestic sales (1994–1996) with the exclusion of foreign investors. The problem with the first method was that it produced diffuse ownership and in the absence of minority shareholder protection rights it provided considerable opportunities for investment fund managers to enrich themselves (Marcincin 2000a, 300–303). As they supported Mečiar's opponents, from 1994 privatization proceeded through a series of direct sales mainly to political allies—the former communist managers (Fisher, Gould, and Haughton 2007, 988). Other aspects of economic policy (state aid, favorable public contracts, state guarantees on loans, lack of bankruptcy enforcement, and creditors' right protection) complemented the political objectives of privatization and helped to preserve the inherited industrial structure (Marcincin 2000b, 331–332).

The result of the above policy was a growing fiscal deficit, although hidden through creative accounting,[45] as well as a steady deterioration of international competitiveness, which was manifested in the worsening current account.[46] The lack of international competitiveness also meant the accumulation of non-performing loans in the banking sector, reaching 41 percent by 1998 (Barto 2000, 365). At the same time the soft policies that postponed restructuring were unable to protect jobs and unemployment remained steadily over 10 percent (Morvay 2000, 22).

The fall of Mečiar however was not primarily due to the economy. The ensuing corruption, disregard of the constitution, criminal methods to deal with opponents, strong nationalist rhetoric, and mistreatment of the Hungarian minority[47] together led to international isolation. In the economy this was shown by the lack of FDI inflows thus making the country reliant on foreign loans to finance the twin deficit (Fisher, Gould, and Haughton 2007, 988). Even more critical was the fact that in contrast to the other Visegrad countries, Slovakia was refused first-wave accession into both the NATO and the European Union.

Building credibility during the first Dzurinda government

International rejection deeply hurt Slovak national pride and undermined Mečiar's capacity to mobilize nationalism for his survival (Greskovits 2008). In 1998, the anti-Mečiar forces won the elections, which mobilized 84.4 percent of the Slovak voters. The new coalition led by Mikulas Dzurinda included 10 political groups which were bound together primarily by their anti-Mečiarism (Keszegh 2006, 173). While the presence of former communists made radical change impossible, the prospect of EU accession held the coalition together and the government succeeded in the most urgent tasks.

---

[45] Tóth (2000) provides data from the Ministry of Finance, showing that after the initial shock of creating a new state, fiscal prudence was observed—after 1994 the budget deficit was never higher than 5 percent (63–64). However, he also notes the unreliability of this information and the difficulties of knowing the real balance (65). In hindsight his analysis was correct—net lending reached -9.9 percent in 1996 and -6.3 percent in 1997.

[46] The current account deficit remained over 9 percent between 1996 and 1998.

[47] On Mečiar's anti-democratic practices see Fish (1999).

The most important task was to regain the confidence of the international organizations. This was done through a very strong cooperation with the European Union during which Slovakia implemented all the necessary measures without asking for exceptions or special treatment during the negotiation process (Fisher, Gould, and Haughton 2007, 990). The international community responded well to Slovakia's efforts and in 1999 the European Commission revised its previous opinion and concluded that Slovakia fulfilled the Copenhagen political criteria. The country also joined the OECD in 2000 and the NATO in 2002.

Besides building international credibility, the government introduced an austerity package to stabilize public finances, which turned out to be in a worse state than expected. In addition to severely restricting government expenditures, the package included a 7 percent import surcharge, which not only meant increased revenues but also contributed to reducing the current account deficit (Suster 2004, 66). The government also encouraged the inflow of FDI through tax and tariff breaks as well as the privatization of banks and state monopolies. The sale of state banks after restructuring, which cost 13 percent of the GDP in 2000, resulted in a 97 percent foreign ownership of total private Slovak banking capital (Suster 2004, 69).

While the reforms were far from popular and unemployment reached its peak at 19.8 percent in 1999, the success of the Dzurinda government in regaining international confidence helped the government in narrowly winning the elections in 2002 and forming an ideologically coherent center-right coalition without the former communists.

Radical reforms by the second Dzurinda government (2002–2006)

Freed from the tasks of European accession, from 2002 the newly elected government embarked on a series of radical reforms that aimed to address the country's desperate employment performance via neoliberal policies. The main principles driving the reforms were to increase incentives for employment, investment, and job creation (Árendás et al. 2006, 229). In order to reach these objectives systemic measures were implemented in public finance and the market regulatory framework. The main elements were the following:[48]

---

[48] Due to space constraint and the nature of the chapter the following overview can only be an incomplete list of the measures rather than an exhaustive analysis. For a detailed summary and evaluation of the reforms see the edited volumes of Zachar (2004) and Zachar (2005).

- *Flat tax*: introduction of a uniform 19% rate for corporate tax, personal income tax, and VAT. The idea behind this measure was to tax all income equally regardless of its source, eliminate the numerous exceptions that characterized the prior system, and simplify tax administration to reduce tax evasion (Árendás et al. 2006, 230–232). Through providing tax bonuses after every child, the system also aimed to motivate employment.

- *Public finance responsibility*: increasing budgetary transparency, introducing program budgeting, and developing a medium-term macroeconomic framework in order to improve the cost-effectiveness of taxpayers' money. As a result of the reforms, Slovakia now has the fourth strongest budgetary framework in the European Union (European Commission 2007, 125).

- *Labor market reforms*: in order to increase the flexibility of the labor market, the power of trade unions was curbed and employment protection regulations eased (Fisher, Gould, and Haughton 2007, 982).

- *Regulatory reforms:* easing the process of establishing and closing a business through simplified procedures and more effective registration of property.

- *Social policy reforms:* aimed to end the situation when under certain conditions receiving aid was more beneficial to a family than gaining employment (Király et al. 2006, 259–260). The length of unemployment insurance was reduced from 9 to 6 months, while the replacement ratio decreased from 60% of the previous wage to 50%. The reform of sickness benefits meant that the first 10 days of sickness was paid by the employer, which gave incentive for better monitoring. Receiving unemployment benefits was tied to actively searching for a job.

- *Pension reform*: in order to deal with the consequences of aging population, the age limit for retirement was raised to 62 years and a three-pillar pension system was introduced.

- *Health care reform*: the reform sought to transform providers into competing businesses and opened up the insurance market to private competitors. Consumers were discouraged to seek unnecessary care through the introduction of copayment fees (Fisher, Gould, and Haughton 2007, 984).

- *Judicial reform*: fight corruption in the legal profession as well as implement a new set of penalties to encourage socially functional behavior (Fisher, Gould, and Haughton 2007, 985).

The reforms were widely hailed among international observers and in 2005 Slovakia was named top reformer by the World Bank (2005). The international acclaim was supported by the strong performance of the economy that could be observed in the acceleration of growth, decreasing unemployment and declining inflation (Figure 5.19).

Figure 5.19. Unemployment, GDP growth and inflation in Slovakia 2003–2008 (%)

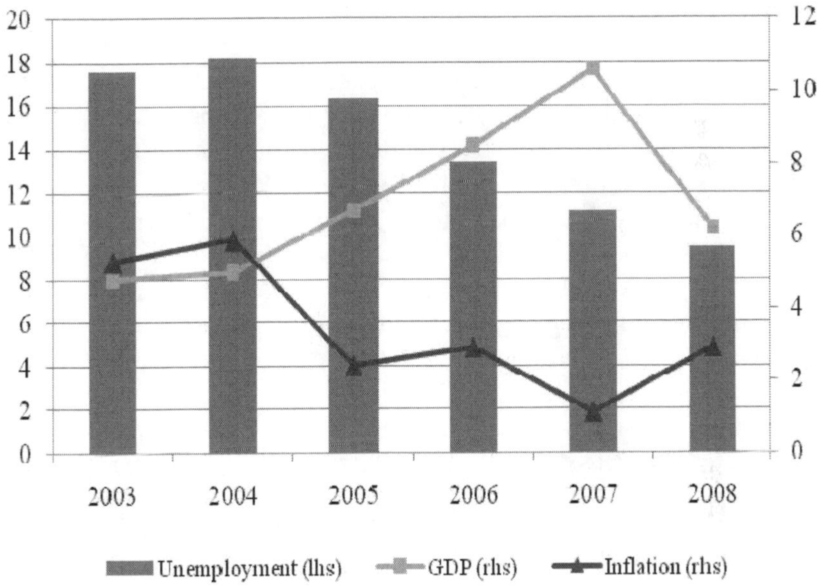

Data: European Commission (2010): 200

The reforms however were not without costs. The low-skilled, the unemployed and the pensioners were especially hard-hit as their benefits were reduced while the prices of food and utilities rose (Moore 2005, 24–27). The food riots and violent demonstrations during 2004 in mainly Roma-populated areas in eastern Slovakia manifested the hardship of the reforms and the unequal regional distribution of benefits. The inequality is also shown by the fact that about two-thirds of employees earn less than the average monthly wage (EIU 2006a, 14). Furthermore, while total unemployment was still high at around 10 percent, in the eastern regions it is steadily over 20 percent (IMF 2007c, 14). The resulting public disaffection was shown during the 2006 elections, where an extremely low turnout (54 percent) produced a convincing majority for the left-wing anti-reform forces led by Robert Fico's SMER.

Mild reversal of reforms, EMU accession, and the subprime crisis

While the populist rhetoric of the new government and the return of Meciar to government provoked speculations about the fate of Dzurinda's reforms, fears of a complete reversal proved to be unfounded. The budget submitted in December 2006 reflected the maintenance of the flat tax system as well as the commitment to EMU accession (Fisher, Gould, and Haughton 2007, 995). At the same time, in spite of maintaining the main elements of the reforms, a gradual softening of policies took place. Immediately after assuming power the Fico-led government abolished the highly unpopular copayment in health care, decreased the VAT rate for foodstuffs, increased state support for utility prices, and ruled out privatization of "strategic" enterprises including the Bratislava airport and the rail transport firm ZSSK Cargo (EIU 2006b, 22–23).

The slight turnaround however did not undermine the reform structure built by the previous government. This was recognized in the European Commission's assessment in May 2008 that Slovakia was ready for the euro. Furthermore the rapid growth and increasing employment made the Fico government highly popular, while Dzurinda remained one of the most unpopular public figures in Slovakia.

However, the subprime crisis changed the Slovakian political landscape. Given the strong export-dependence of Slovakia's economy, the GDP contracted by 4.7 percent in 2009 while unemployment increased to 12 percent. As 2010 was also an election year, it is unsurprising that budget deficit rose to 6.4 percent of GDP. At the same time, the economic downturn eroded support for the governing coalition, and in spite of expectations, after the 2010 elections a coalition of center-right parties led by Iveta Radicova returned to power (EIU 2010, 5). Her government was committed to the continuation of economic reforms and fiscal responsibility, which involved a harmonization of social security contributions as well as the further strengthening of fiscal institutions (IMF 2011b, 11–12). While investor confidence remained strong and the economy grew by 4 percent in 2010, the European debt crisis still led to the collapse of government—in October 2011 Radicova lost the vote of confidence in relation with Slovakia's contribution to the European crisis mechanism. In the April 2012, Fico came back to power with an absolute majority.

Overall, Slovakia entered the subprime crisis in a very different state than Hungary. Implementing structural reforms during the period of international economic boom allowed the country to introduce the euro, which provided substantial protection against market forces at a time when other countries in the region struggled to keep the value of their currency. Given its strong export dependency, Slovakia could not avoid being hit by the crisis, however, it quickly recovered and is expected to grow by 4 percent in the medium term (IMF 2011b, 1).

5.5.4. The political economy of reforms in a low-trust environment

The experiences of almost two decades of transition in Hungary and Slovakia allow some general inferences regarding the conditions under which reforms become possible even in an environment where lack of trust is likely to increase resistance to reforms. As both of these countries face a very similar external environment, I will not discuss global markets and the EU separately as I did in the previous chapter after the case studies. Instead I will focus on specific internal factors, which can be considered as decisive in the different outcomes: crisis, reformers' credibility, and elite consensus. These also allow placing the role of EU and EMU into a domestic context.

Crisis played an important role in reforms both in Hungary and Slovakia. In Hungary the fear of an imminent collapse was instrumental in the implementation of the Bokros package, while in Slovakia the international isolation as a result of Meciar's policies was seen as critical. Crisis however was conspicuously lacking in Hungary between 2000 and 2006 when the international financial markets contributed to the irresponsibility of Hungarian politicians by providing financing for the imbalances.

When discussing the role of crisis in reforms, Rodrik (1996, 27) calls such explanations problematic as they are both tautological and non-falsifiable: if the economy in crisis is not reformed, then the explanation that the crisis has not been severe enough is rather unsatisfying. This criticism was already mentioned in the previous chapter with regard to the cases of Portugal and Sweden. It is valid in these cases as well, and leads us to recognize that any crisis-based explanation is necessarily based on perceptions rather than objective reality. This means that it is impossible to tell the degree of deterioration that is necessary for politicians and the electorate to initiate change in previously followed policies. In 1995, there was no need for collapse of the Hungarian economy and the government implemented the stabilization package as a preventive measure. In Slovakia the fear of being left out from the EU was instrumental in generating the perception of crisis.

The subprime crisis is a further illustration of the limits of crisis-based arguments. In both cases, the economic downturn led to a change in government but this can hardly be interpreted as a popular mandate for large-scale reforms. Although in Hungary it led to the implementation of large-scale fiscal consolidation, the radical measures taken by the center-right government clearly indicate that not all reforms should be considered as progress.

Reformers' credibility was also instrumental for the success of reforms in both cases. The personal commitment and ability of Bokros and Dzurinda to implement a liberal reform agenda were not questioned even by their harshest opponents. Their critics at home rather focused on the necessity of such reforms, while investors were convinced about the advantages as manifested by the accelerating investment activity after the reforms. The failure of the Gyurcsány government after 2006 to implement structural reforms also underlines the importance of credibility. As Gyurcsány admitted in the infamous lie speech[49] the responsibility for the near-crisis situation in 2006, his motivation for reform was called into serious doubt. The over 80 percent rejection of the three symbolic elements of reform at the referendum in March 2008 signaled that the public was unwilling to accept restrictions from politicians primarily responsible for the need for such measures.

Elite consensus played an important but marginal role in reforms both in Hungary and in Slovakia. In Hungary the early consensus that characterized the transition was instrumental in hardening the budget constraints and privatization to foreigners. With such a consensus in place there was no need for a crisis to implement the necessary policies. Lacking such consensus, it took almost a decade of experimenting for Slovakia to follow this course. However, the disillusionment from the transition and its exploitation by the major parties led to the collapse of the early consensus in Hungary. Following the 2010 elections, the consensus appeared to be returning given the large majority in government, but this was mostly an anti-reform consensus, which is well in line with the theory predicting the difficulties of structural change in a low-trust environment.

Consensus has been even more absent in Slovakia during the nearly two decades of transition. The only important exception is the introduc-

---

[49] After the successful elections, in May 2006 Ferenc Gyurcsány gave a speech to the Socialist party members of the newly elected Parliament at Balatonőszöd. In the speech he admitted lying day and night about the true state of the country in order to win the elections. The speech was secretly recorded and on September 17 it was broadcasted on Hungarian Radio. The content and obscenity of the speech ignited mass protests around Hungary and riots in Budapest in the following months.

tion of the euro, to which Fico remained committed in spite of his populist discourse. However, even in this case consensus did not mean discussions on policy and shared responsibility but rather the response to pressures from business interest groups who had a stake in introducing the common currency and sustaining the reforms (Fisher, Gould, and Haughton 2007, 995).

Summing up the results of the comparison between Hungary and Slovakia, the following reform dynamic appears. In the absence of an elite consensus, a perception of crisis by the elite is necessary for changing unsustainable policies. Once a window of opportunity appears for reforms, the human factor becomes critical in the quality and quantity of the measures. If these reforms are successful, an elite consensus might emerge on the necessity to maintain them. This dynamics implies that the main difference between Hungary and Slovakia in the past decade was that in the latter case all three factors have prevailed, while in the former all of them were lacking, not least due to the previous success of the transition, which provided sufficient international credibility for irresponsible policies to go unpunished. Finally, luck also has seems to have a role favoring Slovakia. The country introduced its reforms at a time of global prosperity, and even as Hungary tries to copy some of those reforms following the subprime crisis, they are unlikely to yield the same rewards.

* * *

The main question of this chapter was how to prevent the emergence of a vicious cycle between low trust, populist economic policies, and low growth or, if present, under what conditions it can be broken. From the overview of the experiences of CEE-10, it appears that there is no easy solution to this problem. While certain shortcuts such as establishing a currency board might prevent large imbalances in the public sector, financial imbalances seem to prevail in a different form—with a few exceptions it appears that fiscal stringency and accumulation of private debt often go together. This implies that the availability of credit might serve as a form of compensation for limited welfare spending. The resulting overheating, asset bubbles, and current account imbalances indicate the heavy price paid for such policies.

In the region, the example of Slovakia stands out as a case where path dependence could be broken and in spite of a difficult start at the beginning of transition, the country has clearly broken out of a vicious cycle. The deeper examination of its reforms indicates both the importance of human agency as well as timing. While most countries delayed structural changes during the boom years of 2002–2007, Slovakia used this time to implement far-reaching changes in its economy. The success of the reforms made the changes sustainable and placed the country on a steady path of growth.

From the overview of both the old and the new post-communist members of the EU, the major lesson is the lasting divergence of economic policies and the continued importance of domestic decision making. In order to check the broader relevance of this finding, in the following chapter, I will discuss the evolution of the subprime crisis at the EU-level and look at whether the cases of Hungary and Slovakia can be generalized, that is, whether pre-crisis evaluation is a good predictor of performance during the crisis.

CHAPTER 6

Financial Crisis in the EU-25

Old and new EU members alike came under severe pressure as the sub-prime crisis swept over the world in 2008. Economic conditions were very different in the various groups, which were discussed in the previous two chapters, and the divergence persisted throughout the crisis. The major question of this chapter is whether the pre-crisis evaluation of economic performance is tenable following the crisis. Are there any unexpected causalities or successes? If so, how does it affect the argument about the relevance of trust for economic outcomes?

In order to answer the above questions, the chapter first provides a brief account of the financial crisis then assesses the costs of the crisis in the various groups examining growth, unemployment, and public debt developments. Through this exercise two major surprises are identified and analyzed in depth—Ireland as an unexpected causality and Poland as an unexpected success story. These cases call attention to the limits of the theory and the need for acknowledging the persistence of fundamental un-certainty even in a seemingly well-functioning institutional environment: overconfidence and complacency caused the collapse in Ireland, while Poland benefited from the prudence understandable in an environment of distrust. These extremes also help to explain the surprising finding from the assessment of performances during the crisis—slow reformers appear to have done better than the pre-crisis star performers.

The chapter proceeds as follows. In the next two sections I will provide an overview about the roots of the subprime crisis and its spread in the EU. Then I will discuss the performance of the seven groups of countries during the crisis and contrast the assessment with the predictions of the theory. In the following I will address the cases of Ireland and Poland, the two major surprises of the crisis. I will conclude the chapter with implications to the theory.

6.1. The origins of the subprime crisis[1]

The subprime crisis, which hit the world in 2008, had its origins in the United States subprime mortgage markets but its roots went deeper than particular market segments. Easy monetary conditions are usually identified as the root of most financial crises (Kindelberger 1989, Reinhart and Rogoff 2009) and the subprime crisis is a prime example of this thesis. Following the collapse of the dotcom bubble in 2000, the very low interest rates in the United States, including a 3-year period of negative real rates between August 2002 and August 2005, as well as the substantial dollar savings from Asian countries, created enormous liquidity on the financial markets. As investors were looking for increasing yields, higher risk-taking became the norm—implying increased leverage and the expansion of loans to consumers, who were previously denied credit. Advances in risk management, most importantly the securitization of loans, made these investments appear safer since risks could be spread across the financial system.[2]

The wide availability of credit started a bubble on the housing markets—as demand for housing grew, and supply followed only with a lag, a steady increase of prices took place (Baker 2008). This made real estate an attractive investment leading to further price hikes. However, once supply caught up with demand and prices started to decline, the process took a reverse turn—credit became constrained, leading to a further fall in prices. For those who had low equity in their house, the drop in prices meant that many owed more than the value of their property, and thus it was a better option to leave the key at the bank than continue paying the mortgage.

The collapse of the housing market led to the deterioration of the balance sheet of financial institutions, which had a stake in the market. Since securitization implied both a widespread ownership of these papers as well as an ambiguity about the precise extent of exposure, trust in the interbank market collapsed, and interest rates increased sharply—first in August 2007, followed by December 2007 and April 2008. For the wider

---

[1] In the following I present a very brief overview about the major causes of the crisis based on my earlier article (Győrffy 2009). There is already an enormous literature on the issue, see for example Brunnermeier (2009), Rajan (2010), Reinhart and Rogoff (2009), and Stiglitz (2010).

[2] For a concise overview of securitization see for example Coval, Jurek, and Stafford (2009) as well as Gorton (2008).

audience however, the crisis really started in September 2008 when Lehman Brothers was allowed to collapse and international financial markets froze as a result. While the U.S. government immediately intervened through fiscal and monetary measures, the crisis could not be contained and already in October it spread to Europe.

6.2. The crisis in the EU

After the collapse of Lehman Brothers, the freezing of the international monetary system transmitted the crisis around the world rapidly. Emerging markets dependent on foreign capital were particularly hard hit as risk premiums increased, new loan syndications dropped, and demand for their exports fell sharply (EBRD 2009, 10–11). As investors became more attentive to fundamentals, Hungary was hit first in the CEE region. As discussed in the previous chapter, Hungary was hit by the crisis given the lack of credibility of the government, high deficit and debt levels, as well as large-scale foreign indebtedness. In order to stop the speculative attack on the currency, the country had to turn to the IMF in October 2008.

As interbank markets froze, regional banks were also hard hit, particularly domestic ones, which had no access to liquidity from foreign parent banks. The Parex Bank in Latvia was a causality of the drying up of the interbank market—since the fixed exchange rate regime made it impossible for Latvia to bail out the bank, the country also had to turn to the IMF for help in December 2008 (Aslund 2010, 27).

The third country in the region, which needed IMF support, was Romania. On paper its fundamentals appeared better with lower level of debt and less foreign indebtedness. However, the maturity structure of its debts raised concerns and the country had difficulty rolling over short-term debt (Aslund 2009, 28). It signed an agreement with the IMF in March 2009.

The rest of the CEE region did not need external assistance for dealing with the crisis. Estonia and Lithuania implemented substantial fiscal cuts and managed the crisis on their own, while the two euro member states, Slovenia and Slovakia, as well as Poland and the Czech Republic, were not hurt by the crisis given sound fundamentals and a foreign owned banking sector (Aslund 2010, 28, 40–42). Maintaining exposure to the region by foreign banks is generally regarded as one of the major stabilizing factors in avoiding a full-blown financial collapse (EBRD 2009, 18).

As the crisis receded in the CEE region, attention started to turn to the indebted members of the euro-zone. By 2010, it became evident that euro-zone membership in itself was not a guarantee against the crisis. The first causality was Greece, which was, similarly to Hungary, an accident waiting to happen. As it could be seen from Chapter 4, Greece had never fulfilled the Maastricht deficit criterion and creative accounting was widespread. This became especially serious as the global crisis hit the world and two major sectors of the Greek economy—tourism and shipping—suffered especially hard. The situation was exacerbated by the policies of the new PA-SOK government, which gained power with promises of greater public spending and more social benefits.[3] As earlier attempts at creative accounting also came to light in November 2009, and the government was forced to present the true figures on public finance (deficit was revised from 3.7 to 12.5 percent of GDP, while public debt approached 120 percent of GDP), investors became concerned about the ability of Greece to repay its debt and interest rates rose substantially. (IMF 2010b, 6–7). However, instead of turning to the IMF the country had to wait for euro-zone governments to agree on a bailout package. This was accomplished in May 2010, when the European Financial Stability Facility (EFSF) was established by the European Commission and the IMF in order to provide financial assistance to euro-zone member states in times of economic difficulties.

Following the bailout of Greece, attention turned to Ireland, which recorded a 32 percent deficit in 2009 and its debt level approached 100 percent by 2010 after the collapse of its housing market and the bailout of its largest bank. Given the increasing difficulty of the government to obtain financing due to sharply rising interest rates, in November 2010 the country accepted an 85 billion euro rescue deal from the EFSF. As Ireland was one of the star performers in the past two decades, the collapse of its financial sector is one of the major surprises of the crisis. Its case will be discussed more in the depth in the second part of the chapter.

The third causality of the crisis was Portugal, which received a 78 billion euro bailout package in May 2011. The country was unable to substantially reduce its fiscal deficit of 10.1 percent in 2009 and recorded a 9.1 percent deficit in 2010. As a consequence, debt grew over 90 percent, and given the country's competitiveness problems, which were discussed in Chapter 4, investors became increasingly anxious about the financing of this debt, especially after the Irish bailout. The increased borrowing

---

[3] According to Visvizi (2012, 21) the increased deficit served the establishment of a solidarity fund, which distributed €800 million to the needy.

costs also affected the liquidity of the banking sector, which carried the danger of the familiar pattern of credit constraints, asset price decline, and worsening bank portfolios. The bailout package aimed to stop such a vicious cycle.[4]

Markets were not calmed however, and the crisis escalated during the summer of 2011. European interbank lending rates greatly increased, and the financing of public debt in Italy and Spain became particularly difficult. Although the European Central Bank used radical measures to maintain liquidity,[5] market confidence remained weak. Spain received a bailout package in June 2012, as the bursting of the real estate bubble brought the stability of the banking system into question and predicted the rise in public debt. The package aimed to break the vicious cycle of bank crisis and debt crisis.[6] At the time of writing the crisis is far from over and the future of the euro-zone remains an open question. However, for the purposes of this book it is safe to conclude that a clear divergence has emerged within the EU during the crisis, which allows the comparative assessment of performance of the various groups.

6.3. Consequences of the crisis in the EU-25

The crisis affected the real economy in Europe through three major channels.[7] First, the crisis was transmitted through the international financial system as losses in particular markets forced institutions to sell assets and withdraw resources from markets not affected by the crisis at the initial stage. Credit constraints thus became widespread and imposed limits on the spending decisions of economic actors. Second, the loss in wealth due to the fall in housing prices forced households to increase savings and postpone investment into consumer durables and housing. This led to a collapse in demand for manufacturing goods, especially for cars, and resulted in cuts in production as well as an increase in unemployment with an adverse feedback effect on the financial sector. Third, world trade collapsed in the last quarter of 2008 not only because of the global fall in demand but also be-

---

[4] See the press release of the IMF on the bailout package: http://www.imf.org/external/np/sec/pr/2011/pr11190.htm.

[5] Radical measures include the buying of government bonds—in clear contradiction with the statutes of the ECB—as well as the long-term refinancing operations, which injected €1 trillion into the European banking system.

[6] For a detailed chronology of the events see IMF (2012a, 5-10).

[7] The following summary is based on European Commission (2009), 24–26.

cause of the unavailability of trade finance as well as the prevalence of global supply chains, which immediately transmitted the crisis.

While these shocks were equally present for all countries, their consequences were diverse. It is thus a legitimate question to ask how the groups, which were formed prior to these events, fared during the crisis. The most interesting question is how strong the link is between performance prior to the crisis and afterwards. In order to assess the consequences of the crisis I will focus on three critical macroeconomic variables: GDP, public debt and unemployment. Examining these variables together provides a more thorough picture about crisis performance than looking at a single indicator because the distribution of the burden of the crisis is partly a matter of policy choice—while increasing fiscal spending might contain the collapse of GDP or unemployment, the effect of a fullblown crisis shows up in the accumulation of public debt and thus the costs have to be borne by future generations. In the following I will first assess the performance of individual countries in terms of the three indicators, then provide a summary assessment on the basis of the three indicators. This analysis will give preliminary answers to the main question of this chapter as well as guide the selection of case studies, which help to refine these answers.

6.3.1. Growth

The most often cited variable about the impact of crisis is the change in economic growth. Figure 6.1 shows the growth rates in the 25 countries under examination during the period from 2007, the last year before the crisis, to 2011. In order to have a sense of the differences among groups, countries are clustered together based on the groupings from the previous two chapters.[8]

Even at first sight it can be seen that performances differed widely both before and during the crisis. There is also some variety in the recovery phase, although slow growth rates are forecasted almost everywhere.

The volatility during this period was the greatest in currency board countries (Group 6), which had excellent growth performance prior to the crisis, but suffered the largest decline in the EU. However, they are expected to grow considerably faster than the EU-25 average by 2011. Re-

---

[8] The only change in the original groupings is to count Estonia as a Group 6 country together with other Baltic states and Bulgaria—as it was able to introduce the euro only in 2011 following the crisis.

covery is also expected in the new EMV member states (Group 5), particularly in Slovakia, which grew by over 4 percent already in 2010. The real surprise of the region however is Poland, which was the only country in the EU that did not experience a recession. As it also grew fast prior to the crisis and recovery is expected to be strong, its cumulative growth performance during the period under analysis is the best in the EU-25 (see Table 6.1. later).

Figure 6.1. Change in GDP in the EU-25 2007–2011

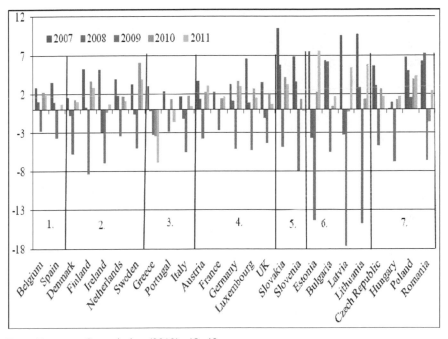

Data: European Commission (2012): 48–49

Among the old member states of the EU, Nordic countries (Group 2) could be expected to fare best on the basis of prior fiscal performance. On the basis of the figure, this is however not the case. While in Group 4 countries (and also in Belgium) the recession lasted for a single year, in Denmark and Sweden it lasted for 2 years, while in the case of Ireland it lasted for three. The good performance of Group 4 is somewhat surprising—these countries experienced the mildest recession among the EU-15, while recovery is expected to be as strong as in Group 2. In this group no countries needed a bailout, while all of them returned to growth by 2010, with Germany growing by 3.7 percent that year.

The weak performance of countries in Group 3 is hardly surprising on the basis of Chapter 4—pre-crisis financial imbalances and a lack of structural change made them vulnerable to the crisis. Greece and Portugal needed a bailout, while recovery is slow in all three countries.

Unlike in the case of Group 3, generalizations about performance are difficult to make for the two countries in Group 1, showing the limits of focusing on groups and necessitating analysis of individual cases. While Belgium shows strong recovery following a single year of recession, Spanish recovery is very slow and the country needed a bailout. While in Chapter 4 the basis for grouping cases was fiscal policy strategy, this strategy overlooked an important difference between the two countries— the presence of a real estate bubble in Spain, which requires a painful readjustment in order to improve competitiveness following the crisis.[9]

6.3.2. Public debt

When looking at the extent of the recession, it is also important to see the costs of potential countermeasures. These costs usually show up in the evolution of public debt (Figure 6.2).

Figure 6.2. Public debt in the EU-25 2007–2011 (% of GDP)

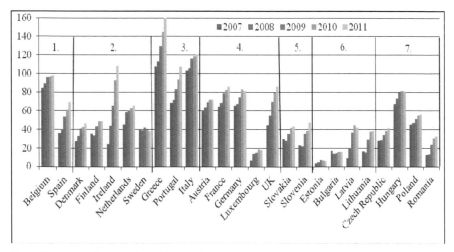

Data: European Commission (2012): 184-185

---

[9] Given the constraints of this chapter, I will not provide a more in-depth account of the real estate bubble in Spain. However, the case shows substantial similarity with Ireland, which will be discussed more in depth in section 6.4. For a comparison of the real estate bubbles in the two countries see FitzGerald (2009).

From Figure 6.2, it is evident that there is a general upward tendency of public debt in the EU, but this tendency is far from being uniform. While some countries experienced an increase of debt over 30 percent, many succeeded in keeping their debt level almost stable.

The performance of the CEE countries compares favorably to EU-15 experiences. Bulgaria and Estonia succeeded in keeping their debt levels stable, and even in countries that experienced a substantial increase in debt (Latvia, Lithuania, and Romania), the low starting level implies that they are still well below the average of the old member states. In the CEE-10, only Hungary has a debt level higher than the Maastricht debt criterion, and that debt was accumulated before the crisis.

In the EU-15, Group 2 countries—with the significant exception of Ireland—could also contain the rise in debt, with Sweden reducing its debt level below 40 percent. With the exception of Luxembourg, countries in the three other groups recorded a large increase, which is likely to be a strong constraint on future economic policy. This is particularly problematic for countries in Group 3, which had a very high initial level of debt. For the two countries in Group 1, debt developments show worrying tendencies, with Belgium projected to pass the 100 percent threshold and Spain the 80 percent threshold in 2012 (European Commission 2012, 184). It is unsurprising that investors have become increasingly worried about such performance.

6.3.3. Unemployment

The surge in unemployment, which is shown in Figure 3, reflects the human costs of the crisis. Similarly to the other two variables, the diversity of performance is the first thing to be noticed.

The largest surge in unemployment occurred in Spain, Ireland, Greece, Slovakia, and the three Baltic states, where the figure is over 14 percent—in the case of Spain it is over 20 percent. In contrast, unemployment in the Netherlands, Austria, and Luxembourg remained below 6 percent even during the crisis—all in the EU-15. In general, EU countries performed better than the CEE countries on this measure, which probably reflects the flexibility of the labor market as well as the constraints of increasing indebtedness in the new member states.

Figure 6.3. Unemployment in the EU-25 2007–2011

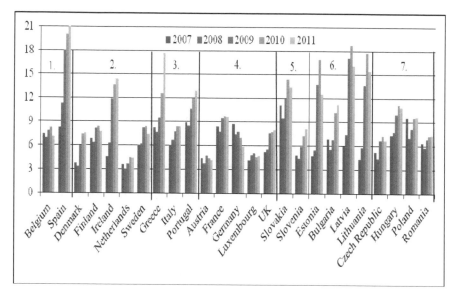

Data: European Commission (2012): 34–35

6.3.4. Assessment of crisis performance

In order to assess overall performance, Table 6.1 summarizes develop-ments in the three indicators discussed above: cumulative GDP, as well as change in debt and unemployment during 2007–2011.

Before analyzing the table, it is important to underline what these numbers imply and to what extent they can be taken as measures of coun-try performance. Among the three measures, cumulative growth can be taken as the most reliable indicator of performance—while the 2007 val-ues might be biased due to the presence of a credit boom, this bias is com-pensated by the collapse of the bubble in 2009 as well as the speed of the recovery. However, the other two measures (change in debt and unem-ployment) strongly depend on the initial values—for example an increase in public debt from 10 percent to 30 percent is not the same as an increase from 60 to 80 percent. It is the same with unemployment—a rise from 4 to 6 percent is different from a rise from 10 to 12 percent. A lower initial valve inplies room for deterioration in hard times, while an increase in the case of a high initial level makes an already serious problem acute. Still, as I mentioned earlier, it is important to look at other indicators than the growth rate, since a relatively good performance can be accompanied by a

sharp rise in debt, and for the assessment of performance the two measures should be considered jointly.

Table 6.1. Summary of crisis performance in the EU-25

Country	Cumulative growth (%) 2007–2011	Change in debt (% of GDP) 2007–2011	Change in unem- ployment (%) 2008–2011
Belgium	5.3	13.9	-0.2
Spain	1.3	32.3	13.4
Denmark	-2.7	19	3.8
Finland	1.1	13.4	0.9
Ireland	-4.5	83.4	9.8
Netherlands	5.1	19.9	0.8
Sweden	7.7	-1.8	1.4
Greece	-10.9	47.9	9.4
Portugal	-0.7	39.5	2.3
Italy	-2.8	17	3
Austria	6.7	12	-0.2
France	2.7	21.6	1.3
Germany	6	16	-2.8
Luxembourg	6.4	11.5	0.6
UK	0.8	41.3	2.7
Slovakia	18.9	13.7	2.4
Slovenia	3.7	24.5	3.3
Estonia	-0.6	2.3	4.3
Bulgaria	9.2	-0.9	7.8
Latvia	-6.2	33.6	10.1
Lithuania	5.2	21.7	11.1
Czech Republic	8.5	13.3	1.4
Hungary	-2.8	13.5	3.5
Poland	21.7	11.3	0.1
Romania	7.9	20.5	1

Source: see Figures 6.1, 6.2, 6.3.

Even with the above caveats we can see that the table reveals several surprises as we look at the highlighted cases, which represent a somewhat arbitrary assessment of the top 3 and bottom 3 performers during the crisis. Based on the three indicators, Poland appears to have fared best during the period, registering the highest level of cumulative growth and almost no rise in unemployment. Its case is a strong contrast to the Irish performance, which registered a negative growth rate during the period and a large surge in debt and unemployment. These two cases clearly contradict the theoretical predictions as well as expectations, which could be formed based on the economic policy analysis of the previous chapters. They will be examined more in depth in the next part of the present chapter. More in line with expectations are the other four cases highlighted (Sweden, Austria, Greece, and Latvia), which have been considered in the previous chapters. Austria and Sweden are high-trust countries with responsible economic management prior to the crisis. Their examples contrast with Greece, the representative case for public finance mismanagement, and Latvia, the representative case for a credit boom. The solid performance of the former two and the need for a bailout in the latter two countries can be explained well by the arguments advanced in the earlier chapters.

In the case of other countries, the answer to the central question of this chapter, whether pre-crisis assessments hold following the crisis, is far from straightforward.

Generally, the policies of countries that were considered clear failures prior to the crisis do not need reassessment. These include countries in Group 3 (Greece, Italy, and Portugal) as well as Latvia and Lithuania, where allowing private indebtedness was a substitute for welfare spending stringency. While Hungary and Romania do not fare particularly poorly based on the three indicators, the need for a bailout in their cases does not allow them to be considered either as surprises to the theory or success stories.

Some reassessment of the theory is needed in the cases of Group 2 and 5, which were considered as examples of policy credibility in the previous chapters. While the performance of Sweden, Finland, the Netherlands, and Slovakia mostly confirm their pre-crisis assessment, Ireland, Denmark, and Slovenia do not fit well into the theory. In all three cases a domestic credit boom could be observed, and its collapse during the crisis caused a sharp decline in output and a surge in debt and unemployment. Analyzing the case of Ireland more in depth will help to accommodate the experiences of these countries with the theoretical framework of the book.

Compared to the evaluation from the previous chapter the good performance of Group 4 as well as part of Group 7 (Czech Republic and Poland) is somewhat surprising. None of these countries needed a bailout, and all of them recorded substantial positive cumulative growth with only a mild increase—in the cases of Austria and Germany a decrease—in unemployment. With the exception of the UK, where the public debt increased by over 40 percent of GDP, the other six countries registered only around 10–20 percent increase. Their experience indicates that an internal commitment to stability, even in the absence of a far-reaching reform agenda and resistance to EU pressures, could maintain an environment that withstands the disturbance caused by the crisis.

Overall, based on the analysis one can find both confirming and disconfirming evidence to the validity of pre-crisis assessment of performance. Even with the caveats, which were mentioned earlier about the constraints of interpreting the data, a clear puzzle emerges, which needs to be addressed. As already mentioned, the sharp contrast between Ireland and Poland requires an explanation. At a more general level however, the major question is the following: why did the star performers of the two regions (Group 2 and 5) record a worse performance than those that were seen as slow reformers (Group 4 and Group 7)? The juxtaposition of Ireland and Poland might help to answer this question and allow the modification of the original theory of the book to better fit reality.

6.4. Surprising cases: Ireland and Poland

Based on World Governance Indicators, Ireland is clearly a case where the public administration can be trusted. Ever since the creation of the index in 1996, the country has consistently ranked in the top 10 percent for all indicators.[10] Poland on the other hand has been only in the top 30 percent for all indicators, and in some years not even above this threshold. As shown in the previous chapter, Polish governance quality is below the CEE-10 average. Consequently, on the basis of the theoretical framework it could be expected that the Polish government would allow the growth of a credit bubble, while financial balance is maintained in the case of Ireland. This is clearly not the case, however. In the following, I will give a brief overview of the two cases then try to give an answer to this central puzzle.

---

[10] Source: World Governance Indicators data base: http://info.worldbank.org/governance/wgi/index.asp.

6.4.1. Ireland

The collapse of the Irish banking sector and the need for a bailout package was perhaps the greatest shock of the financial crisis in Europe. Ireland is one of the greatest success stories of the European Union and its failure during the crisis poses uncomfortable questions about whether it can still be considered a model case for emerging economies. In order to answer to this question, it is necessary to look at the roots of the crisis in Ireland and see, which elements of the Irish model could be held responsible for its collapse. In the following, first I will discuss the main features of the successful Irish model then look at the evolution of the crisis.

The Celtic Tiger

Following the Social Pact of 1987, which put an end to a period of fiscal imbalances and low growth, Ireland stepped on a rapid growth path characterized by export-led growth and macroeconomic stability. While there is substantial controversy about the individual contribution of various elements that underlined the model, the success of Ireland is generally attributed to the following factors:[11]

- FDI-led growth model: Attracting foreign direct investment was a conscious policy choice of the government from the 1950s, led by the Industrial Development Agency (IDA). IDA consciously selected specific sectors for investment in Ireland—for example in the 1980s electronics and financial services were selected (Barry 2006). The inflow of FDI boomed in the 1990s with the IT revolution and the progress of fiscal consolidation. According to Ó Riain (2000, 160), between 1989 and 1998 employment in the foreign-owned manufacturing sector increased by 24.8 percent, while in financial and internally traded services it rose by 384.5 percent. What made Ireland special is that the FDI-dominated segment of the economy did not remain isolated and a strong indigenous industry could also develop in parallel with employment growing by 10.4 percent in manufacturing and 197.7 percent in internationally traded services (Ó Riain 2000, 161).

---

[11] Due to the constraints of the chapter, I do not aim at a full review of the debate about the literature on Irish development. In the following I will just briefly summarize the most often mentioned elements of the success relying primarily on Powell (2003) and Ó Riain (2000).

- Investment into human capital: A low-cost, English speaking work-force was one of the major advantages of Ireland in attracting in-vestment from the US. The quality of this workforce was further improved by conscious government policy—starting in the 1960s a system of Regional Technical Colleges was developed, producing engineering, science, and computer graduates, all of whom made Ireland particularly attractive for high-tech investment (Barry 2007).
- European regional funds: Ireland made more efficient use of cohe-sion funds than the southern European countries during the 1980s. As the country was treated as one region, resources were distributed by the national government and channeled primarily into human capital development (Boltho 2000).
- Social pact: From 1987 to 2009 social partners could agree in fiscal consolidation measures, as well as wage setting and other labor market issues. This created a stable and peaceful environment for business planning (Boltho 2000).
- Fiscal consolidation: As discussed in Chapter 4, starting from 1987, Ireland implemented an expenditure-led fiscal consolidation and re-duced its level of debt from over 100 percent to below 40 percent by 2000. Cutting both expenditures and taxes, state redistribution also fell sharply from 51 to 31 percent during the same period.[12]
- Increased economic freedom: In parallel with fiscal consolidation, considerable institutional reforms took place aimed at increased economic freedom, meaning the ability of actors to engage in mutu-ally advantageous transactions. These imply removing restrictions on trade, capital flows, protecting property rights, as well as ensur-ing legal security and the rule of law. According to Powell (2003, 438) increasing economic freedom can be considered a major ex-planation for the success of Ireland.

As a result of these arrangements, in the two decades following the origi-nal social pact, Ireland could emerge from the periphery of Europe to a model case of development. In 2007, just before the crisis, GDP per capita adjusted for purchasing power parity stood at 147 percent of EU average, and the country was second on this indicator after Luxembourg.

---

[12] Unless otherwise noted the source of statistical data is from European Commission (2010).

The road to the crisis

By 2010, it had become evident that much of the recent development in Ireland was led by a bubble in the real estate sector. However, it is much less evident which elements of the original model were responsible for the growth of the bubble and to what extent the crisis invalidates the model. In the following, I will provide a brief account of the origins of the crisis then try to answer these questions.

Figure 6.4. Irish inflation and ECB policy rate 1999–2010

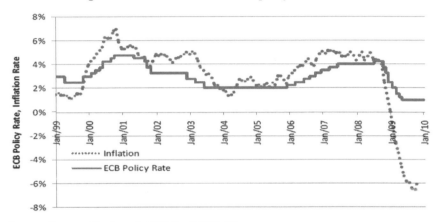

Source: Connor, Flavin and, O'Kelly (2010): 12

Similarly to other cases of bubbles, the origins of the crisis can be traced back to easy monetary conditions.[13] Between 1999 and 2008, real interest rates were negative for almost 10 years, evidence that the interest rate set by the ECB was too low for Ireland, which had an inflation rate higher than the euro-area average (Figure 6.4). This was a clear sign of overheating of the economy, which was the result of buoyant investment, rising private consumption, erosion of wage moderation due to emergent labor shortages, as well as government policy, which involved both increased spending and tax cuts.[14] The resulting negative real interest rates

---

[13] For the classic exposition of this thesis see Kindelberger (1989). The term "capital flow bonanza" is used in the recent book of Reinhart and Rogoff (2009) for the same phenomenon.

[14] The overheating of the Irish economy did not go unnoticed. In 2001, the European Commission publicly reprimanded Ireland for lack of budgetary discipline, while the IMF also noted the dangers associated with labor shortages and easy monetary policy (IMF 2000a).

strongly encouraged borrowing, which was made even easier given the enormous inflows of foreign savings, especially following the introduction of the euro (Honohan 2009, 210).

The availability of cheap credit led to an easing of lending standards, which made mortgages available to those segments of the population that previously did not have access—100 percent loan-to-value ratios were not unusual, making negative equity widespread once prices started to decline (Honohan 2009, 216). Given the widespread increase in credit, housing prices soared (Figure 6.5), which started a bubble as expectations about further price increases boosted current prices and investment into real estate increased further.

Figure 6.5. Irish housing prices 1970–2008

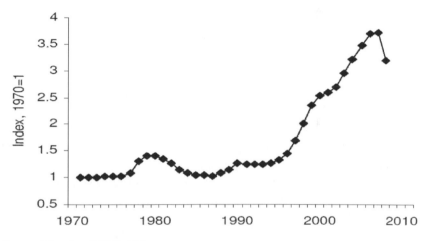

Source: Honohan (2009): 211

One of the major questions of the Irish story is why the regulatory authorities did not attempt to counter these tendencies. Traditional measures of risk were sidelined—Honohan (2009, 217) mentions a widely used warning sign, which triggers actions by regulators if the balance sheet of a financial institution grows faster than 20 percent per year. Thus, the lack of action against the Anglo-Irish Bank, which registered over 36 percent annual growth for a decade between 1998 and 2007, begs an explanation.[15]

---

[15] As Connor, Flavin and, O'Kelly (2009, 15) recounts the institution was also involved in multiple cases of fraudulent accounting, which was also ignored or even condoned by authorities and illustrates the failure of supervision. It is unsurprising that at the bust of the crisis the head of the regulatory authority retired.

Following the crisis the Irish government asked the governor of the central bank to give a report on the failure of regulatory authorities to foresee and prevent the crisis. In the report, Honohan (2010) points to three major factors:

- The regulatory approach chosen by authorities emphasized the supervision of systems of governance and the verification of risk assessment models rather than an individual assessment of risk based on quantitative indicators. The underlying philosophy behind this approach was that well-governed banks would remain sound (Honohan 2010, 8). However, competition forced banks to adopt ever lower lending standards thus accumulating substantial risk.
- Due to the institutional separation of banking supervision from the Central Bank, which was responsible for overall financial stability, both actors were prone to complacency. According to Honohan (2010, 11), "if regulators had realized how risky the macroeconomic picture was for the banks they might have concluded that forceful action was needed; conversely, if the analysts dealing with financial stability had had a fuller understanding of how dependent banks' solvency was on the property market holding up, they might have looked at the stress tests with a more skeptical eye."
- As the presence of the bubble became evident for authorities, postponement of action was due to fears about upsetting the market: "rocking the boat and swimming against the tide of public opinion would have required a particularly strong sense of the independent role of a central bank in being prepared to spoil the party and withstand possible strong adverse public reaction" (Honohan 2010, 16).

Letting the bubble grow unimpeded in the real estate market resulted in a familiar cycle of overheating. From 2001 onwards, the Irish growth model began to change as construction took over the lead from exports—it peaked at 24.5 percent of GNP in 2006 (NESC 2009, 18). Employment in construction illustrates the fast growth of the sector—between 1993 and 2007 it more than doubled growing from less than 6 percent to over 13 percent as a share of total employment (Honohan 2009, 212).

The sharp rise in domestic demand also drove up wages, which led to inflation. This was disastrous in the euro-zone given the lack of recourse to devaluation. As labor costs increased, Ireland steadily lost its competitive position on the international markets, which was reflected in a worsening current account position (Figure 6.6).

Figure 6.6. Wage costs and current account in Ireland 1995–2012

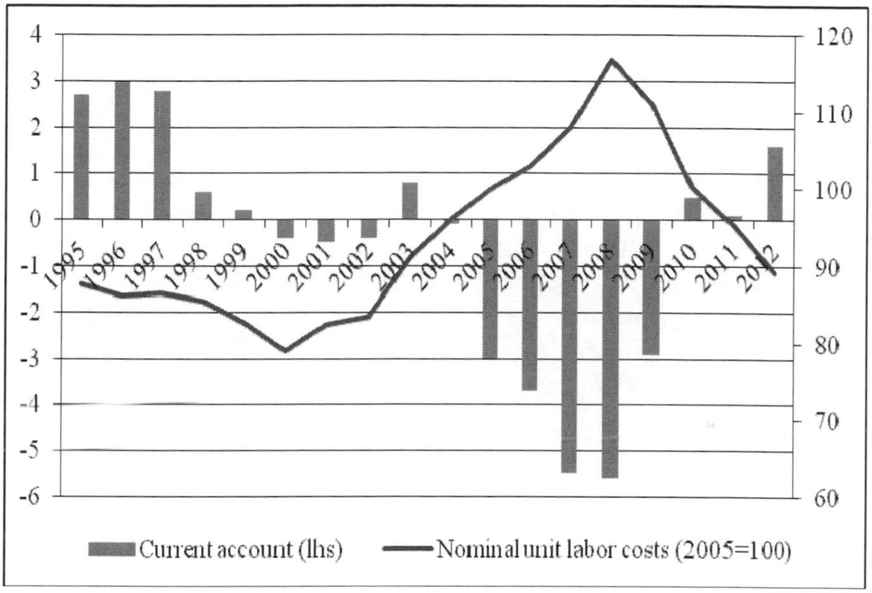

Current account (lhs)   Nominal unit labor costs (2005=100)

Data: European Commission (2012): 98, 116

Vulnerability to crisis was further exacerbated by the fiscal policy of the government. Starting from the 1990s, a substantial shift took place in the composition of tax revenue: the share of cyclically sensitive taxes such as stamp duties, capital gains tax, and corporation tax increased from 8 percent to 30 percent (Regling and Watson 2010, 27). In explaining this shift, Dellepiane and Hardiman (2010, 10) point to the role of social part-nership in wage-setting—through the reduction of personal income tax, trade union members could enjoy an increase in real wages, while the government could collect revenues from the boom in housing. The reli-ance on revenues from the housing sector might be an explanation why the government also took actions to fuel the boom—the ceiling on the income tax deductibility of mortgage interest for owner-occupiers was increased in 2000, 2003, 2007, and 2008 (Honohan 2010, 31).

Given the interests of governments and households, the reluctance of the regulatory authorities to "ruin the party" becomes understandable. However, once the crisis hit, the pitfalls of this arrangement became evi-dent overnight. As Honohan (2010, 32) argues, the bubble would have burst even without the international crisis as house prices had been falling for 18 months prior to the collapse of Lehman Brothers. The banks involved in real estate lending were thus on the road to insolvency. The contribution of the international crisis to the domestic problems was that soft landing became impossible.

Once the international financial markets froze and the banks could not rollover their short-term debt, immediate government intervention became necessary for saving the financial system. Measures included the guarantee of all bank accounts, the nationalization of Anglo-Irish Bank, as well as the recapitalization of the two largest banks—Allied Irish Bank (AIB) and Bank of Ireland (BoI). According to the latest estimates, the total cost of these measures was over 40 percent of the GDP at 50 billion euros (IMF 2011a, 4). At the same time, the international crisis depressed foreign trade as well, thus domestic and external demand both collapsed, leading to a sharp fall of GDP—a drop of 3.5 percent in 2008 followed by 7.6 percent in 2009—and an increase in unemployment to over 12 percent. The subsequent collapse of revenues and the rise in expenditures together with the costs of bank consolidation resulted in a fiscal deficit of 32 percent of GDP in 2009, while public debt passed 100 percent in 2011 from 25 percent in 2007. All these developments led to doubts about Ireland's ability to pay its liabilities, and a vicious cycle of high interest rates and increased skepticism about debt service developed. In order to stop the cycle the country was given an 85 billion euro bailout in November 2010.

Assessment of the Irish model

Overall the crisis in Ireland is a classical boom-bust cycle, similar to the Swedish banking crisis in the early 1990s. While the decision to bail out the banks is subject to an intense debate in Ireland, the situation meant that the authorities lacked good options—the banks were both too big to fail and too big to save. Thus, the crucial question is not whether the collapse is the result of poor judgment by the government, but rather what elements of the Irish model can be held responsible for such a situation to develop in the first place.

The most important element of the Irish model, which directly contributed to the crisis, is probably the decision of the government in the 1980s to become a major offshore financial center in Europe by providing a low-tax environment and light-touch regulation. Eventually this arrangement earned Ireland the dubious distinction of becoming "the wild west of European finance" (Connor, Flavin, and O'Kelly 2009, 14–15).

The crisis also called into question the tax system, which evolved in response to the boom. Relying on less cyclical revenues, rolling back some of the tax reductions of the last decade as well as introducing new taxes is likely to be necessary (Lane 2009, 245). Strengthening fiscal institutions and medium-term planning are also likely to be necessary to avoid a similar situation in the future.

Many of the elements of the original model however remain relevant and provide hope that Ireland will recover from the crisis. A skilled, English-speaking labor force is still present to attract investment, and wages have started to fall, which should help restore competitiveness. With the recovery of global trade, Ireland can return to its export-oriented growth model. Third, social partnership is also likely to be an important asset in recovery in coordinating expectations and sharing the burden of adjustment fairly.

At the time of writing, developments in Ireland appear to justify positive expectations. In spite of a change in government in 2011, there was little change in the determination of Irish authorities in managing the crisis and international institutions applaud the country for its performance.[16] The over 60 percent "Yes" vote in the referendum over the European Fiscal Compact[17] in May 2012 signals the acceptance of fiscal austerity by the public. The sharing of burdens is also strongly in line with expectations—according to Callan et al. (2012, 53), the composition of Irish fiscal adjustment is by far the most progressive among the crisis countries. As a visible sign of the efforts, nominal unit labor costs fell substantially, leading to a considerable improvement in the current account (Figure 6.6). An increase in FDI is also expected to help this process (IMF 2012, 10). While an export-led recovery is by its very nature conditional upon the health of the main trading partners, Ireland appears on its way to recovering from the crisis.

6.4.2. Poland

While for Ireland the major issue was how a former star performer could be so badly hit by a crisis, in Poland we have to answer the opposite question— how a former laggard country could emerge from the crisis unscathed.

---

[16] IMF (2012b) acknowledges strong progress on fiscal, financial sector, and structural reforms. In the first report on the progress on Euro Plus commitments, Ireland ranked third in adjustment progress and is considered the "star performer of the periphery crisis countries" (Lisbon Council 2011, 55).

[17] Treaty on Stability, Coordination, and Governance in the Economic and Monetary Union, which was adopted by the European Council on March 2, 2012. The Treaty commits participants to keeping the budget close to balance or surplus and facing fines if they do not comply. Full text is available: http://european-council.europa.eu/media/639235/st00tscg26_en12.pdf.

Prior to the crisis, Poland was far from being a star performer even among Central European countries. With the victory of the Law and Justice Party in 2005, the country essentially gave up fast accession of the euro, which led to the postponement of macroeconomic stabilization. Growth performance was also far from spectacular by regional standards—as shown by Figure 5.2, GDP per capita in PPS in 2007 was the lowest among the eight CEE countries that joined the EU in 2004, even though there was an acceleration of growth from 2005 due to the effects of EU accession and increasing capital inflows (Gorzelak 2010, 140). Poland also scored the lowest among the CEE8 on the corruption perception index—in 2007 it ranked 61st out of 179 countries.[18] The picture was not much brighter if prospects for growth were considered—according to the 2007 *Doing Business* report, Poland ranked 75 out of 175 countries, the lowest among EU member states and just after Pakistan (World Bank 2007, 6). The low ranking was driven by poor performance on measures for starting a business (ranked 114), dealing with licenses (146), registering property (86), trading across borders (102), and enforcing contracts (112). Besides these fields, the EBRD (2010, 135) also calls attention to the pervasive involvement of the state in the economy, particularly in the fields of power, natural resources, and the banking sector.

Against this background, it appears rather surprising that Poland was the only country in the EU that avoided a recession during the subprime crisis. As it can be seen from Figure 6.7, although a slowing of growth could be observed in comparison to pre-crisis performance, a strong rebound took place already in 2010. During the pre-crisis years, unemployment dropped substantially,[19] and there was only a mild reversal during the crisis. Finally, while fiscal deficit increased substantially during 2009–2010, in 2012 it is expected to drop to 3 percent. The question thus naturally emerges—what lies behind the Polish success? In the following I will provide an overview of the major factors that allowed Poland to escape the crisis, then compare its experience to that of Ireland.

---

[18] Rankings are available on the website of Transparency International at www. transparency.org.

[19] According to Gorzelak (2010, 140), the drop in unemployment was partly due to the recovery of the economy, but also to outward migration following EU accession, when an estimated 1.5 million workers left the country.

Figure 6.7. Selected macroeconomic indicators in Poland 2005–2012

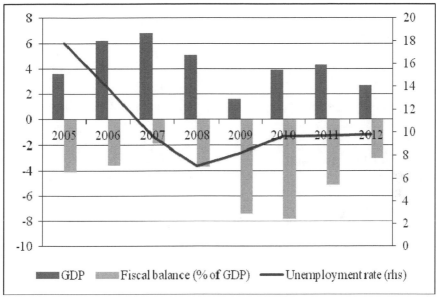

Data: European Commission (2012): 211

Weak credit growth prior to the crisis

One of the major factors that allowed Poland to avoid a crisis similar to the one in Ireland or the Baltics was the absence of a credit boom prior to the crisis. During the years prior to the crisis, the Czech Republic and Poland had the lowest rate of credit inflows among the CEE countries (IMF 2010c; 5). Prior to the crisis this performance in financial deepening gave rise to concerns about falling behind the rest of the region. Discussing the roots of this problem, an IMF study pointed to three major factors (IMF 2007a): first, low demand and supply of credit given weak economic activity after 2000; second, weaknesses in the institutional environment concerning the enforcement of pledges and collateral; third, strong policies aimed at containing credit growth, especially mortgages in foreign currency. In the following, I will provide a brief overview of these factors.

Poland experienced considerable slowdown during 2001 and 2002, recording just over 1 percent growth, which affected both the demand and supply for credit. Slow economic activity implied low demand for credit, especially from corporations. Although growth recovered in 2003, corporate credit remained sluggish as high liquidity allowed internal financing. At the same time banks were also more cautious in lending as the share of non-performing loans increased from 13 percent in 1998 to almost 30 percent by 2003 due to the lax lending standards during the previous period of credit expansion (IMF 2007a, 4–5). Furthermore, as emphasized by Strojwas (2010, 2), since 44 percent of Poles still do not own a bank account, fees and commissions of basic banking services generate satisfactory profits for financial institutions, thus there has been no need for taking excessive risks.

Beyond cyclical factors however, a weak institutional framework for the enforcement of pledges and collateral provides a deeper explanation for the absence of a credit surge. The costs and uncertainties involving the reception of payments from pledged or mortgaged assets in case of a default strongly affect whether or not credit is available and at what costs (Dahan and Simpson 2005, 3). This is particularly the case for small- and medium-sized enterprises, which are generally seen as highly risky by banks.[20] One rule, which makes mortgage financing difficult, is that eviction is possible only if an alternative place to live is found for the evicted. In a regional comparison, Poland is by far the worst in the CEE-10 concerning the time, costs, and simplicity of enforcing pledges and collateral (Dahan and Simpson 2005, 29).[21]

Finally, policymaking also contributed to the absence of a credit boom in Poland. In an environment of overall slow credit growth, housing loans were the fastest growing components of private sector credit, and similarly to other countries in the region, much of these loans were denominated in foreign currency. However, as shown by Figure 6.8, the growth of foreign currency lending was rather moderate until 2007, which was the result of several different policy measures.

According to Bethlendi (2011, 212), Poland used several instruments to slow the rise of foreign indebtedness. The most successful tool was monetary policy—letting the exchange rate float freely alleviated the need for maintaining a high interest rate and thus decreased the extra costs associated with loans in zloty, while the volatility of the exchange rate increased the awareness of risks associated with foreign currency loans. Second, prudential and supervisory measures were implemented, including the increase of

---

[20] Indeed, resolving the problems of financing these enterprises is one of the major post-crisis challenges for Poland according to the EBRD (EBRD 2010, 135).

[21] For a more detailed description of the inefficiencies of the Polish legal system concerning the weakness of the secured credit market see Dahan and Simpson (2006).

capital requirements for foreign currency loans, as well as setting minimum standards for risk management. Third, risk awareness campaigns were conducted, addressing both the public as well as the banks. An important institutional precondition for these measures was that unlike in Ireland, financial supervision was not separated from the monetary authority, which allowed comprehensive and decisive action on different fronts.

Figure 6.8. Housing loan balance in Poland 2002–2009

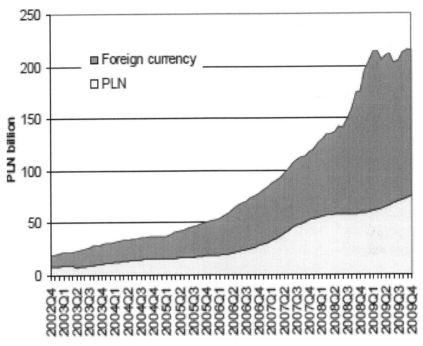

Source: NBP (2010): 37

As shown by Figure 6.8, the above measures could hinder the growth of foreign currency lending only temporarily. However, it proved to be sufficient for Poland to avoid a serious crisis as the sharp rise, which started in 2007, was soon stopped by the financial crisis.

The consequences of the crisis

Following the collapse of Lehman Brothers, Poland was not immune from the loss of confidence that prevailed on the international financial markets. Although to a lesser extent than in other countries of the region, CDS spreads increased substantially, from less than 100 basis points to around 400 basis points in February 2009 (IMF 2009, 8). Loss of confidence was also signaled by the sharp depreciation of the zloty, which lost about 50 percent of its value to the euro from its July 2008 peak to April 2009 (Strojwas 2010, 4).

In order to restore confidence, stop the depreciation of the zloty, and boost reserves, Poland turned to the IMF in April 2009 and asked for a one-year flexible credit line (FCL) arrangement in the amount of $20.3 billion. This arrangement is designed for countries that have strong fundamentals but might face a loss of confidence due to contagion from other countries. The IMF approved Poland's application noting its sustainable external position, continued access to private capital markets, sustainable public debt position, sound monetary and exchange rate arrangements, as well as effective financial supervision (IMF 2009, 16–17). This step was successful in stopping a further depreciation of the exchange rate.

Besides the FCL arrangement, Poland also benefitted from having a largely foreign-owned banking sector similar to other countries in the region. With the freezing of the international financial markets, a sudden stop of capital flows, similar to what happened in the Asian countries, was a real threat to the CEE region. However, as parent banks refinanced their subsidiaries, capital outflows were smaller than might be expected (Berglöf et al. 2009).[22]

While the above factors helped Poland to avoid a systemic banking crisis, the resilience of domestic demand—even in 2009 it grew by 2 percent (EC 2010, 211)—maintained a positive growth rate throughout the crisis. This had a number of elements. The rise in fiscal deficit contributed to the resilience of demand primarily through tax cuts taken in 2006 and 2007, as well as the working of automatic stabilizers on the expenditure side (IMF 2010c, 4). In the construction sector, EU funds remained available for financing infrastructure investment—Poland is now the largest beneficiary of EU cohesion funds reaching 3.3 percent in GDP in 2009 (OECD 2010, 4). Finally, the preparation for the Euro 2012 football championship also helped in maintaining investment (Gorzelak 2010, 144).

Overall, from the deeper examination of the factors that helped Poland avoid a recession, the main conclusion is that we can hardly talk about a

---

[22] In this process, the Vienna initiative by the European Commission and the international financial institutions was probably critical—through seeking a commitment from financial institutions to maintain exposure to the region, it helped to coordinate the behavior and expectations of private actors (EBRD 2010, 36).

miracle. While prudent financial policy was important in avoiding a credit boom, the outcome also reflects initial weaknesses such as the underdevelopment of the institutional environment and the stance of the economic cycle, as well as structural factors including a large domestic market, utilization of EU cohesion funds as well as the Euro 2012 preparations. Lack of recession in Poland is the joint result of all these factors.

6.4.3. Implications for the theory

At first sight, the cases of Ireland and Poland appear to contradict the theory, which emphasizes that long-term planning can be expected in a high-trust environment and populist measures are more likely in a low-trust regime. Still, a credit bubble evolved in high-trust Ireland and not in Poland.

From the overview, however, we can give an interpretation to the events that is not incompatible with the theory. In the case of Ireland, a decade of unimpeded success gave rise to overly optimistic expectations regarding future developments as well as to a strong belief in prevailing economic fashions concerning financial regulation. With the evolving global financial crisis, the home-grown bubble proved to be fatal and a soft landing became impossible. However, the crisis did not invalidate the results of the Celtic tiger, which transformed Ireland from a periphery country to a model of economic development. Even after the real estate bubble burst, Irish GDP per capita in PPS is 128 percent of the EU-27 average—only Luxembourg and the Netherlands can claim a higher measure.[23] Furthermore, the experiences with crisis management so far indicate that the country is handling the crisis considerably better than other countries that needed a bailout.

The case is just the opposite in Poland. Given low expectations about the economic outlook, a credit bubble was less likely at the outset. This was reinforced by a more prudent approach to risk management than in Ireland, which probably reflected the conservative convictions of Leszek Balcerowicz, president of the National Bank of Poland until January 2007. Once he left office, a sharp rise in credit did take place, which is in line with the theoretical predictions. Escaping the crisis unscathed for such reasons does not make Poland a model case to follow—even without a recession, its GDP per capita in PPS is 63 percent of EU-27 average.

---

[23] The source for GDP per capita in PPS data is the homepage of Eurostat: http://epp.eurostat.ec.europa.eu/portal/page/portal/eurostat/home.

While this is a strong improvement on its pre-crisis measure at 54 percent in 2007, it is still less than half the Irish performance. Thus, building institutions that allow long-term planning for economic actors is certainly a non-avoidable task.

However, even with such interpretation one cannot overlook an important lesson from the two cases concerning trust. As in other areas in life, overconfidence and complacency can be dangerous. Distrust also has its benefits and the Polish story is an example of the prudence that seems necessary in a risky environment. Keeping this in mind and avoiding overreaction to temporary tendencies or intellectual fashions might be an error on the side of conservative policies, but it can save the economy from excessive volatility. The strong performance of Group 4 countries also supports these insights.

* * *

The main objective of this chapter was to conduct a robustness test of the theory proposed in the book. The 2008–2010 financial crisis allowed addressing the question about whether pre-crisis evaluations of economic performance are tenable following the crisis. On the basis of analyzing the performance of seven groups of countries as well as the two case studies, one can answer the basic question with a qualified yes. Generally, countries, which were considered as clear failures prior to the crisis fared very poorly during the crisis. Most of the success stories also showed relatively good performance in a radically changed environment. The even better performance of countries that were not at the forefront of reforms, suggests that avoiding major policy mistakes goes a long way in ensuring growth and avoiding excessive volatility. This also implies that policy-making with an eye on potential pitfalls appears to be more effective in hindsight than policies maximizing growth rates or other aggregate variables.

At the same time, there were major surprises during the crisis—most importantly the collapse of Ireland and the success of Poland. When one takes a deeper look at these issues, we can see that Ireland basically became a victim of its former success, while Poland gained because of its earlier failures. Their cases shed further light on why Group 4 countries fared so well during the crisis—avoiding overconfidence, the subsequent credit boom, and complacency are likely to be important reasons. However, in assessing the Irish and the Polish cases, it is important to place these performances into a broader framework than a five-year growth performance under extreme global conditions. The still existing difference in their level of development in itself speaks against a major revision of the basic theory.

Overall, while the robustness test for the theory largely confirms the evaluation of economic policy from the previous chapters, the significant exceptions cannot be overlooked either. In the closing chapter of this book I will return to the original hypotheses of this study, reexamine the theoretical framework, and consider the policy implications of the research.

CHAPTER 7

The Relevance of Trust for Economic Outcomes

In the previous chapters, I have examined how institutional trust matters in economic policymaking in the EU-15 and the CEE-10 within the context of euro-zone accession. The experiences of various members during the subprime crisis represent an important test for the sustainability of policies. As we could observe, while most countries fared according to expectations, there were also important exceptions that call for a modification of the original theoretical framework.

The aim of this closing chapter is to integrate the findings into a coherent narrative and answer the original question of the project: how and when does trust matter in economic policymaking? Understanding the conditions under which trust can exert its influence gives policymakers a proper perspective on when its significance is either underestimated or overestimated by the presence of prominent examples for either position.

The chapter proceeds as follows. First, I will briefly summarize the main findings of individual chapters then provide a comparative assessment of the role of trust in the old and new member states of the EU. Afterwards, I will revisit the hypotheses from Chapter 3 on the expected paths of economic development in high- and low-trust environments. In the following section, I will summarize the main factors, which are responsible for deviation from the hypotheses. In the closing part of the chapter, I will discuss some of the policy implications of the research.

7.1. Summary of findings

While it has been recognized that trust matters for economic outcomes, the problem of causality has remained underexplored. This book has attempted to contribute to filling this gap through focusing on the role of institutional trust in influencing economic policy. By narrowing the question to policies associated with the euro, I also aim at contributing to the ongoing debates about the future of the common currency.

In order to provide a theoretical framework for assessing how trust might matter to economic policies, in Chapter 2 I situated the subject in the broadly understood institutionalist school of economics, which is able to handle both rational and non-rational motives in human decision making. Through integrating insights from Post-Keynesian, Austrian, and new institutional economics, as well as modern political philosophy, it has been proposed that the presence or absence of institutional trust creates virtuous and vicious cycles in law-abidance, which critically influence the possibility for economic agents to have realistic long-term plans. In a low-trust environment the uncertainty surrounding the functioning of institutions results in a tendency towards having a short-term focus in decision making.

The major question of Chapter 3 was to assess how and when a prevailing tendency among economic actors towards short-term decision making affects the decisions of policymakers. Within the context of the creation of the euro-zone it has been suggested that while trust does not necessarily affect unique decisions, in repeated situations without clear external pressures the presence or absence of institutional trust clearly has a role in policymaking. Several hypotheses were proposed on how lack of trust might matter in decisions over economic policy, including populist fiscal measures, suboptimal strategies for consolidation, as well as the postponement of structural reforms. As a consequence of such policies, it was hypothesized that low-trust countries are likely to fare poorly in and outside of the euro-zone, while high-trust countries were expected to fare well regardless of their decision over the euro.

In order to assess the hypotheses empirically, first fiscal policies prior and after the creation of the euro-zone were examined in the EU-15. In Chapter 4, it was found that in spite of the motive for consolidation due to the Maastricht criteria, the EU had a clear influence on fiscal policy in only five countries out of the 15. In contrast, institutional trust—as approximated by the World Governance Indicators—proved to be a good predictor of what type of fiscal consolidation was implemented. In high-trust countries consolidation focused primarily on the expenditure side, while in low-trust countries tax increases and savings from debt service contributed the most to the improvement of the fiscal balance. Through the divergent cases of Sweden and Portugal, the mechanisms behind this outcome were also shown—while in Sweden a nationwide cooperation on optimal fiscal policy measures could be achieved, in Portugal, consolidation was achieved within the constraint of ensuring the least possible cost for vested interest groups. As a result, the consolidation was not lasting, while the status quo undermined competitiveness at a time when considerable structural change took place in the world economy.

The experiences of Central Europe represent an important contrast to cases from Western Europe. As shown in Chapter 5, in the CEE-10—with the exception of Hungary—fiscal policy did not show a populist orientation in spite of the low level of trust, which is the heritage of communism and the transition. This finding is somewhat surprising since euro-zone accession had even less influence than in the EU-15—it had a clear influence only in Slovakia—thus one could have expected substantial pressures on policymakers to increase wellbeing on the short-term. In fact, once we consider the almost unrestrained growth of private indebtedness, there is a reality to this expectation. Private credit can be viewed as a substitute for public spending: it has the potential of increasing consumption and it also makes a country vulnerable to turbulences on the international financial markets. Still, as the contrast of Hungary and Slovakia indicates, low-level trust does not necessarily lead to short-term policies—a window of opportunity for change might open and in case of a committed and capable political leadership, path dependency can be broken. In spite of its weak institutional framework, Slovakia became the second CEE country to successfully introduce the euro.

The experiences of the subprime crisis, which were examined in Chapter 6, provide further elements to the solution of the puzzle on how and when trust plays a role in economic outcomes. The overview of crisis performance indicates that while countries that were considered clear failures prior to the crisis were heavily hit and needed a bailout, there were some exceptions. The cases of Hungary, Latvia, Greece, and Portugal are hardly surprising in light of the findings from earlier chapters. However, the situation is much less clear in the case of successful countries—while the majority of them fared well, overconfidence in several cases led to the overheating of the economy and a painful experience during the crisis. The two most surprising cases were Poland and Ireland, which were examined in depth. Their experiences have clearly shown that sometimes underdevelopment has its benefits, while overconfidence can be very dangerous. I will return more in depth to these claims in a later section of the chapter.

7.2. Differences between East and West in the EU

The different influence of trust on economic policy in the EU-15 and the CEE-10 indicates that even within the same external framework we should be careful about generalizing regional experiences. In the following, I will review the main similarities and differences of the experiences of the two regions. In the next section, I will attempt to list the main factors responsible for this divergence.

The most important difference between the two regions lies in their attitude toward the external framework. In the EU-15, not joining the euro-zone was viewed as a luxury for those countries that have strong institutions to protect against the turbulence of the financial markets. The popularity of the euro was extremely high in the southern countries, while similarly low-trust countries in the CEE-10 were much less eager to join. The much lower level of indebtedness and thus lower potential saving on debt service might be an important reason for this difference; however, it is far from the whole story as this was also true for the three CEE countries that did introduce the euro. In the rest of the region, a much greater debate prevailed about the costs and benefits of euro-zone accession than in the southern states, and the population was much less enthusiastic about the prospect. Eventually these issues could be resolved only in the two countries with the highest quality institutions in the region (Slovenia and Estonia) as well as Slovakia, which counts as an exception.

While attitudes toward the euro differed substantially between East and West, the limited influence of the EU on economic policy choices is a shared feature. In the EU-15, it had a clear influence only in five out of the 15 countries, and even where it mattered, the composition of fiscal consolidation was sub-optimal. In the CEE-10, the EU had a critical influence only in Slovakia, but even there it was more of an anchor for domestic aspirations than a trigger for a particular policy path. In the majority of the countries, domestic priorities determined policy, and in predicting the differences trust had a relatively good explanatory power.

At the same time the particular manifestation of short-term decision making over economic policy differed greatly between East and West. In the EU-15, the level of trust proved to be a good predictor for the composition of fiscal stabilization—in accordance with the theory, low-trust countries were unwilling to cut welfare spending and implement structural change. In contrast, the picture is much less straightforward among CEE-10 countries, where a low level of welfare spending was often cut even further—particularly in those countries that opted for a currency board to gain credibility. In these states, the primary method of meeting public expectations for immediate wellbeing had been an unconstrained credit boom.

In spite of the different manifestations of short-term orientation in economic policymaking, the consequences were very similar and the subprime crisis exposed the unsustainability of these policies clearly. Countries with very different problems needed a bailout—the source of crisis in Greece was indebtedness, Portugal suffered for its lack of competitiveness, while Ireland for its banking crisis. With these considerations in mind I will now revisit the hypotheses from Chapter 3 about expected economic performance following the decision over accession to the eurozone.

7.3. Institutional trust and economic consequences

In Chapter 3, several hypotheses were proposed regarding trust and economic performance within the context of the euro. Most importantly it was suggested that it is not the exchange rate regime that matters, but rather the ability of countries to manage the different challenges presented by the various regimes. In this ability, trust was hypothesized to play a critical role.

Table 7.1 below shows four groups of countries based on the ranking for rule of law according to the world governance indicators and whether the country introduced the euro or not.[1] High-trust countries are defined as ranked in the top 10 percent of countries, while low-trust countries rank below—the numbers shown range from 0 to 100, with 90 to 100 representing the top 10 percent.[2] In the table I use data from 2004—it is the year of accession for CEE countries, but it can also be identified as the

---

[1] While looking only at the rule of law indicator in this case might seem arbitrary, for the simple separation of countries into high- and low-trust regimes it is the closest indicator from the perspective of the theoretical framework. Control of corruption is also very close to the theory but looking at the data shows that rankings on the two are almost identical—this is not surprising as corruption can be interpreted as the subversion of the rule of law. Other variables might be more prone to bias, such as government effectiveness or the danger of political violence. On the problems of these indicators see the sources from Chapter 1.

[2] Naturally this is a rather crude differentiation especially in light of the divergence of low-trust countries, but as a first approximation to illustrate the validity of theoretical predictions its simplicity is a benefit.

starting point for the build-up of vulnerability prior to the subprime crisis. While the choice of year is certainly arbitrary, given the relative stability of the indicator, classification would not differ substantially if data from a different year would be used. In Table 7.1 included the rule of law indicator in parenthesis.

The major objective of the table is to give a first approximation on the validity of the hypotheses before going into more detail by group. In order to help the assessment of the theory, countries that deviate from its predictions—high-trust countries faring poorly or low-trust countries performing well during the crisis—are listed in bold characters. Evaluation of performance is based on the assessment of the previous chapter—poor performance is signaled by a bailout, a fall in cumulative GDP between 2007 and 2011, or an increase of public debt over 30 percent of GDP during the same period.[3]

Table 7.1. Trust and the euro: surprises to the theory

	EURO-ZONE	NON EURO-ZONE
High trust	Austria (96), Belgium (90), Finland (99), France (92), Germany (93), **Ireland** (93), Luxembourg (98), Netherlands (95)	**Denmark** (99), Sweden (97), **UK** (94)
Low trust	Greece (81), Italy (70), Portugal (87), Estonia (79), **Slovakia** (67), **Slovenia** (83), Spain (86)	**Czech Republic** (73), **Poland** (64), Romania (51), Hungary (81), **Bulgaria** (54), Latvia (69), Lithuania (71)

As we can see from the table, the most we can say about the hypotheses is that more countries confirm them than not. At the same time, surprises are present in every group, which underlines the limitations of focusing on one factor in analyzing economic outcomes. Before identifying the other factors at work in bringing about the outcome, I will examine the hypotheses from Chapter 3 more in depth for the different groups.

---

[3] Naturally, these measures are also somewhat arbitrary, but as mentioned in the previous footnote, the exercise primarily serves illustrative purposes.

7.3.1. High-trust countries in the euro-zone

These countries were expected to benefit the most from the euro given their ability to maintain financial stability as well as implement structural reforms needed for competitiveness. Based on the assessment from the previous chapter, the majority of these countries was among the least hit by the crisis and recovered rapidly. However, when judging performance it is important to look at longer trends and put performance during the crisis in perspective. GDP per capita in purchasing power parity between 1998 and 2009 is shown in Figure 7.1. From the figure, we can see considerable divergence in relative performance, but the most important issue to notice is that with the exception of France, these countries have mostly been able to maintain their relative advantage in their level of development. Ireland is a special case in this group—for almost a decade it not only preserved its relative position but was able to improve it substantially. While the crisis eroded much of the gains, in 2010 it was still in a better position than in 1998. Naturally, given the costs of the banking bailout, it is a question for the future whether it will be able to preserve its position.

Figure 7.1. GDP per capita PPS in high-trust euro-zone countries (1998–2010)

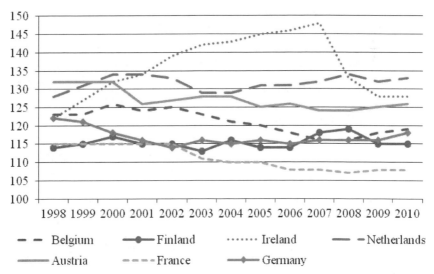

Notes: EU-27 average=100. From the figure Luxembourg is excluded given the different scale of its development—in 1998 its GDP per capita PPS was 218 percent of EU-27, in 2010 it was 271 percent.
Data: Eurostat http://epp.eurostat.ec.europa.eu/tgm/table.do?tab=table&init=1&plugin=1&language=en&pcode=tec00114

7.3.2. High-trust countries outside the euro-zone

These countries were expected to fare well outside of the euro-zone given their ability to maintain a stable currency as well as implement structural reforms for enhancing competitiveness. Having their own currency could also have been an advantage in the case of unexpected shocks. In their fiscal policies these countries confirmed the hypotheses as all three of them succeeded in reducing their debt below 45 percent and keeping their deficit below 3 percent of GDP. However, as shown by Figure 7.2, such a strong fiscal performance was insufficient to maintain their relative lead over their competitors—a clear loss of relative position can be observed in the case of the UK and Denmark, and only Sweden was able to maintain its relative position. While their level of development is still considerably higher than the EU-27 average, these trends differ considerably from those observed in the previous group of countries (Figure 7.1).

Figure 7.2. GDP per capita PPS in Denmark, Sweden, and the UK (1998–2010)

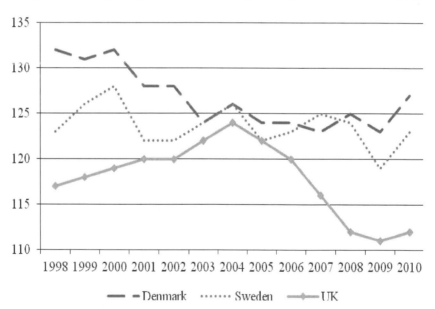

Notes: EU-27 average=100.
Data: Eurostat http://epp.eurostat.ec.europa.eu/tgm/table.do?tab=table&init=1&plugin= 1&language=en&pcode=tec00114

Although we should be careful not to generalize on the basis of only three countries, especially because we know that Denmark and the UK suffered a credit boom, it appears that not joining the euro-zone entails considerable economic costs even for countries that can manage an independent currency. The fact, that the relative decline started well before the subprime crisis adds further support to this claim. Still, the experiences of these countries do not invalidate the relevance of trust in economic performance, as none of them needed a bailout package and at the time of writing both Denmark and the UK appear successful in stabilizing their economies after being hit by the crisis.

7.3.3. Low-trust countries in the euro-zone

Southern members of the EU as well as the three CEE countries that succeeded in introducing the euro, belong here.[4] According the hypotheses from Chapter 3, this is the most dangerous quadrant, since these countries do not have recourse to devaluation, while their lack of ability to maintain financial discipline and implement structural reforms imply considerable vulnerabilities in terms of financing and competitiveness. In the subprime crisis all have been hit very hard with the exception of Slovakia. The reasons however were different: while Portugal, Greece, and Italy suffered from public finance imbalances and lack of structural reforms, in Spain, Slovenia and Estonia credit bubbles developed. The case of Slovakia however indicates that even in this quadrant there is no determinacy and under certain conditions—to which I will return in the next section—good performance is possible. At the same time, when looking at longer-term trends the chances seem slight: Italy has been steadily losing its relative position during the period; Portugal stagnated at 80 percent of the EU-27 average, while the apparently good performance of Greece and Spain proved to be unsustainable given the public and private indebtedness which accompanied it. In the group, only Slovakia shows steady convergence, while the progress of Slovenia and Estonia was halted by the crisis.

---

[4] Although Estonia introduced the euro only in 2011, its currency board arrangement essentially implied very similar constraints to having the euro thus its performance can be analyzed in this context.

Figure 7.3. GDP per capita in PPS in low-trust euro-zone countries (1998–2010)

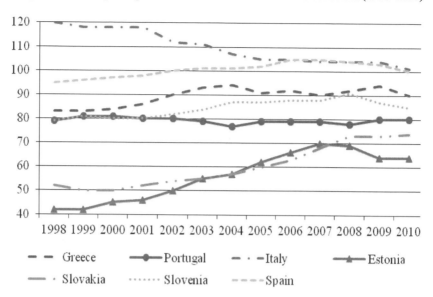

Notes: EU-27 average=100.
Data: Eurostat http://epp.eurostat.ec.europa.eu/tgm/table.do?tab=table&init=1&plugin=
1&language=en&pcode=tec00114

7.3.4. Low-trust countries outside the euro-zone

In low-trust countries, large macroeconomic volatility was expected given the populist pressures on economic policy and the subsequent exposure to international market sentiments. The boom and bust cycle in the Baltics is representative of the sudden stop phenomenon,[5] while the case of Hungary provides an excellent illustration for populist pressures on fiscal policy. Romania also became victim of changing market sentiment in spite of its relatively low level of indebtedness. While these cases support the original hypothesis, the experiences of the remaining three countries—Czech Republic, Poland, and Bulgaria—strongly contradict the theory, as these have been among the best performers during the crisis in the EU-25. Through implementing harsh fiscal stabilization measures, Bulgaria was able to overcome the overheating of its economy without giving up its

---

[5] Sudden stop means a large fall in capital inflows relative to its past trajectory, causing significant disruption in economic activity. For an overview of its basic mechanisms see Calvo (1998).

currency board or needing a bailout,[6] while substantial devaluation as well as limited foreign indebtedness helped the Czech Republic and Poland avoid the worst consequences of the crisis.

The picture is also far from clear-cut when looking at the development of GDP per capita in PPS (Figure 7.4). As we can see, steady convergence could be observed in all countries except Hungary prior to the subprime crisis. Although this process was halted by the crisis in all countries except Poland, the possibility for growth in spite of persistent distrust in these countries cannot be denied.

Figure 7.4. GDP per capita in PPS in CEE-7 (1998–2010)

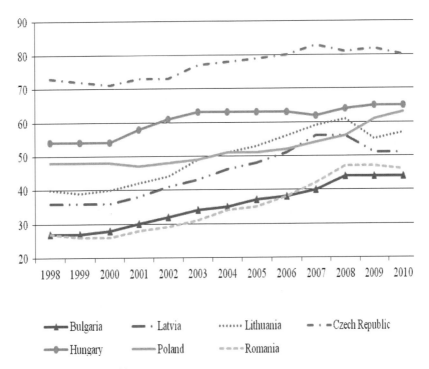

Notes: EU-27 average=100.
Data: Eurostat http://epp.eurostat.ec.europa.eu/tgm/table.do?tab=table&init=1&plugin=
1&language=en&pcode=tec00114

Overall, while we can find evidence confirming the predictions of the theory, in all four groups there are surprises that add up to more than sim-

---

[6] For an overview of the influence of crisis on Bulgaria see IMF (2010a).

ple outliers. This implies that besides trust other factors are clearly at work in shaping long-term economic outcomes. In the following section I will summarize the major factors that mitigate the significance of trust for economic performance.

7.4. Factors moderating the role of trust

On the basis of the case studies, deviations from the theoretical predictions can be explained by five factors: low level of initial development, international financial market pressures, overconfidence, fashions in economic thinking, and leadership. In the following I will provide a brief overview about the role of these factors and through them tie in the broader literature on development.

7.4.1. Initial level of development

In the theory advanced in Chapter 2 and 3, there was no indication that the proposed mechanisms would have different implications for developed and developing countries. However, on the basis of the empirical chapters as well as from the figures on GDP per capita, we can see that lack of trust in itself does not necessarily represent an obstacle to convergence. In Figure 7.4, we can see a steady convergence up to the financial crisis among CEE countries that have not introduced the euro. In spite of lower levels of trust than in the core EU member states, these countries have been able to catch up considerably on the leaders.

Although this outcome contrasts with the predictions of the theory from Chapter 3, in a sense it is far from surprising. From the literature on economic growth we know that countries far from the technological frontier have the chance to step on a transition path, which facilitates a period of high growth rate and catching up (Barro and Sala-i-Martin 1997). Stepping on a transition path might come from a variety of factors. Examples include the adoption of more advanced technology as well as economic policies oriented toward strengthening the market allocation of resources such as opening markets and increasing the export-orientation of the economy.[7] However, once countries approach the technological frontier trust appears to assume increasing importance. This is indicated by the experi-

---

[7] One method to find the needed reform is to target the most binding constraint on growth through the use of growth diagnostics. See: Hausmann, Rodrik, and Velasco (2008).

ences of the southern countries in the EU-15. As we have seen on Figure 3, loss of relative position or stagnation characterizes these countries.

The above considerations require a qualification to the original theory. It appears that institutional trust is likely to matter more for countries that are close to the technological frontier and which have used the potential for stepping on a temporary transition path of fast growth. This does not mean that lack of trust is irrelevant for less developed countries, since as we could see in the case of Hungary, using the possibility of a transition path is far from evident, and low trust can strongly hinder a country even at a relatively low level of development. However, the possibility of a transition path does imply that considerable improvement can be achieved by policies, which are much easier to implement than increasing institutional trust.

7.4.2. International financial market pressures

One factor that can force a low-trust country to implement painful economic reforms is pressure from international financial markets. Among the CEE-10 countries, those with the weakest institutions—the Baltic states in the 1990s as well as Bulgaria—were forced to implement measures to boost their credibility. Such a straightjacket proved to be effective in avoiding not only classical populist measures, which could be seen in Hungary or the southern states, but also in implementing a radical neoliberal agenda of market reforms. Although the emerging credit boom reflected market optimism over these developments as well as served to appease the public, the disciplining force of the market on economic policies was evident.

The pressure from international financial markets is far from uniform, however. While it represents a strong force for countries with the weakest institutions, the situation has been very different for countries with somewhat better institutions, i.e., the Visegrad group and the southern member states of the EU. These countries had stable access to international financial markets without a need for an extreme commitment to stability, as manifested by a currency board. To what extent they used or abused this access was a matter of domestic politics to which I will return.

Overall, the pressures from international markets differ substantially depending on the strength of institutions. This finding relates to the concept of debt intolerance (Reinhart, Rogoff, and Savastano 2003), which refers to the phenomena that the safe thresholds of debt differ substantially among countries based on the strength of financial institutions. It should be also noted that following the financial crisis markets started to strongly differentiate and constrained access not only for countries with the weakest institutions but—as we could see in Chapter 5—also for those with weak fundamentals. This implies the possibility that the disciplinary effect of markets might increase in the future.

7.4.3. Overconfidence

The assessment of the influence of trust is further complicated by the fact that too much trust can be as bad as lack of trust. This is a form of optimism that Keynes called "animal spirits." Its combination with cheap financing lies behind the build-up of bubbles, when the availability of financing and expectations about asset price developments reinforce one another. During this process, prices increasingly deviate from fundamentals although even at the peak of the bubble investors try to rationalize their decision (Kindelberger 1989, Shiller 2000, Reinhart and Rogoff 2009). Such bubbles were behind the crisis in Ireland, Spain, Denmark, the UK, and the Baltic states. In all cases favorable fiscal indicators lay behind the optimism.

Given the problems bubbles cause when they burst, it appears a natural conclusion that there is an optimal level of trust and more trust is not necessarily better. This resonates with the findings of Butler, Guiliano, and Guiso (2009), who found that the relation of individual income to the individual level of trust is hump-shaped—people with excessive or too little trust pay a price comparable to the costs of foregoing a college education.

While optimism might explain the growth of the bubble, in Chapter 5, lack of government action against its development was interpreted as a measure to appease the public for stringent fiscal policies. At the same time, in Chapter 6 it was considered more of a genuine mistake by authorities in the case of Ireland. The two interpretations are not necessarily exclusive—the bubble was very important for Irish fiscal performance—but in order to understand them a look at prevailing economic ideas is necessary.

7.4.4. Economic ideas

Prior to the subprime crisis a general sense of complacency could be observed in mainstream economic thinking. The coexistence of low inflation and high rates of growth generated a considerable literature regarding the causes of this phenomenon, named the Great Moderation. While researchers agreed that several factors together are likely to be responsible for it, including structural changes such as the spread of information technology, as well as good luck, a leading explanation was better understanding of monetary policymaking (Bernanke 2004). After about three decades of macroeconomic stability in advanced countries, many economists were convinced that the problem of large cyclical fluctuations in the economy have been solved for all practical purposes, and methods of fine-tuning require researchers' attention (Lucas 2003).

In this new era of economic development, prices were seen as unlikely to deviate from fundamentals or at least there was no reason for policy intervention if it occurred. According to Mishkin (2011, 19–21) such stance rested on three major premises. First, on the basis of equilibrium economics, a bubble could not develop—or at least the central bank does not have an informational advantage over market players to know if it did. According to this view, if market players knew there was a bubble, it would burst. Second, monetary policy was not seen as an effective tool to fight a bubble either because it had no tools for the abnormal conditions represented by a bubble or because the bubble focused on one sector in the economy, while policy affects the entire economy. Finally, it was also believed that instead of preventing the growth of a bubble, monetary policy has more tools to deal with it afterwards. In his autobiography (Greenspan 2007), which was published right before the crisis, the former head of the Fed gives a firsthand account about how such ideas shaped his monetary decision making.

As both Shiller (2000) and Reinhart and Rogoff (2009) show, new era thinking is a characteristic feature of developing bubbles. While an explanation could stop here, it has to be noticed that such thinking was very convenient for policymakers. As we could see in the Baltics, increased consumption could substitute for public spending, while in Ireland it gave rise to a trend that made the budget dependent on revenues from the real estate boom. Implementing serious measures to stop the boom would have been highly damaging to the governments in both cases.

Making errors is human, thus we should not underestimate the chance for genuine policy mistakes based on prevailing economic ideas. At the same time when such mistakes benefit a government so well—at least in the short-run—we have to keep in mind the potential for opportunistic motivations. When judging bubbles, both considerations should be taken into account, which means that trust exerts its influence on policy through a credit boom with the support of economic fashions. Once a high-trust country has experienced the bust of a bubble such as Sweden in the 1990s, policymakers tend to recognize the inherent dangers of letting bubbles grow unimpeded and implement the necessary regulations. Developments in Ireland and Denmark suggest a similar path.

7.4.5. Leadership

While some countries managed fall into crisis in spite of an environment characterized by trust, other countries—most notably Poland—avoided the fate of several other low-trust countries. Still others such as Slovakia managed to perform considerably better than could be expected on the basis of the theory. In both cases the personality of the leaders played a critical role—in Slovakia, Dzurinda was able to push through reforms that prepared the country for EMU accession, while the National Bank of Poland (NBP) led by Leszek Balcerowicz implemented steps to save the country from the emerging credit boom in spite of the prevailing economic fashions. Naturally, the role they played in countering short-term tendencies in policy was conditional on several other factors—lack of a strong opposition in Slovakia, underdevelopment in Poland, and the institutional autonomy of the NBP.

It is also notable that personalities could play a role countering short-term pressures primarily in the CEE countries. While it naturally requires more research into the subject, a possible explanation for this phenomenon might be that in new democracies with a less professionalized political class, highly-skilled, idealistic leaders might sometimes gain power and resist short-term pressures from the environment. However, in more established democracies, the attitude of the elites is likely to increasingly reflect the values of the masses, thus less resistance from pressures is expected.[8] This might be the reason why the hypotheses fit so much better in the EU-15 countries.

While the above five factors can considerably modify the extent to which the consequences of low trust manifest themselves in economic outcomes, they do not invalidate the core argument of the book, which claims that in low-trust environments there is a tendency towards short-term decision making, which undermines prospects for sustainable economic development. Once we accept the presence of such a tendency, it is important to consider some of its implications.

---

[8] The close correlation between the attitudes of the masses and elite quality is shown by Welzel (2002).

7.5. Implications for policy

While there might be numerous potential implications for the theory, in the following I will focus on three major issues, which are closest to the subject of the empirical chapters: the future of the euro-zone, the accession by CEE countries, and the political economy of policy reforms.

7.5.1. The future of the euro-zone

The theory proposed in the book does not predict an easy future for the euro-zone. At the time of writing, it seems uncertain whether the various measures will succeed in keeping troubled states in the euro-zone. Based on the previous chapters, it can be argued that even if these packages are successful in preventing exit, without a comprehensive overhaul of the institutional environment, imbalances are likely to reemerge in the future. Given the difficulties of building a trustworthy state, especially in times of crisis, recovery is unlikely to be fast. This implies that conditional bailout packages are unlikely to work, and a move toward corner solutions—stronger fiscal union or exit—appears necessary.

A stronger fiscal union would spread risks across the EU, while an exit would make a more fitting monetary policy possible for the exiting country. Both of these solutions have serious drawbacks however. A stronger fiscal union in the form of Eurobonds[9] or larger redistribution across the EU could give rise to significant moral hazard problems, weaken the incentives to reform in the periphery, and be very expensive for the core. An exit could undermine the credibility of the claim about the irrevocable fixing of the exchange rate, and would not really solve the institutional problems in the exiting country. Neither of these solutions can thus be considered optimal, and choosing between them is a political and not an economic question. However, from an economic perspective either is likely to be less harmful than disregarding the inherent divergence within the euro-zone and maintaining considerable uncertainty by not making the choice.

The alternative to the corner solutions is the improvement of economic governance. The Sixpack, which was adopted in 2011, aims to improve

---

[9] Eurobonds would be government bonds issued in euros by the 17 euro-zone countries, which would limit the country risk faced by individual investors. The precise arrangements, which would limit the problem of moral hazard, are subject to considerable debates, see for example Delpla and Weizsäcker (2010) and Muellbauer (2011).

the enforcement of the Stability and Growth Pact, broaden macroeconomic surveillance, and include more automatic trigger mechanisms to impose fines on countries that breach the rules.[10] While a greater commitment to responsible economic policy is certainly welcome, the package is not very different in structure from the earlier Stability and Growth Pact—instead of focusing on the roots of imbalances, it outlaws them through the possibility of fines. This implies that the basic incentive structure for governments is not going to change—they will continue to weigh electoral considerations and external pressure together, and it is unlikely that the calculation will lead to radically different results than prior to the crisis. This is especially true if the EU is presented as a scapegoat for austerity, so its warnings are dismissed by the population. Based on the previous chapters fundamental change has to come from internal sources. While given the lessons of the crisis this possibility cannot be completely excluded, until it happens the need for choice over the two corner solutions remains pressing.

7.5.2. Accession of CEE countries to the euro-zone

Recognizing the link between low trust and short-term orientation in economic policymaking also has implications for the accession of the remaining CEE countries to the euro-zone. While the possible danger of repeating the experiences of the southern states should serve as a warning when considering the costs and benefits of accession, the experiences of high-trust countries outside the euro-zone strengthen the case for joining.

The combination of short-term orientation in decision making with the availability of financing requires caution for preventing public and private overspending. The consideration of factors, which were listed in the previous section as mitigating the importance of trust, implies that the dangers might be lessened. The greater pressures from the international markets have forced most CEE countries to conduct sustainable fiscal policies. The labor market is also much more flexible than in the southern member states (Darvas and Szapáry 2008, 29–30). Following the crisis, the recognition of the dangers of a credit boom is likely to contribute to implementing stricter financial regulations. These factors reduce the danger of repeating the Southern experience and might allow the development

---

[10] For a comprehensive overview of the measures in this package see the website of the European Commission: http://ec.europa.eu/economy_finance/economic_governance/index_en.htm.

of a positive cycle of good policies, good performance, and increasing trust, which have taken place in Slovakia.

The positive scenario however should not be taken for granted. The negative cycle of erroneous policies, weak performance and increasing distrust is also a possibility. Even if it does not materialize in the form of financial imbalances given international financial market constraints, distrust might influence policies outside the economic sphere—blaming minorities, the poor, or foreigners are well-known tactics of vote gathering for politicians in the region.

The question naturally arises whether the negative scenario is more or less likely in the euro-zone. While having an anchor for responsible economic policy is certainly helpful in saving a country from the worst policy mistakes and its consequences, based on the experiences of the financial crisis we can find success and failure both within and outside the euro-zone. It is thus hard to avoid the conclusion that the fate of CEE countries does not primarily depend on whether and when they introduce the euro but rather on the development of an internal commitment to long-term thinking and responsibility. While an elite conviction about the benefits of stability is indispensable, building institutional trust provides a lasting foundation for such commitment.

7.5.3. The political economy of policy reforms

During the transition from socialism, one of the major debates concerned the issue of shock therapy versus gradualism. In policy discourse, shock therapy came to imply radicalism in reforms, which was seen as a value in its own right, while gradualism was equated with timidity and unwillingness to change. As Csaba (2009b, 385–386) discusses, the original meaning of gradualism was the very opposite: "taking the long view, setting a timetable and dosing the measures so that the synergies could work out." Such debate has not lost its relevance after the transition, since at a time of acute economic difficulties there is a general temptation—especially for governments with a strong mandate—toward offering simple solutions to complex problems and implementing them through authoritarian methods. These might range from lack of consultation with relevant interest groups to retroactive laws.

The theory proposed in this book strongly advises against such practices. It helps to recognize that solutions that might be economically advisable but undermine trust in the institutional framework might cause more problems than they resolve. Respecting the mechanisms for democratic decision making is thus an important constraint on economic policy. While it might slow down decision making and delay solutions to acute problems, the sense of stability such rules provide should be an important consideration, and their role in long-term planning in society should be respected.

A sense of stability or consensual decision making on policy reforms is obviously hard to expect in the majority of new democracies. However, even in this context it is important to follow a strategy that does not go directly against the possibility of eventually reaching these goals. From the perspective of this book it implies that even in difficult situations governments should adhere to at least the formal principles of the rule of law in the Hayekian sense, which means governing through public, prospective laws with the qualities of generality, certainty, and equality of application.

7.6. Conclusions

The original objective of this research was to discover the mechanisms through which institutional trust might influence economic policies and economic growth. Through making a connection between law abidance and the prevailing time horizon in decision making, I have shown why a short-term orientation can become persistent in economic decision making in spite of clear evidence about its consequences. The argument does not imply that trust should be viewed as a fundamental source of economic growth, but rather as an enabling factor, which facilitates the reaching of a country's growth potential. Its real significance lays in the specific context of globalization—in an era of intense global competition and interdependence, the consequences of errors, which can be traced to distrust in policymakers, are magnified.

Although the research has argued for the importance of trust both on theoretical and empirical grounds, it should also be emphasized that the presence or absence of trust creates only a tendency towards certain kinds of policies rather than acts as a determinate force. Based on the case studies, several factors have been noted, which might contribute to countering the dangers of low-level trust. Given the difficulties of building institutional trust in the short-term, the presence of these factors can help to keep a low-trust country on a convergence path. Such a path, however, should not obscure the need to build institutional trust eventually and thus facilitate long-term orientation in decision making for all actors.

As countries around the world struggle to rebuild their economies following the subprime crisis, building a trustworthy state should be high on the agenda. During a period of austerity this might appear an impossible task. However, if we are able to believe that trust has other sources than material welfare, policies addressing concerns of fairness in distributing the burden of adjustment as well as measures focusing on the impartial provision of public services might go a long way. There is probably no universal guideline to complete these objectives and this book certainly does not claim to have given one. Still, it is hard to escape the conclusion that without a genuine commitment from policymakers, the public is unlikely to perceive the Leviathan as a benign creature.

Bibliography

Ábel, István, and Szakadát László. 1997. "A bankrendszer átalakulása Magyarországon 1987–1996 között." [The transformation of the banking system in Hungary between 1987 and 1996] *Közgazdasági Szemle* 44 (7–8): 635–552.

Afonso, Antonio, Werner Ebert, Ludger Schuknecht, and Michael Thöne. 2005. "Quality of Public Finances and Growth." European Central Bank Working Paper No. 438.

Alesina, Alberto, and Roberto Perotti. 1995. "Fiscal Expansions and Fiscal Adjustments in OECD Countries." NBER Working Paper No. 5214.

Alesina, Alberto, Roberto Perotti, and Jose Tavares. 1998. "The Political Economy of Fiscal Adjustments." *Brookings Papers on Economic Activity* 18 (1): 197–266.

Almond, Gabriel A., and Sidney Verba. 1963. *The Civic Culture*. Princeton: Princeton University Press.

Andreoni, James, Brian Erard, and Jonathan Feinstein. 1998. "Tax Compliance." *Journal of Economic Literature* 36 (2): 818–860.

Antal László. 1985. *Gazdaságirányítási és pénzügyi rendszerünk a reform útján.* [Our system of economic and financial management on the path of reform] Budapest: Közgazdasági és Jogi Könyvkiadó.

Appel, Hilary, and John Gould. 2000. "Identity Politics and Economic Reform: Examining Industry–State Relations in the Czech and Slovak Republics." *Europe-Asia Studies* 52 (1): 111–131.

Arcalean, Calin, et al. 2007. "The Causes and Nature of the Rapid Growth of Bank Credit in the Central, Eastern and South-eastern European Countries." In *Rapid Credit Growth in Central and Eastern Europe: Endless Boom or Early Warning?*, ed. Charles Enoch and Inci Ötker-Robe, 13–46. Houndmills and New York: Palgrave Macmillan.

Ardagna, Silvia. 2004. "Fiscal Stabilizations: When Do They Work and Why." *European Economic Review* 48 (5): 1047–1074.

Árendás, Csaba, Tamás Dudás, Gábor Illés, and Marianna Szinek Kékesy. 2006. "The Tax Reforms in Slovakia in 2004—the Year of 19%." In *Gazdasági váltás Szlovákiában— Economic Reforms in Slovakia*, ed. Béla Keszegh, and Tamás Török, 223–256. Komárom/Komárno: Kempelen Farkas Társaság.

Aslund, Anders. 2007. *How Capitalism was Built: the Transformation of Central and Eastern Europe, Russia, and Central Asia*. Cambridge: Cambridge University Press.

————. 2010. *The Last Shall Be the First: the East European Financial Crisis 2008–10*. Washington, DC: Peterson Institute for International Economics.

Balmaseda, Manuel, Miguel Sebastian, and Patry Tello. 2002. "Spain Accession to the EMU: A Long and Hilly Road." *The Economic and Social Review* 33 (2): 195–222.

Baker, Dean. 2008. "The Housing Bubble and the Financial Crisis." *Real-world Economics Review* 46: 73–81.

Barrios, Salvador, and Andrea Schaechter. 2008. "The Quality of Public Finances and Economic Growth." Economic Papers No. 337. Brussels: Directorate General for Economic and Financial Affairs.

Barro, Robert J., 1974. "Are Government Bonds Net Wealth?" *Journal of Political Economy* 82 (6): 1095–1117.

Barro, Robert J., and David B. Gordon. 1983. "Rules, Discretion and Reputation in a Model of Monetary Policy." *Journal of Monetary Economics* 12 (1): 101–120.

Barro, Robert J. and Xavier Sala-i-Martin. 1997. "Technological Diffusion, Convergence, and Growth." *Journal of Economic Growth* 2 (1): 1–26.

Barry, Frank. 2006. "Foreign Direct Investment and Institutional Co-Evolution in Ireland." Centre for Economic Research Working Paper. http://www.ucd.ie/economics/research/papers/2006/WP06.03.pdf (accessed on September 27, 2012).

Barto, Martin. 2000. "Banking Sector in the Slovak Republic." In *Economic Policy in Slovakia 1990–1999,* ed. Anton Marcincin and Miroslav Beblavy, 358–375. Bratislava: INEKO.

Barry, Frank. 2007. "Third-Level Education, Foreign Direct Investment and Economic Boom in Ireland." *International Journal of Technology Management* 38 (3): 198–219.

Barry, Frank, Nuno Crespo, and M. Paula Fontoura. 2004. "EU Enlargement and the Portuguese Economy." *World Economy* 27 (6): 781–802.

Beetsma, Roel M., and Xavier Debrun. 2007. "The New Stability and Growth Pact: A First Assessment." *European Economic Review* 51 (2): 453–477.

Benczes, István. 2008. *Trimming the Sails: The Comparative Political Economy of Expansionary Fiscal Consolidations*. Budapest and New York: CEU Press.

Berggren, Niclas, Mikael Elinder, and Henrik Jordahl. 2008. "Trust and Growth: A Shaky Relationship." *Empirical Economics* 35 (2): 251–74.

Bergh, Andreas, and Christian Bjorskov. 2011. "Historical Trust Levels Predict the Current Size of the Welfare State." *Kyklos* 64 (1): 1–19.

Berglöf, Eric, Yevgeniya Korniyenko, Alexander Plekhanov, and Jeromin Zettelmeyer. 2010. "Understanding the Crisis in Emerging Europe." *Public Policy Review* 6 (6): 985–1008.

Bernát, Ildikó. 2009. "A 'Piacgazdaság normatív keretei (gazdaság és kultúra)' című kutatás adatfelvételének gyorselemzése." [First analysis of survey results for the research on 'The normative framework of market economy—economics and culture'] http://www.tarki.hu/hu/research/gazdkult/gazdkult_gyorselemzes_bernat.pdf (accessed on September 27, 2012).

Bernanke, Ben. 2004. "The Great Moderation." Remarks at the meetings of the Eastern Economic Association, Washington, D.C., February 20, 2004. http://www.federalreserve.gov/BOARDDOCS/SPEECHES/2004/20040220/default.htm (accessed on September 27, 2012).

Bethlendi, András. 2011. "Policy Measures and Failures on Foreign Currency Household Lending in Central and Eastern Europe." *Acta Oeconomica* 61 (2): 193–223.

Blondal, Jon R. 2001. "Budgeting in Sweden." *OECD Journal on Budgeting* 1 (1): 27–57.

Bohle, Dorothee. 2010. "East European Transformations and the Paradoxes of Transnationalization." EUI Working Paper SPS No. 2010/01. Badia Fiasolana: European University Institute.

Bohle, Dorothee, and Béla Greskovits. 2007. "Neoliberalism, Embedded Neoliberalism and Neocorporatism: Towards Transnational Capitalism in Central-Eastern Europe." *West European Politics* 30 (3): 443–466.

Boltho, Andrea. 2000. "What Matters for Economic Success? Greece and Ireland Compared." In *Small Economies Adjustment to Global Tendencies*, ed. Bara Zoltán and László Csaba, 150–169. Budapest: Aula.

Bönker, Frank. 2006a. *The Political Economy of Fiscal Reform in Eastern Europe: Hungary, Poland, and the Czech Republic from 1989 to EU accession*. Cheltenham, UK: Edward Elgar.

———. 2006b. "From Pacesetter to Laggard: the Political Economy of Negotiating Fit in the Czech Republic." In *Enlarging the Euro Area: External Empowerment and Domestic Transformation in East Central Europe*, ed. Kenneth Dyson, 160–177. Oxford: Oxford University Press.

Braithwaite, Valerie. 2009. *Defiance in Taxation and Governance: Resisting and Dismissing Authority in a Democracy*. Cheltenham, UK: Edward Elgar.

Brender, Adi, and Allan Drazen. 2005. "Political Budget Cycles in New versus Established Democracies." *Journal of Monetary Economics* 52 (7): 1271–1295.

Brown, Martin, Karolin Kirschenmann, and Steven Ongena. 2010. "Foreign Currency Loans—Demand or Supply Driven?" CEPR Discussion Paper No. 7952.

Brunnermeier, Markus K. 2009. "Deciphering the Liquidity and Credit Crunch 2007–2008." *Journal of Economic Perspectives* 23 (1): 77–100.

Buchanan, James M., and Richard E. Wagner. 1977. *Democracy in Deficit: The Political Legacy of Lord Keynes*. San Diego and London: Academic Press.

Buckley, Francis H. 2005. "Perfectionism." *Supreme Court Economic Review* 13, 133–163.

Buiter, Willhem H., Giancarlo M. Corsetti, and Paolo A. Pesenti. 1998. "Interpreting the ERM Crisis: Country-specific and Systemic Issues." Princeton Studies in International Finance No. 84.

Buti, Marco. 2006. "Will the New Stability and Growth Pact Succeed? An Economic and Political Perspective." Economic Papers No. 241, Brussels: Directorate General for Economic and Financial Affairs.

Buti, Marco and Lucio R. Pench. 2004. "Why Do Large Countries Flout the Stability Pact? And What Can Be Done About It?" *Journal of Common Market Studies* 42 (5): 1025–1032.

Butler, Jeffrey, Paola Guiliani, and Luigi Guiso. 2009. "The Right Amount of Trust." NBER Working Paper No. 15344.

Butos, William N., and Roger G. Koppl. 1997. "The Varieties of Subjectivism: Keynes and Hayek on Expectations." *History of Political Economy* 4 (3): 59–80.

Callan, Tim, Claire Keane, Michael Savage, and John R. Walsh. 2012. "Distributional Impact of Tax, Welfare and Public Sector Pay Policies: 2009–2012." In *Quarterly Economic Commentary Winter 2011/Spring 2012*, ed. David Duffy, Joseph Durkan, and Cormac O'Sullivan, 47–55. Dublin: Economic and Social Research Institute. http://www.esri.ie/UserFiles/publications/QEC2011Win.pdf (accessed on September 27, 2012).

Calvo, Guillermo. 1998. "Capital Flows and Capital-Market Crises: The Simple Economics of Sudden Stops." *Journal of Applied Economics* 1 (1): 35–54.

Carabelli, Anna, and Niccolo De Vecchi. 2001. "Hayek and Keynes: From a Common Critique of Economic Method to Different Theories of Expectations." *Review of Political Economy* 13 (3): 269–285.

Cerra, Valerie, and Sweta Chaman Saxena. 2005. "Eurosclerosis or Financial Collapse: Why Did Swedish Incomes Fall Behind?" IMF Working Paper No. 05/29.

Chang, Michele. 2006. "Reforming the Stability and Growth Pact: Size and Influence in EMU Policymaking." *European Integration* 28 (1): 107–120.

Chari, V. V. 1999. "Nobel Laurate Robert E. Lucas, Jr: Architecht of Modern Macroeconomics." *Federal Reserve Bank of Minneapolis Quarterly Review* 23 (2): 2–12.

Chavance, Bernard. 2009. *Institutional Economics*. New York: Routledge.

Clift, Ben. 2006. "The New Political Economy of *Dirigisme*: French Macroeconomic Policy, Unrepentant Sinning and the Stability and Growth Pact." *British Journal of Politics and International Relations* 8 (3): 388–409.

Coelho, Cesar, Francisco Jose Veiga, and Linda G. Veiga. 2006. "Political Business Cycles in Local Employment: Evidence from Portugal." *Economic Letters* 93 (1): 82–87.

Connor, Gregory, Thomas Flavin, and Bryan O'Kelly. 2010. "The U.S. and Irish Credit Crises: Their Distinctive Differences and Common Features." Irish Economy Note No. 10. Available at http://www.irisheconomy.ie/Notes/IrishEconomyNote10.pdf (accessed on September 27, 2012).

Constancio, Vitor. 2005. "European Monetary Integration and the Portuguese Case." In *The New EU Member States: Convergence and Stability*, ed. Carsten Detken, Vitor Gaspar, and Gilles Noblet, 204–216. Frankfurt: European Central Bank.

Coval, Joshua, Jakub Jurek, and Erik Stafford. 2009. "The Economics of Structured Finance." *Journal of Economic Perspectives* 23 (1): 3–25.

Csaba, László. 1995. *The Capitalist Revolution in Eastern Europe: a Contribution to the Economic Theory of Systemic Change*. Cheltenham: Edward Elgar.

———. 1998a. "A Decade of Transformation in Hungarian Economic Policy: Dynamics, Constraints and Prospects." *Europe-Asia Studies* 50 (8): 1381–1391.

———, ed. 1998b. *The Hungarian SME Sector Development in Comparative Perspective*. Washington and Budapest: CIPE/USAID and Kopint Datorg.

———. 2007. *The New Political Economy of Emerging Europe*. 2nd ed. Budapest: Akadémiai Kiadó.

———. 2009a. *Crisis in Economics?* Budapest: Akadémiai Kiadó.

———. 2009b. From Sovietology to Neo-institutionalism. *Post-Communist Economies* 21 (4): 383–398.

———. 2012. "Haladás vagy hanyatlás? Avagy miért marad le Magyarország?" [Progress or recess? Or why is Hungary falling behind?]. In *Földobott kő? Tények és tendenciák a 21. században*, ed. László Muraközy, 282–312. Budapest: Akadémiai Kiadó.

Csepeli, György, Antal Örkény, Mária Székelyi, and Ildikó Barna. 2004. "Blindness to Success: Social Psychological Objectives Along the Way to a Market Economy in Eastern Europe." In *Creating Social Trust in Post-Socialist Transition*, ed. János Kornai, Bo Rothstein, and Susan Rose-Ackerman, 213–240. New York: Palgrave Macmillan.

Cunha, Miguel Pina, Stewart R. Clegg, and Rego Arménio. 2008. "The Institutions of archaic post-modernity and their organizational and managerial consequences: the case of Portugal." FEUNL Working Paper Series No. 528. Available at http://fesrvsd. fe.unl.pt/WPFEUNL/WP2008/wp528.pdf (accessed on September 27, 2012).

Dahan, Frédérique, and John L. Simpson. 2005. "The Impact of the Legal Framework on the Secured Credit Market in Poland." EBRD report initiated by the National Bank of Poland. http://www.nbp.pl/en/publikacje/raporty_ebor/raport_ebor_en.pdf (accessed on September 27, 2012).

Darvas, Zsolt. 2009. "The Impact of the Crisis on Budget Policy in Central and Eastern Europe." Bruegel Working Paper No. 2009/5.

Darvas, Zsolt and Valentina Kostyleva. 2011. "The Fiscal and Monetary Institutions of CESEE Countries." Bruegel Working Paper No. 2011/2.

Darvas, Zsolt and György Szapáry. 2008. "Euro Area Enlargement and Euro Adoption Strategies." Economic Papers No 304. Brussels: Directorate General for Economic and Financial Affairs.

Davidson, Paul. 1982–1983. "Rational Expectations: a Fallacious Foundation For Studying Crucial Decision-Making Processes." *Journal of Post-Keynesian Economics* 5 (2): 182–196.

Dellepiane, Sebastian, and Niamh Hardiman. 2010. "Governing the Irish Economy: From Boom to Bust." Conference paper at ECPR Standing Group on Regulatory Governance Biennial Conference "Regulation in the Age of Crisis." Dublin, 17–19 June 2010. Available: http://regulation.upf.edu/dublin-10-papers/2A2.pdf (accessed on September 27, 2012).

Delpla, Jacques, and Jakob von Weizsäcker. 2010. "The Blue Bond Proposal." Bruegel Policy Brief No. 2010/3.

Dequech, David. 1999. "Expectations and Confidence Under Uncertainty." *Journal of Post-Keynesian Economics* 21 (3): 415–430.

———. 2000. "Fundamental Uncertainty and Ambiguity." *Eastern Economic Journal* 26 (1) 41–60.

———. 2006. "The New Institutional Economics and the Theory of Behaviour Under Uncertainty." *Journal of Economic Behavior and Organization* 59 (1): 109–131.

Dimitrov, Vesselin. 2006. "From Laggard to Pacesetter: Bulgaria's Road to the EMU." In *Enlarging the Euro Area: External Empowerment and Domestic Transformation in East Central Europe*, ed. Kenneth Dyson, 145–159. Oxford: Oxford University Press.

Drees, Burkhart, and Ceyla Pazarbasioglu. 1998. "The Nordic Banking Crisis: Pitfalls in Financial Liberalization?" IMF Occasional Paper No. 161.

Durlauf, Steven N. 2001. "Econometric Analysis and the Study of Economic Growth: A Skeptical Perspective." In *Macroeconomics and the Real World*, ed. Roger Backhouse and Andrea Salanti, 249–262. Oxford: Oxford University Press.

Durlauf, Steven N., and Marcel Fafchamps. 2005. "Social capital." In *Handbook of Economic Growth*, ed. Philippe Aghion and Steven N. Durlauf, 1639–1699. Amsterdam: Elsevier.

Dyson, Kenneth H. 1994. *Elusive Union: The Process of Economic and Monetary Union in Europe*. London: Longman.

Dyson, Kenneth H., and Kevin Featherstone. 1999. *The Road to Maastricht: Negotiating Economic and Monetary Union*. Oxford: Oxford University Press.

Dyson, Kenneth H., and Lucia Quaglia. 2010. *European Economic Governance and Policies: Commentary on Key Historical and Institutional Documents*. Oxford: Oxford University Press.

Easton, David. 1965. *A Systems Analysis of Political Life*. New York: Wiley

Ebeling, Richard. 1983. "An Interview with G. L. S. Shackle." *Austrian Economics Newsletter* 4 (1): 1–7.

EBRD. 2007. *Life in Transition: A Survey of People's Experiences and Attitudes*. London: EBRD.

EBRD. 2009. *Transition Report 2009: Transition in Crisis?* London: EBRD.

EBRD. 2010. *Transition Report 2010: Recovery and Reform*. London: EBRD.

EBRD. 2011. *Life in Transition: After the Crisis*. London: EBRD.

ECB. 2010. *Financial Stability Review June 2010*. Frankfurt am Main: European Central Bank.

Eichengreen, Barry. 1991. "Is Europe an Optimal Currency Area?" NBER Working Paper No. 3579.

———. 2000. "The EMS Crisis in Retrospect." NBER Working Paper No. 8035.

Eichengreen, Barry, and Ricardo Hausmann, eds. 2005. *Other People's Money: Debt Denomination and Financial Instability in Emerging Market Economies*. London and Chicago: University of Chicago Press.

EIU. 2006a. *Country Report Slovakia August 2006*. London: Economist Intelligence Unit.

EIU. 2006b. *Country Report Slovakia November 2006*. London: Economist Intelligence Unit.

EIU. 2010. *Country Report Slovakia August 2010*. London: Economist Intelligence Unit.

Elster, Jon. 2007. *Explaining Social Behavior: More Nuts and Bolts for the Social Sciences*. Cambridge: Cambridge University Press.

Eurobarometer. 2006. *Introduction of the Euro in the New Member States*. Brussels: European Commission Directorate General for Communications.

Eurobarometer. 2009. *Introduction of the Euro in the New Member States*. Brussels: European Commission Directorate General for Communications.

———. 2012. *Introduction of the Euro in the More Recently Acceded Member states*. Brussels: European Commission Directorate General for Communications.

Eurofound. 2004. *Life Satisfaction in an Enlarged Europe*. Dublin: European Foundation for the Improvement of Living and Working Conditions.

European Commission. 2000. *The EU Economy: 1999 Review*. Brussels: Directorate General for Economic and Financial Affairs.

European Commission. 2006a. "Measuring administrative costs and reducing administrative burdens in the European Union." Commission Working Document No. 2006 (691).

European Commission. 2006b. *Public Finance in EMU: 2006*. Brussels: Commission of the European Communities Directorate General for Economic and Financial Affairs.

European Commission. 2007. *Public Finances in EMU: 2007*. Brussels: Directorate General for Economic and Financial Affairs.

European Commission. 2008. *EMU@10. Successes and Challenges after 10 Years of Economic and Monetary Union*. Brussels: Directorate General for Economic and Financial Affairs.

European Commission. 2009. *Economic Crisis in Europe: Causes, Consequences and Responses*. Brussels: Directorate General for Economic and Financial Affairs.

European Commission. 2010. *Statistical Annex of European Economy, Spring*. Brussels: Directorate General for Economic and Financial Affairs.

European Commission. 2012. *Statistical Annex of European Economy, Spring*. Brussels: Directorate General for Economic and Financial Affairs.

Evans, George W., and Seppo Honkapohja. 2005. "An Interview with Thomas J. Sargent." *Macroeconomic Dynamics* 9 (4): 561–83.

Fabrizio, Stefania, and Ashoka Mody. 2009. "Breaking the Impediments to Budgetary Reforms: Evidence from Europe." In *Achieving and Sustaining Sound Fiscal Positions*, ed. Martin Larch, 32–59. Economic Papers No. 377. Brussels: Commission Directorate General for Economic and Financial Affairs.

Fama, Eugene. 1970. "Efficient Capital Markets: a Review of Theory and Empirical Work." *Journal of Finance* 25 (2): 383–417.

Fatas, Antonio, and Ilian Mihov. 2003. "The Case for Restricting Fiscal Policy Discretion." *Quarterly Journal of Economics* 118 (4): 1419–1447.

Fatas, Antonio, Jürgen von Hagen, Andrew Hughes Hallett, Rolf R. Strauch, and Anne Sibert. 2003. *Stability and Growth in Europe: Towards a Better Pact*. London: Center for Economic Policy Research.

Fehr, Ernst. 2009. "On the Economics and Biology of Trust." *Journal of the European Economic Association* 7 (2–3): 235–266.

Feld, Lars P., and Bruno S. Frey. 2007. "Tax Compliance as a Result of a Psychological Tax Contract: The Role of Incentives and Responsive Regulation." *Law and Policy* 29 (1): 102–120.

Feldmann, Magnus. 2006. "The Baltic States: Pacesetting on EMU Accession and the Consolidation of Domestic Stability Culture." In *Enlarging the Euro Area: External Empowerment and Domestic Transformation in East Central Europe*, ed. Kenneth Dyson, 127–144. Oxford: Oxford University Press.

————. 2008. "Baltic States: When Stability Culture is not Enough." In *The Euro at 10: Europeanization, Power and Convergence*, ed. Kenneth Dyson, 243–257. Oxford: Oxford University Press.

Fish, Steven. 1999. "The End of Meciarism." *East European Constitutional Review* 8 (1–2): 47–55.

Fischer, Jonas, Lars Jonung, and Martin Larch. 2007. "101 Proposals to Reform the Stability and Growth Pact. Why so Many? A Survey." Economic Paper No. 267. Brussels: Directorate General for Economic and Financial Affairs.

Fisher, Sharon, John Gould, and Tim Haughton. 2007. "Slovakia's Neoliberal Turn." *Europe-Asia Studies* 59 (6): 977–998.

FitzGerald, John. 2009. "Blowing Bubbles—and Bursting Them: The Case of Ireland and Spain." Euroframe conference presentation, London, 12th June, 2009. Available at http://www.euroframe.org/fileadmin/user_upload/euroframe/docs/2009/EUROF09_FitzGerald.pdf (accessed on September 27, 2012).

Fleming, Marcus J. 1962. "Domestic Financial Policies Under Fixed and Floating Exchange Rates." *IMF Staff Papers* 9: 363–380.

Flyvberg, Bent. 2006. "Five Misunderstanding About Case-Study Research." *Qualitative Inquiry* 12 (2): 219–245.

Förster, Michael, and Marco M. d'Ercole. 2005. "Income Distribution and Poverty in OECD Countries in the Second Half of the 1990s." Social, Employment and Migration Working Papers No. 22. Paris: OECD.

Frederick, Shane, George Loewenstein, and Ted O'Donoghue. 2002. "Time Discounting and Time Preference: A Critical Review." *Journal of Economic Literature* 40 (2): 351–401.

Friedman, Eric, Simon Johnson, Daniel Kaufmann, and Pablo Zoido-Lobaton. 2000. "Dodging the Grabbing Hand: the Determinants of Unofficial Activity in 69 countries." *Journal of Public Economics* 76 (3): 459–493.

Frydman, Roman, and Michael D. Goldberg. 2007. *Imperfect Knowledge Economics.* Princeton and Oxford: Princeton University Press.

FSA. 2009. *The Turner Review. A regulatory response to the global banking crisis.* London: Financial Services Authority.

Fukuyama, Francis. 1995. *Trust: the Social Virtues and the Creation of Prosperity.* London: Hamish Hamilton.

Gamble, Andrew, and Gavin Kelly. 2002. "Britain and EMU." In *European States and the Euro: Europeanization, Variation and Convergence,* ed. Kenneth Dyson, 97–119. Oxford: Oxford University Press.

Gamson, William A. 1968. *Power and Discontent.* Homewood, Il: The Dorsey Press.

Geddes, Barbara. 1990. "How the Cases You Choose Affect the Answers You Get: Selection Bias in Comparative Politics." In *Political Analysis,* ed. James A. Stimson, 131–150. Ann Arbor: University of Michigan Press.

Gemmel, Norman. 2001. "Fiscal Policy in a Growth Framework." UNU Wider Discussion Paper No. 2001/84.

George, Alexander L., and Andrew Bennett. 2005. *Case Studies and Theory Development in the Social Sciences.* Cambridge, Mass.: MIT Press.

Gerrard, Bill. 1994. "Beyond Rational Expectations: A Constructive Interpretation of Keynes Analysis of Behavior Under Uncertainty." *Economic Journal* 104 (423): 327–337.

Giavazzi, Francesco, and Marco Pagano. 1990. "Can Severe Fiscal Consolidations be Expansionary? Tales of Two Small European Countries." NBER Working Paper No. 3372.

Gilley, Bruce. 2009. *The Right to Rule: How States Win and Lose Legitimacy.* New York: Columbia University Press.

Gleich, Holger. 2003. "Budget Institutions and Fiscal Performance in Central and Eastern European Countries." Working Paper No. 215. Frankfurt: European Central Bank.

Gloria-Palermo, Sandye. 1999. "An Austrian Dilemma: Necessity and Impossibility of a Theory of Institutions." *Review of Austrian Economics* 11 (1): 31–45.

Goldman, Alan H. 2006. "The Rationality of Complying with Rules: A Paradox Resolved." *Ethics* 116 (3) 453–470.

Goodfriend, Marvin. 2007. "How the World Achieved Consensus on Monetary Policy." NBER Working Paper No. 13580.

Goodhart, Charles A. 1989. *Money, Information, and Uncertainty.* 2nd ed. London: Macmillan.

Gorton, Gary B. 2008. "The Subprime Panic." NBER Working Paper No. 14398.

Gorzelak, Grzegorz. 2010. "The (Non-Existing?) Polish Crisis." In *Financial crisis in Central and Eastern Europe: from similarity to diversity,* ed. Grzegorz Gorzelak and Chor-Ching Goh, 139–149. Warsaw: Naukowe Scholar.

Greenspan, Alan. 2007. *The Age of Turbulence: Adventures in a New World.* New York: Penguin.

Greskovits, Béla. 2008. "Hungary and Slovakia: Compliance and its Discontents." In *The Euro at 10: Europeanization, Power and Convergence,* ed. Kenneth Dyson, 274–291. Oxford: Oxford University Press.

Gulde, Anne-Marie. 1999. "The Role of Currency Board in Bulgaria's Stabilization." IMF Policy Discussion Paper No. 99/03.

Győrffy, Dóra. 2007. *Democracy and Deficits: The New Political Economy of Fiscal Management Reforms in the European Union.* Budapest: Akadémiai Kiadó.

———. 2008. "Political Trust and the Success of Fiscal Consolidations: Lessons from Sweden and Hungary." *Zeitschrift für Staats- und Europawissenschaften* 6 (1): 75–100.

———. 2009a. "Enduring Lure of Socialism: The Political Economy of the Subprime Crisis." *Zeitschrift für Staats- und Europawissenschaften* 7 (2): 250–275.

——— 2009b. "Structural Change Without Trust. Reform Cycles in Hungary and Slovakia." *Acta Oeconomica* 59 (2): 147–177.

Hall, Peter A. 2005. "Preference Formation as a Political Process: The Case of Monetary Union in Europe." In *Preferences and Situations: Points of Intersection Between Historical and Rational Choice Institutionalism,* ed. Ira Katznelson and Barry R. Weingast, 129–160. New York: Russel Sage Foundation.

Hallerberg, Mark. 2004. *Domestic Budgets in a United Europe: Fiscal Governance from the End of Bretton Woods to EMU.* Ithaca: Cornell University Press.

Hardin, Russel. 1999. "Do We Want to Trust the Government?" In *Democracy and Trust,* ed. Mark E. Warren, 22–41. Cambridge: Cambridge University Press.

Hausmann, Ricardo, Dani Rodrik, and Andres Velasco. 2008. "Growth Diagnostics." In *The Washington Consensus Reconsidered: Towards a New Global Governance,* ed. Narcis Serra and Joseph Stiglitz. Oxford: Oxford University Press.

Havrylyshyn, Oleh. 2006. *Divergent Paths in Post-Communist Transformation: Capitalism for All or Capitalism for the Few?* Basingstoke: Palgrave Macmillan.

Hayek, Friedrich A. von. 1944. *The Road to Serfdom.* London: Routledge.

———. 1952. *The Sensory Order: An Inquiry into the Foundation of Theoretical Psychology.* London: Routledge.

———. 1973. *Law, Legislation and Liberty, Vol. 1. Rules and Order.* London: Routledge.

———. 1976. *Law, Legislation and Liberty, Vol. 2. The Mirage of Social Justice.* London: Routledge.

Hellman, Joel and Daniel Kaufmann. 2004. "The Inequality of Influence." In *Building a Trustworthy State in Post-Socialist Transition,* ed. János Kornai and Susan Rose-Ackerman, 100–132. New York: Palgrave Macmillan.

Hesse, Joachim Jens. 2007. "Redefining Statehood? In Search of Good Governance, Regulated Markets and Workable Democratic Procedures—an Outline." In *The Public Sector in Transition: East Asia and the European Union Compared,* ed. Joachim Jens Hesse, Jan-Erik Lane, and Yoichi Nishikawa, 13–19. Baden Baden: Nomos.

Hetherington, Marc J. 1998. "The Political Relevance of Political Trust." *American Political Science Review* 92 (4): 791–808.

———. 2004. *Why Trust Matters: Declining Political Trust and the Demise of American Liberalism.* Princeton: Princeton University Press.

Hilbers, Paul, Inci Ötker-Robe, and Ceyla Pazabasioglu. 2007. "Analysis of and Policy Responses to Rapid Credit Growth." In *Rapid Credit Growth in Central and Eastern Europe: Endless Boom or Early Warning?,* ed. Charles Enoch and Inci Ötker-Robe, 84–136. Houndmills and New York: Palgrave Macmillan.

Hochreiter, Eduard, and George E. Tavlas. 2004. "Two Roads to the Euro: The Monetary Experiences of Austria and Greece." Conference presentation: Euro Adoption in the

Accession Countries—Opportunities and Challenges, Prague, February 2–3, 2004. Available at http://www.cgu.edu/include/Hochreiter1.pdf (accessed on September 28, 2012).

Hodgson, Geoffrey M. 2004. *The Evolution of Institutional Economics: Agency, Structure and Darwinism in American Institutionalism.* London: Routledge.

Honohan, Patrick. 2009. "Resolving Ireland's Banking Crisis." *The Economic and Social Review* 40 (2): 207–231.

———. 2010. *The Irish Banking Crisis: Regulatory and Financial Stability Policy 2003–2008.* A Report to the Minister for Finance from the Governor of the Central Bank. Dublin: Central Bank. Available at http://www.bankinginquiry.gov.ie/The%20Irish %20Banking%20Crisis%20Regulatory%20and%20Financial%20Stability%20Policy%20 2003-2008.pdf (accessed on September 28, 2012).

Horvath, Julius. 2003. "Optimal Currency Area Theory. A Selective Review." BOFIT Discussion Papers No. 2003/15.

Hudecz, András. 2012. "Párhuzamos történetek. A lakossági devizahitelezés kialakulása és kezelése Lengyelországban, Romániában és Magyarországon" [Parallel stories. The development and management of foreign currency household lending in Poland, Romania, and Hungary] *Közgazdasági Szemle* 59 (4): 349–411.

Hughes-Hallett, Andrew, and John Lewis. 2008. "European Fiscal Discipline Before and After the EMU: Crash Diet or Permanent Weight Loss?" *Macroeconomic Dynamics* 12 (3): 404–424.

Hurd, Ian. 1999. "Legitimacy and Authority in International Politics." *International Organization* 53 (2): 379–408.

IMF. 1998. "Sweden: Selected Issues." IMF Country Report No. 98/124.

IMF. 2000a. "Ireland: Staff Report for Article IV Consultation." Country Report No. 00/97.

IMF. 2000b. "Portugal: 2000 Article IV Consultation Staff Report." IMF Country Report No. 00/152.

IMF. 2001. "Sweden: Selected Issues. The Role of Government." IMF Country Report No. 01/169.

IMF. 2005a. "Spain: Selected Issues." IMF Country Report No. 05/57.

IMF. 2005b. "The IMF's Approach to Promoting Good Governance and Combating Corruption—A Guide." http://www.imf.org/external/np/gov/guide/eng/index.htm (accessed on September 28, 2012).

IMF. 2006. "Portugal: 2006 Article IV Consultation Staff Report." IMF Country Report No. 06/377.

IMF. 2007a. "Republic of Poland: Financial Sector Assessment Program Technical Note—Credit, Growth, and Financial Stability." IMF Country Report No. 07/160.

IMF. 2007b. "Portugal: 2007 Article IV Consultation Staff Report." IMF Country Report No. 07/341.

IMF. 2007c. "Slovak Republic: 2007 Article IV Consultation." IMF Country Report No. 07/226.

IMF. 2008. "Hungary: Request for Stand-By Arrangement—Staff Report." IMF Country Report No. 08/361.

IMF. 2009. "Republic of Poland: Arrangement Under the Flexible Credit Line." IMF Country Report No. 09/138.

IMF. 2010a. "Bulgaria: 2010 Article IV Consultation." IMF Country Report No. 10/160.

IMF. 2010b. "Greece: Staff Report on Request for Stand-By Arrangement." IMF Country Report No. 10/110.

IMF. 2010c. "Republic of Poland: Arrangement Under the Flexible Credit Line." IMF Country Report No. 10/207.

IMF. 2011a. "Ireland: First and Second Reviews Under the Extended Arrangement and Request for Rephasing of the Arrangement." IMF Country Report No. 11/109.

IMF. 2011b. "Slovak Republic: 2011 Article IV Consultation." IMF Country Report No. 11/122.

IMF. 2012a. "Euro Area Policies: 2012 Article IV Consultation—Selected Issues." Country Report No. 12/182. Washington: IMF.

IMF. 2012b. "Ireland: Fifth Review Under the Extended Arrangement." IMF Country Report No. 12/48.

Inglehart, Ronald, and Christian Wenzel. 2005. *Modernization, Cultural Change, and Democracy: the Human Development Sequence*. Cambridge: Cambridge University Press.

Jacoby, Wade. 2006. "Inspiration, Coalition and Substitution: External Influences on Postcommunist Transformations." *World Politics* 58 (4): 623–651.

Jalali, Carlos, and Marco Lisi. 2009. "Weak Societal Roots, Strong Individual Patrons? Patronage and Party Organization in Portugal." *Revista Enfoques* 7 (11): 441–470.

James, Harvey S. 2002. "The Trust Paradox: A Survey of Economic Inquiries Into the Nature of Trust and Trustworthiness." *Journal of Economic Behavior and Organization* 47 (3): 291–307.

Kahneman, Daniel, and Amos Tversky. 1979. "Prospect Theory: An Analysis of Decision under Risk." *Econometrica* 47 (2): 263–291.

Kato, Junko, and Bo Rothstein. 2006. "Government Partisanship and Managing the Economy: Japan and Sweden in Comparative Perspective." *Governance* 19 (1): 75–97.

Kaufmann, Daniel, Aart Kraay, and Massimo Mastruzzi. 2010. "The Worldwide Governance Indicators: Methodology and Analytical Issues." World Bank Policy Research Working Paper No. 5430.

Kazakos, Panos. 1994. "Introduction" in Panos Kazakos and Panayotis C. Ioakimidis, eds. *Greece and EC Membership Evaluated*. London: Pinter, 13–23.

Kenen, Peter. 1969. "The Theory of Optimum Currency Areas: An Eclectic View." In *Monetary Problems in the International Economy*, ed. Robert Mundell and A. Swoboda, 41–60. Chicago: University of Chicago Press.

Keszegh, Béla. 2006. "The Political Background and the Prerequisites for the Reforms." In *Gazdasági váltás Szlovákiában—Economic Reforms in Slovakia*, ed. Béla Keszegh and Tamás Török, 169–176. Komárom/Komárno: Kempelen Farkas Társaság.

Keynes, John M. 1936. *The General Theory of Employment, Interest and Money*. New York: Harcourt, Brace.

Keynes, John M. 1937. "The General Theory of Employment." In *The Collected Writings of John Maynard Keynes* XIV: 109–123. London: Macmillan.

Kindleberger, Charles P. 1989. *Manias, Panics and Crashes*. 2nd ed. Houndmills and London: Macmillan Press.

Király, Zsolt, Péter Kürthy, Péter Sidó, and Krisztina Száraz. 2006. "Reform of the Social Security System in Slovakia." In *Gazdasági váltás Szlovákiában—Economic Reforms in Slovakia*, ed. Béla Keszegh and Tamás Török, 257–288. Komárom/Komárno: Kempelen Farkas Társaság.

Kirman, Alan P. 1992. "Whom or What Does the Representative Individual Represent?" *Journal of Economic Perspectives* 6 (2): 117–136.

Kis, János. 2004. *A politika mint erkölcsi probléma.* [Politics as a moral problem.] Budapest: Élet és Irodalom. Published in English as *Politics as a Moral Problem.* 2008. Budapest–New York: Central European University Press.

Knack, Stephen, and Philip Keefer. 1997. "Does Social Capital Have an Economic Payoff? A Cross-Country Investigation." *Quarterly Journal of Economics* 112 (4): 1251–1288.

Knight, Frank H. 1921. *Risk, Uncertainty and Profit.* New York: Reprints of Economic Classics, 1964.

Kocenda, Evzen, Ali Kutan, and Taner Yigit. 2008. "Fiscal Convergence and Discipline in Monetary Unions: Evidence from the European Union." Working Paper No. 61. International Policy Center: University of Michigan.

Kornai, János. 1971. *Anti-Equilibrium.* Fairfield: Augustus M. Kelley.

———. 1980. *Economics of Shortage.* Amsterdam: North-Holland.

———. 1992. *The Socialist System: The Political Economy of Communism.* Oxford: Clarendon Press.

———. 2006. "The Great Transformation of Central Eastern Europe: Success and Disappointment." *Economics of Transition* 14 (2): 207–244.

———. 2011. *Gondolatok a kapitalizmusról.* [Thoughts about Capitalism] Budapest: Akadémiai Kiadó.

Kraan, Dirk-Jan, Daniel Bergvall, Ian Hawkesworth, and Philipp Krause. 2007. "Budgeting in Hungary." *OECD Journal on Budgeting* 6 (3): 1–61.

Krugman, Paul. 1979. "A Model of Balance-of-Payments Crisis." *Journal of Money, Credit and Banking* 11 (3): 311–325.

———. 2009. "How Did Economists Get It So Wrong?" *The New York Times.* September 2.

Kurkchiyan, Marina. 2003. "The Illegitimacy of Law in Post-Soviet Societies." In *Law and Informal Practices: The Post-Communist Experience,* ed. Marina Kurkchiyan and Denis J. Galligan, 25–45. Oxford: Oxford University Press.

Kydland, Finn E., and Edward C. Prescott. 1977. "Rules Rather than Discretion: The Inconsistency of Optimal Plans." *Journal of Political Economy* 85 (3): 473–491.

———. 1982. "Time to Build and Aggregate Fluctuations." *Econometrica* 50 (6): 1345–1370.

Lachmann, Ludwig M. 1971. *The Legacy of Max Weber.* Berkley: Glendessary Press.

———. 1976. "From Mises to Shackle: An Essay on Austrian Economics and the Kaleidic Society." *Journal of Economic Literature* 14 (1): 54–62.

———. 1978. *Capital and its Structure.* Kansas City: Sheed Andrews and McMeel.

Laki, Mihály and Júlia Szalai. 2006. "The Puzzle of Success: Hungarian Enterpreneurs at the Turn of the Millenium." *Europe-Asia Studies* 58 (3): 317–345.

Lámfalussy, Sándor. 2000. *Financial Crises in Emerging Markets: an Essay on Financial Globalisation and Fragility.* New Haven: Yale University Press.

Lane, Philip R. 2009. "A New Fiscal Strategy for Ireland." *The Economic and Social Review* 40 (2): 233–253.

Langbein, Laura, and Stephen Knack. 2008. "The Worldwide Governance Indicators and Tautology: Causally Related Separable Concepts, Indicators of a Common Cause, or Both?" World Bank Policy Research Working Paper No. 4669.

Larch, Martin, and Alessandro Turrini. 2008. "Received Wisdom and Beyond: Lessons from Fiscal Consolidation in the EU." Economic Paper No. 320. Brussels: Directorate General for Economic and Financial Affairs.

László, Csaba. 2001. "Vargabetűk az államháztartási reform tízéves történetében 1988–1997." [Twists and turns in the ten-year history of Hungarian public finance reforms 1988–1997] *Közgazdasági Szemle* 48 (10): 844–864.

Levi, Margaret. 1998. "A State of Trust." In *Trust and Governance*, ed. Valerie A. Braithwaite and Margaret Levi, 77–101. New York: Russel Sage Foundation.

Lindahl, Rutger, and Daniel Naurin. 2005. "Sweden: The Twin Faces of a Euro-Outsides." *Journal of European Integration* 27 (1): 65–87.

Lindbeck, Assar. 1997. "The Swedish Experiment." *Journal of Economic Literature* 35 (3): 1273–1319.

Lisbon Council. 2011. *The 2011 Euro Plus Monitor: Progress Amid the Turmoil.* Brussels: Lisbon Council. http://www.lisboncouncil.net//index.php?option=com_downloads&id =595 (accessed on September 28, 2012).

Lucas, Robert E. 1977. "Understanding Business Cycles." Carnegie-Rochester Conference Series on Public Policy (5): 7–29.

————. 1981. *Studies in Business Cycle Theory.* Cambridge, MA: MIT Press.

————. 2003. Macroeconomic Priorities. *American Economic Review* 93 (1): 1–14.

Lundberg, Erik. 1985. "The Rise and Fall of the Swedish Model." *Journal of Economic Literature* 23 (1): 1–36.

Macedo, Jorge Braga de. 2003. "Portugal's European Integration: The Good Student with a Bad Fiscal Constitution." In *Spain and Portugal in the European Union: The First 15 Years*, ed. Sebastian Royo and Paul Christopher Manuel, 169–194. Southgate, UK and Portland, US: Frank Cass and Co.

Magone, José M. 2004. *The Developing Place of Portugal in the European Union.* New Brunswick, N.J.: Transaction Publishers.

Mahoney, James. 2010. "After KKV: The New Methodology of Qualitative Research." *World Politics* 62 (1): 120–147.

Marchionatti, Roberto. 1999. "On Keynes's Animal Spirits." *Kyklos* 52 (3): 415–439.

Marcincin, Anton. 2000a. "Privatization." In *Economic Policy in Slovakia 1990–1999*, ed. Anton Marcincin and Miroslav Beblavy, 292–319. Bratislava: INEKO.

————. 2000b. "Enterprise Restructuring." In *Economic Policy in Slovakia 1990–1999*, ed. Anton Marcincin and Miroslav Beblavy, 320–357. Bratislava: INEKO.

Marcussen, Martin. 2002. "EMU: A Danish Delight and Dilemma." In *European States and the Euro: Europeanization, Variation and Convergence*, ed. Kenneth Dyson, 120–144. Oxford: Oxford University Press.

McIntyre, Robert J., and Bruno Dallago, eds. 2003. *Small and Medium Enterprises in Transitional Economies.* London and New York: Palgrave Macmillan.

McKinnon, Ronald. 1963. "Optimum Currency Areas." *American Economic Review* 53 (4): 717–724.

McNamara, Kathleen. 1997. *The Currency of Ideas: Monetary Politics in the European Union.* Ithaca, NY: Cornell University Press.

Mihályi, Péter. 2001. "The Evolution of Hungary's Approach to FDI in Post-Communist Privatization." *Transnational Corporations* 10 (3): 61–74.

Mises, Ludwig Von. 1949. *Human Action: a Treatise on Economics.* 4th Edition. San Francisco: Fox and Wilkes, 1996.

Mishkin, Frederic S. 2011. "Monetary Policy Strategy: Lessons from the Crisis." NBER Working Paper No. 16755.

Mishler, William, and Richard Rose. 2001. "What are the Origins of Political Trust? Testing Institutional and Cultural Theories in Post-Communist Societies." *Comparative Political Studies* 34 (1): 30–62.

Molander, Per. 2000. "Reforming Budgetary Institutions: The Swedish Experiences." In *Institutions, Politics and Fiscal Policy*, ed. Rolf Strauch and Jürgen Von Hagen, 191–214. Dordrecht, Netherlands and Norwell, US: Kluwer Academic Publishers Group.

Molnár, György and Zsuzsa Kapitány. 2007. "Bizonytalanság és a jövedelmek újraelosztása iránti igény Magyarországon." [Uncertainty and demands for state redistribution in Hungary] *Közgazdasági Szemle* 54 (3): 201–232.

Moore, David. 2005. "Slovakia's 2004 Tax and Welfare Reforms." IMF Working Paper No. 05/133.

Morvay, Karol. 2000. "Overall Macroeconomic Development." In *Economic Policy in Slovakia 1990–1999*, ed. Anton Marcincin and Miroslav Beblavy, 18–59. Bratislava: INEKO.

Muellbauer, John. 2011. "Resolving the Eurozone Crisis: Time for Conditional Eurobonds." CEPR Policy Insight No. 59.

Mundell, Robert A. 1961. "A Theory of Optimum Currency Areas." *American Economic Review* 51 (4): 657–665.

―――. 1963. "Capital Mobility and Stabilization under Fixed and Flexible Exchange Rates." *Canadian Journal of Economics and Political Science* 29 (4): 475–485.

Muraközy, László. 2012. *Államok kora: az európai modell* [The era of states: the European model]. Budapest: Akadémiai Kiadó.

Muth, John F. 1961. "Rational Expectations and the Theory of Price Movements." *Econometrica* 29 (3): 315–335.

NBH [National Bank of Hungary]. 2012. "Jelentés a pénzügyi stabilitásról" [Report on financial stability]. Budapest: NBH.

NBP [National Bank of Poland]. 2010. "Report on the Polish Residential Market 2002–2009." Warsaw: NBP. Available at http://www.nbp.pl/en/publikacje/inne/residential_2002_2009.pdf (accessed on September 29, 2012).

NESC [National Economic and Social Council]. 2009. *Ireland's Five-Part Crisis: An Integrated National Response*. Dublin: NESC.

Newton, Ken. 2008. "Trust and Politics." In *The Handbook of Social Capital*, ed. Castiglione, Dario, Jan W. van Deth, and Guglielmo Wolleb, 241–272. Oxford: Oxford University Press.

North, Douglass C. 1990. *Institutions, Institutional Change and Economic Performance*. Cambridge: Cambridge University Press.

―――. 2005. *Understanding the Process of Economic Change*. Princeton: Princeton University Press.

O'Driscoll, Gerald P. Jr. 1979. "Rational Expectations, Politics and Stagflation." In *Time, Uncertainty and Disequilibrium: Exploration of Austrian Themes*, ed. Mario J. Rizzo, 153–186. Lexington, MA and Toronto: Lexington Books.

OECD. 2008. *Reforms for Sustainable Growth: An OECD Perspective on Hungary*. Paris: OECD.

OECD. 2009. *Society at a Glance 2009—OECD Social Indicators*. Paris: OECD.

OECD. 2010. "Economic Survey of Poland 2010—Policy Brief." Paris: OECD.

Offe, Claus. 1999. "How Can We Trust Our Fellow Citizens?" In *Democracy and Trust*, ed. Mark E. Warren, 42–87. Cambridge: Cambridge University Press.

Ohnsorge-Szabó László and Balázs Romhányi. 2007. "Hogy jutottunk ide: magyar költségvetés, 2000–2006." [How we got here: Hungarian fiscal policy 2000–2006] *Pénzügyi Szemle* 52 (2): 239–285.

O'Neill, Onora. 2002. *A Question of Trust.* Cambridge: Cambridge University Press.

Ó Riain, Seán. 2000. "The Flexible Developmental State: Globalization, Information Technology, and the 'Celtic Tiger.'" *Politics and Society* 28 (2): 157–193.

Papadimitriu, Dimitris. 2006. "Persistent Laggard: Romania as Eastern Europe's Sysphus." In *Enlarging the Euro Area: External Empowerment and Domestic Transformation in East Central Europe*, ed. Kenneth Dyson, 215–233. Oxford: Oxford University Press.

Patterson, Orlando. 1999. "Liberty Against the Democratic State: On the Historical and Contemporary Sources of American Distrust." In *Democracy and Trust*, ed. Mark E. Warren, 151–207. Cambridge: Cambridge University Press.

Powell, Benjamin. 2003. "Economic Freedom and Growth: the Case of the Celtic Tiger." *Cato Journal* 22 (3): 431–448.

Putnam, Robert D. 1988. "Diplomacy and Domestic Politics: The Logic of Two-Level Games." *International Organization* 42 (3): 427–460.

———. 1993. *Making Democracy Work.* With Robert Leonardi and Raffaella Y. Nanetti. Princeton: Princeton University Press.

———. 2000. *Bowling Alone: The Collapse and Revival of American Community.* New York: Simon and Schuster.

Rajan, Raghuram. 2010. *Fault Lines: How Hidden Fractures Still Threaten the World Economy.* Princeton: Princeton University Press.

Regling, Klaus, and Max Watson. 2010. "A Preliminary Report on the Sources of Ireland's Banking Crisis." Dublin: Government Publications Office. http://www.rte.ie/news/2010/0609/reglingwatson.pdf (accessed on September 29, 2012).

Reinhart, Carmen M., and Kenneth S. Rogoff. 2009. *This Time is Different: Eight Centuries of Financial Folly.* Princeton: Princeton University Press.

Reinhart, Carmen M., Kenneth S. Rogoff, and Miguel A. Savastano. 2003. "Debt intolerance." *Brookings Papers on Economic Activity* 23 (1): 1–62.

Rodrik, Dani. 1996. "Understanding Economic Policy Reform." *Journal of Economic Literature* 34 (1): 9–41.

Rogoff, Kenneth. 1985. "The Optimal Degree of Commitment to a Monetary Target." *Quarterly Journal of Economics* 100 (4): 1169–1190.

Rogoff, Kenneth S., Aasim M. Husain, Ashoka Mody, Robin Brooks, and Nienke Oomes. 2003. "Evolution and Performance of Exchange Rate Regimes." IMF Working Paper No. 03/243.

Rosanvallon, Pierre. 2008. *Counter-Democracy: Politics in an Age of Distrust*, trans. Arthur Goldhammer. Cambridge: Cambridge University Press.

Rose, Richard. 2006. "Diverging Paths of Post-Communist Countries: New Europe Barometer Trends since 1991." Studies in Public Policy No. 418. Glasgow: Centre for the Study of Public Policy.

———. 2009. *Understanding Post-communist Transformation: A Bottom Up Approach.* London: Routledge.

Rosenberg, Christoph, and Marcel Tirpák. 2008. "Determinants of Foreign Currency Loans in the New Member States of the EU." IMF Working Paper No. 08/173.

Roth, Felix. 2009. "Does Too Much Trust Hamper Economic Growth?" *Kyklos* 62 (1): 103–28.

Rothstein, Bo. 1998. *Just Institutions Matter: The Moral and Political Logic of the Universal Welfare State*. Cambridge: Cambridge University Press.

———. 2005. *Social Traps and the Problem of Trust*. Cambridge: Cambridge University Press.

———. 2011. *The Quality of Government: Corruption, Social Trust and Inequality in International Perspective*. Chicago: Chicago University Press.

Rothstein, Bo, and Dietling Stolle. 2008. "The State and Social Capital: an Institutional Theory of Generalized Trust." *Comparative Politics* 40 (4): 441–67.

Rothstein, Bo, and Jan Teorell. 2008. "What is the Quality of Government? A Theory of Impartial Government Institutions." *Governance* 21 (2): 165–190.

Rousseau, Denise M., Sim B. Sitkin, Ronald S. Burt, and Colin Camerer. 1998. "Not So Different After All: A Cross-discipline View of Trust." *Academy of Management Review* 25 (3): 393–404.

Rudolph, Thomas J., and Jillian Evans. 2005. "Political Trust, Ideology, and Public Support for Government Spending." *American Journal of Political Science* 49 (3): 660–671.

Sargent, Thomas J. 1993. *Bounded Rationality in Macroeconomics*. Oxford: Oxford University Press.

Schick, Allen. 2004. "Fiscal Institutions versus Political Will." In *Rules-Based Fiscal Policy in Emerging Markets*, ed. George Kopits, 81–94. New York: Palgrave Macmillan.

Schucknecht, Ludger. 2004. "EU Fiscal Rules: Issues and Lessons from Political Economy." ECB Working Paper No. 421.

Sent, Esther-Mirjam. 1997. "Sargent versus Simon: Bounded Rationality Unbound." *Cambridge Journal of Economics* 21 (3): 323–338.

Shackle, G. L. S. 1955. *Uncertainty in Economics and Other Reflections*. Cambridge: Cambridge University Press.

———. 1972. *Epistemics and Economics*. Cambridge: Cambridge University Press.

Shiller, Robert J. 2000. *Irrational exuberance*. Princeton: Princeton University Press.

Sinn, Hans-Werner. 2002. "Germany's Economic Unification: An Assessment after Ten Years." *Review of International Economics* 10 (1): 113–128.

Solow, Robert. 1956. "A Contribution to the Theory of Economic Growth." *Quarterly Journal of Economics* 71 (1): 65–94.

Soros, George. 2006. *The Age of Fallibility: Consequences of the War on Terror*. New York: PublicAffairs.

Spahn, Heinz-Peter. 2002. *From Gold to Euro: On Monetary Theory and the History of Currency Systems*. Berlin and New York: Springer.

Stiglitz, Joseph E. 2010. *Freefall: America, Free Markets, and the Sinking of the World Economy*. New York: W.W. Norton.

Strojwas, Michal. 2010. "The Polish Banking System: Hit by the Crisis or Merely by a Cool Breeze?" ECFIN Country Focus 7 (2) Brussels: Directorate General for Economic and Financial Affairs.

Suster, Martin. 2004. "Developments of Slovakia's Economy since 1990." In *The Slovak Economy and EU Membership*, ed. Bruno S. Sergi and William T. Bagatelas, 48–85. Bratislava: IURA.

Swensson, Torsten, Masaru Mabuchi, and Ryunoshin Kamikawa (2006): "Managing the Bank-system Crisis in Coordinated Market Economies: Institutions and Blame Avoidance Strategies in Sweden and Japan." *Governance* 19 (1): 43–74.

Szakolczai, György. 2009. "A magyar makrogazdasági egyensúly helyreállításának kísérlete." [An attempt to restore macroeconomic equilibrium in Hungary] *Pénzügyi Szemle* 54 (2–3): 258–302.

Szalai, Júlia. 2007. *Nincs két ország...? Társadalmi küzdelmek az állami (túl)elosztásért a rendszerváltás utáni Magyarországon.* [No two countries? Social struggles for state (over)redistribution in post-transition Hungary] Budapest: Osiris.

Szentkirályi, Balázs. 2011. "Ki a felelős a devizahitelezésért?" (Who is responsible for foreign currency lending?) Index.hu, October 18. http://index.hu/gazdasag/magyar/2011/10/18/ki_a_felelos_a_devizahitelezesert (accessed on May 22, 2012).

Tamanaha, Brian. 2004. *On the Rule of Law: History, Politics, Theory.* Cambridge: Cambridge University Press.

Teorell, Jan. 2009. "The Impact of Quality of Government as Impartiality: Theory and Evidence." APSA 2009 Toronto Meeting Paper. Available at SSRN: http://ssrn.com/abstract=1449173

Thomas, M. A. 2010. "What Do the Worldwide Governance Indicators Measure?" *European Journal of Development Research* 22 (1): 31–54.

Tonkiss, Fran. 2009. "Trust, Confidence and Economic Crisis." *Intereconomics* 44 (4): 196–202.

Török Ádám. 2007. "A versenyképesség egyes jogi és szabályozási feltételei Magyarországon." [Legal and regulatory conditions of competitiveness in Hungary] *Közgazdasági Szemle* 54 (12): 1066–1084.

Tóth, István György. 2003. "Jövedelemegyenlőtlenségek—tényleg növekszenek, vagy csak úgy látjuk?" [Income inequalities—are they really increasing or we just perceive so?] *Közgazdasági Szemle* 50 (3): 209–234.

Tóth, Ján. 2000. "Fiscal Policy." In *Economic Policy in Slovakia 1990–1999*, ed. Anton Marcincin and Miroslav Beblavy. 60–93. Bratislava: INEKO.

Tsebelis, George. 1990. *Nested Games: Rational Choice in Comparative Politics.* Berkley: University of California Press.

Tyler, Tom R. 2006. *Why People Obey the Law.* Princeton: Princeton University Press.

UN ECE. 2003. *Economic Survey of Europe 2003 No. 2.* Geneva, Switzerland: United Nations Economic Commission for Europe.

Uslaner, Eric M. 1999. "Democracy and Social Capital." In *Democracy and Trust*, ed. Mark E. Warren, 121–150. Cambridge: Cambridge University Press.

———. 2008. "Trust as a Moral Value." In *The Handbook of Social Capital*, eds. Dario Castiglione, Jan W. van Deth, and Guglielmo Wolleb, 101–121. Oxford: Oxford University Press.

———. 2010. "Trust and the Economic Crisis of 2008." *Corporate Reputation Review* 13 (2): 110–123.

Vanberg, Viktor. 2001. *The Constitution of Markets: Essays in Political Economy.* London and New York: Routledge.

Veiga, Linda Gonçalves, and Maria Manuel Pinho. 2007. "The Political Economy of Intergovernmental Grants: Evidence From a Maturing Democracy." *Public Choice* 133 (3–4): 457–477.

Visvizi, Anna. 2012. "The Crisis in Greece and the EU–IMF Rescue Package: Determinants and Pitfalls." *Acta Oeconomica* 62 (1): 15–39.

Von Hagen, Jürgen. 1992. "Budgeting Procedures and Fiscal Performance in the EC." Economic Papers No. 96. Brussels: Directorate General for Economic and Financial Affairs.

———. 2003. "Fiscal discipline and Growth in Euroland: Experiences with the Stability and Growth Pact." ZEI Working Paper No. B06/2003.

Voszka, Éva. 2003. *Versenyteremtés alkuval* [Creating competition through bargaining] Budapest: Akadémiai Kiadó.

Wagner, Alexander F., Friedrich Schneider, and Martin Halla. 2009. "The Quality of Institutions and Satisfaction with Democracy in Western Europe—A Panel Analysis." *European Journal of Political Economy* 25 (1): 30–41.

Whiteley, Paul. 2000. "Economic Growth and Social Capital." *Political Studies* 48 (3): 443–466.

Winiecki, Jan, ed. 2009. *Competitiveness of New Europe*. London and New York: Routledge.

Wojcik, Cezary, and Peter Backé. 2004. "The Unilateral Euroisation Debate in Central and Eastern European EU Accession Countries." *Acta Oeconomica* 54 (2): 123–157.

World Bank. 2002. *World Development Report 2002: Building Institutions for Markets*. Washington: World Bank.

World Bank. 2005. *Doing Business in 2005: Removing Obstacles to Growth*. Washington: World Bank.

World Bank. 2007. *Doing Business 2007: How to Reform*. Washington: World Bank.

World Bank. 2008. *Doing Business in 2008*. Washington: World Bank.

Zachar, Dusan. 2004. *Reforms in Slovakia 2003–2004*. Bratislava: INEKO.

Zachar, Dusan. 2005. *Reforms in Slovakia 2004–2005*. Bratislava: INEKO.

Zettelmayer, Jeromin, Piroska M. Nagy, and Stephen Jeffrey. 2010. "Addressing Private Sector Currency Mismatches in Emerging Europe." EBRD Working Paper No. 115.

Zubek, Radoslav. 2008. "Poland: from Pacesetter to Semi-permanent Outsider?" In *The Euro at 10: Europeanization, Power and Convergence*, ed. Kenneth Dyson, 292–306. Oxford: Oxford University Press.

Index

administrative costs, 47, 133
ambiguity, 22, 148
animal spirits, 20, 190
Austria, 61–2, 64–5, 72–3, 79, 155, 157–9, 182
Austrian economics, 13n1, 25n15, 27

bailout, 12, 42, 89, 135, 150–1, 153–4, 158–60, 166, 173, 179, 181–3, 185, 187, 193
Bajnai, G., 135
Balcerowicz, L., 173, 192
banking crisis, 92, 172
    in Bulgaria, 112
    in Ireland, 166, 181
    in Latvia, 149
Belgium, 61–2, 65–7, 119, 153–5, 157, 182
Bokros, L.,
    package, 130, 143
Bretton Woods system, 40
Bundesbank, 40–1
business environment, 47–8, 133

case study method, 10
Celtic Tiger, 160, 173
Central Europe, 100, 103, 179
central planning, 96
checks and balances, 28, 135–6
competitiveness, 38–9, 47, 53, 56, 61, 83, 85, 88–9, 123, 131, 138, 150, 154, 167, 179, 181, 183–5

compliance,
    sources of, 13–4
    with fiscal rules, 10–1, 28–9, 34
    with SGP, 60, 92
commitment,
    to consolidation, 77,
    to financial stability, 43
complacency, 147, 164, 174, 190
consensus, 92, 102–3, 105, 107, 114, 128–30, 132, 137, 143–5
constitution,
    in Hungary, 135–6
convergence in CEE-10, 101
corruption, 9, 29, 33, 47, 76, 84, 91, 97, 100, 109, 128, 138, 140, 168, 181n1
creative accounting,
    in Greece, 70, 150
    in Hungary, 133n34
    in Slovakia, 138
credibility, 9, 16, 28, 38, 40–2, 44, 50–1, 53, 55, 63, 87–8, 91–2, 104, 109, 113–4, 116, 123, 125, 134, 138–9, 143–5, 149, 158, 181, 189, 193
credit boom,
    in Ireland, 158
    in Latvia, 158
    in Poland, 170, 173, 192
    in Portugal, 88, 91
    in Sweden, 84
credit constraints, 151

crisis, 1–2, 4–6, 10, 12, 18–9, 40–1, 50, 56, 59–61, 63, 66–70, 73–4, 79, 81, 84–6, 88–9, 91–3, 102–4, 106n11, 108, 111–3, 115–7, 123, 125, 130–1, 134–5, 137, 142–6, 147–74, 177, 179, 181–3, 185–8, 190–5, 197
culture of fear, 83
currency board, 108–9, 111–3, 116, 118, 121, 123, 125, 145, 152, 180, 185n4, 187, 189
currency crisis, 102, 112
current account deficit,
    in the CEE-10, 111
    in Latvia, 111
    in Slovakia, 138–9
Czech Republic, 113–5, 117–8, 124–5, 137, 149, 158, 169, 182, 186–7

decision-making,
    time horizon, 11, 13, 34, 35–6, 44, 55–6, 196
    recurrent, 11, 35–7, 44, 56
    unique, 11, 36–8, 44, 56, 117, 178
Delors Plan, 41
democracy, 9, 31, 98, 103, 129
Denmark, 43, 52, 61–2, 65, 67–70, 79, 81, 153, 157–8, 182, 184–5, 190, 192
de-politicization of economic policy, 43
devaluation,
    in Portugal, 88, 91
    in Sweden, 85, 91
dictatorship, 66, 70–1, 83
distrust, 2, 4, 33–4, 35, 94, 95–6, 100–1, 117, 126, 128, 137, 147, 174, 187, 195–6
Dzurinda, M., 108, 138–9, 142, 144, 192

Economic and Financial Council (Ecofin), 43n6, 63–4
Economic and Monetary Union (EMU), 11, 35, 37, 42, 44, 53–4, 56–7, 59, 63, 65, 68, 72–3, 76–7, 79, 81, 91–3, 95–6, 106, 108–9, 113–8, 125, 142–3, 167n17, 192
economic freedom,
    in Ireland, 161

economic growth,
    theory, 196
education,
    in Portugal, 83, 89–90
efficient market theory, 15
employment protection laws, 89–90
employment rate,
    in Hungary, 133
enforcement,
    of rules, 9, 138
    of SGP, 194
equilibrium theory, 16, 19n6, 19n7, 191
exchange rate policy, 37–41
export-led growth,
    in Hungary, 129
    in Ireland, 160
external anchor, 5, 65–7, 73, 91, 132, 137
external pressure, 28, 53, 59–60, 65, 70–2, 75–7, 94, 178, 194
EU-15, 3, 5, 11–2, 59–60, 62, 65, 75, 77–8, 80, 84, 87, 90, 94, 104, 114, 153, 155, 177–80, 189, 192
euro, 3, 12, 34, 35–8, 40, 41, 43, 44, 55–7, 59, 63, 64, 66, 68, 70, 71, 72, 73, 76, 77, 79, 81, 88, 92, 104–10, 113–7, 122, 125, 126, 134, 142, 145, 149, 150, 163, 166, 168, 172, 178, 179, 180–6, 188, 195
Eurobonds, 193
European Central Bank (ECB), 42, 45n9, 151
European Commission, 131, 139, 142, 150
European debt crisis, 142
European Fiscal Compact, 167
European economic governance, 5, 42, 193
European Financial Stability Facility (EFSF), 150
European Monetary System (EMS), crisis, 60
European regional funds,
    in Ireland, 161
    in Poland, 172–3
exchange rate policy, 37–41
expectations,
    Austrian theory of, 14, 19–20, 25–7
    post-keynesian theory of, 14, 19–20, 24, 25n15
    rational, 14–9

export-led growth,
    in Hungary, 129
    in Ireland, 160
external anchor, 5, 65–7, 73, 91, 132, 137
external pressure, 28, 53, 59–60, 65, 70–2,
    75–7, 94, 178, 194

Fico, R., 141–2, 145
financial supervision,
    in Hungary, 134n38
    in Ireland, 171
    in Poland, 172
Finland, 61–2, 65, 67–9, 79, 81, 157–8,
    182
fiscal consolidation,
    expenditure-based, 11, 52, 76
    revenue-based, 52
    sustainability of, 76
Fiscal Council,
    in Hungary, 135–6
fiscal deficits, 46, 67, 70–1, 113, 115
fiscal expenditure, 46
fiscal illusion,
    in Hungary, 133
fiscal institutions,
    in Sweden, 83, 86–7
fiscal policy,
    and growth, 84–7, 94
    quality, 47, 90
flat tax in Slovakia, 140, 142
flexible credit line (FCL), 172
floating exchange rate, 106, 113, 125
foreign currency lending,
    in the CEE-10, 124
    in Hungary, 134
    in Poland, 170–1
foreign direct investment (FDI),
    in Hungary, 129
    in Ireland, 160
    in Slovakia, 138–9
    in Portugal, 172
France, 41, 61, 64–5, 72–3, 79, 183
Freiburg school, 26n17
fundamental uncertainty – see uncertainty

GDP per capita trends, 161, 168, 173, 183,
    187

Germany, 40–1, 44, 61, 63–5, 72–4, 79,
    153, 159, 182
    unification, 41, 61
governance,
    good, 9, 76
    quality of, 75–6, 107, 109, 110, 113–4
gradualism, 195
Great moderation, 190
Greece, 63, 65, 70, 77, 90, 93, 119, 150,
    154–5, 158, 179, 181–2, 185
Greenspan, A., 191
growth see economic growth
Gyurcsány, F., 134, 144

Hayek, F., 20–1, 25–7
herd behavior, 18
housing boom,
    in Ireland, 163
    in Latvia, 111
    in Sweden, 85
Hungary, 5, 12, 33n23, 95–6, 99, 103, 113–
    8, 121–2, 124–30, 133–7, 142–6, 149–
    50, 155, 158, 179, 182, 186–7, 189

IMF, 89–90, 116, 135, 149–50, 169, 172
impartiality, 29
inequality,
    in Central Europe, 98
    in Hungary, 99–100, 126
    in Portugal, 84
    in Slovakia, 141
    in Sweden, 84
inflation,
    in Germany, 41
    in Hungary, 124, 131
    in Latvia, 111
    in Lithuania, 111, 117
    in Romania, 116, 124
informal economy, 90–1, 97, 133
institutional economics, 24n14, 27n18,
    178
institutions, 2–3, 7–11, 13–4, 24, 25n15,
    26–34, 42, 51, 55–6, 82, 86, 94, 103,
    113–4, 117, 122–8, 131, 133, 142, 148,
    151, 167, 170, 172n22, 174, 178, 180,
    189–90
interest expenditure, 81

interest rate, 28, 41, 81, 104n9, 110n12, 112, 124, 134, 162, 170
international financial markets, 102–3, 109, 123, 133, 143, 149, 166, 171–2, 179, 189
Ireland, 6, 12, 52, 65, 67–9, 79, 81, 90, 147, 150, 153, 155, 158–69, 171, 173–4, 179, 181–3, 190–2
Italy, 61, 65, 70, 77, 93, 119, 151, 158, 182, 185

Kaczinsky, J., 115
Klaus, V., 137
Keynes, J. M., 18n4, 20–2, 24–6, 190
Keynesianism, 39
knowledge, 6–7, 17–27, 32
Kornai, J., 6n4, 19n7, 36, 96, 97, 127,

Lachmann, L., 18, 21, 23, 26, 28
Latvia, 109–12, 123–4, 149, 155, 158, 179, 182
law-abidance, 11, 178
leadership, 11, 96, 179, 188, 192
learning, 17–8, 21, 36–7, 40, 73
legitimacy, 8–9, 28–9
Lehman Brothers, 1, 135, 149, 165, 171
lending standards, 163–4, 170
liquidity, 102–3, 118, 148–9, 151, 170
Lithuania, 109–12, 117, 149, 155, 158, 182
Lucas critique, 54
Luxembourg, 61, 65, 72–4, 79, 155, 161, 173, 182

Maastricht,
    criteria, 42–3, 55, 59, 61, 63, 65–7, 73–4, 76, 104, 107, 113–4, 118, 178
    process, 68–71, 95, 104, 106n11
    Treaty, 42, 62, 66–7, 72
Meciar, V., 108, 137–8, 142
Mises, L., 22n10, 120
Molander, P., 93
monetary policy, 16, 37, 39, 40–4, 52–4, 110, 113, 162, 170, 191, 193
money,
    functions, 37–8
    and sovereignty, 37

National Bank of Poland (NBP), 173, 192
neo-corporatism, 73
Netherlands, 64–5, 67–9, 79, 81, 155, 158, 173, 182
new era thinking, 191
non-ergodicity, 27
North, D., 25n16, 27, 28
Norway, 61

oil crisis, 40, 66, 68, 70, 74
open-economy trilemma, 39n3
optimal currency area (OCA) theory, 38n2
Orbán, V., 135
ordoliberalism, 26n17
original sin, 124
overconfidence, 147, 174, 179, 188, 190
over-regulation, 100

paternalism, 96
Poland, 6, 12, 113–5, 117, 123–5, 129, 133, 147, 149, 153, 158–9, 167–74, 179, 182, 186–7, 192
policy ineffectiveness proposition, 15, 45
political business cycles,
    in Hungary, 101
    in Portugal, 93
popularity of euro,
    in the Czech Republic, 114
    in Greece, 70
    in Italy, 70
Portugal, 5, 11, 60–1, 63, 65, 70–1, 77, 79, 81–4, 87–94, 143, 150, 154, 158, 178–9, 181, 182, 185
Post-Communist transition, 101, 128
Post-Keynesianism, 25n15
poverty level, 84
privatization,
    in Central Europe, 100
    in Hungary, 128–9, 131, 132n30, 144
    in Slovakia, 137–9, 142
procedural justice, 29–30
prospect theory, 33n24
public administration,
    in Portugal, 89, 93
    in Sweden, 83–4

public debt,
    in the CEE-10, 120–1
    in the EU-15, 80–1
    in the EU-25, 147, 154–6, 182
    in Hungary, 114, 132
    in Sweden, 69
public investment, 45, 52

Radicova, I., 142
rationality, 27, 36, 79, 96
rational expectations, see expectations
Real business cycle theory, 15
Research and development (R&D),
    in Portugal, 90
Ricardian equivalence, 15
risk,
    management in Ireland, 173
Romania, 113–6, 118–9, 121, 123–4, 149,
    155, 158, 182, 186
Rothstein, B., 7, 10n8, 29, 83, 92
rules, 9–10, 13–4, 21, 24–30, 32–4, 36, 44,
    47–8, 52–3, 59, 63–4, 66, 68, 71–4, 84,
    86, 91, 93, 97–8, 100, 135–6, 194, 196
rule compliance, see law abidance
rule of law, 9, 25, 29, 96–8, 100, 103, 161,
    181–2, 196

Sargent, T., 15–8, 19n6
securitization, 148
self-interest, 28, 29n20
Shackle, G., 20–1, 23, 26
Single Market, 39, 56–7, 60, 88
size of the state, 46
skepticism, 43, 54, 92, 128, 166
soft law, 64
Slovakia, 5, 12, 95–6, 103, 105–9, 115–8,
    125–8, 136–46, 149, 153, 155, 158,
    179, 180, 182, 185, 192, 195
small and medium enterprises, 85, 100,
    133, 170
social partnership, 69, 165, 167
social transfers, 46, 52–4, 78, 81, 119
soft budget constraint, 112
sound money paradigm, 43–4, 55
Soviet system, 61
Spain, 61, 66–7, 77–9, 81, 88, 151, 154–5,
    157, 182, 185, 190

spontaneous orders, 25
Stability and Growth Pact (SGP), 43, 60,
    63–4, 66–7, 71, 73–4, 77, 89, 92, 194
stability culture, 73, 108–9, 111, 116
stabilization, see fiscal consolidation
structural reforms, 44, 50, 51, 55, 76, 79,
    86, 88, 91, 104, 112, 114, 130, 133,
    142, 144, 167n16, 178, 183–5
subjectivity, 8, 19
subprime crisis, 1–2, 4–6, 10, 12, 19, 66,
    69–70, 74, 81, 89, 101, 102n4, 104,
    106n11, 108, 113, 115–7, 123, 125,
    134–5, 142–3, 145–6, 147–8, 168, 177,
    179, 181–2, 185, 187, 190, 197
surprise value, 24
Sweden, 5, 11, 43, 60–1, 65, 67, 69–70, 79,
    81–5, 87–8, 91–4, 143, 153, 155, 158,
    178, 182, 184, 191

tax,
    compliance, 14, 29–31, 48
    composition, 165
    revenue, 165
    systems, 47
Thatcher, M., 74
time inconsistency, 16
transformational recession, 98, 111, 126,
    130
trust, 1–12, 13, 14, 16, 17, 31–4, 35, 36, 44,
    45, 47, 48, 49, 50, 53–7, 59, 60, 65, 75,
    82, 83, 84, 91, 93, 95, 102, 106, 109,
    113, 117, 123, 125–8, 132–4, 136, 137,
    143, 144, 147, 148, 173, 174, 177–97
    and growth, 45
    forms of, 7
    origins, 7
Tusk, D., 115
Tyler, T., 29

uncertainty, 10–1, 13–4, 20–8, 31–4, 35–6,
    38, 45n8, 48, 51, 56, 61, 82, 90, 98, 99,
    136, 147, 178, 193
unemployment, 39, 61, 62, 98, 126, 130,
    138–42, 149, 151, 152, 166, 168
    in the EU, 155–9
    in Portugal, 88
    in Sweden, 85–6

United Kingdom (UK), 43, 61, 72, 74, 159,
    182, 184–5, 190
United States (US), 1, 38–9, 54, 148–9

Visegrad group, 189
Von Hagen, J., 64, 93
vulnerability,
    as aspect of trust, 6, 13, 17
    to crisis, 165

wage moderation,
    in Ireland, 162
    in Sweden, 85
welfare state,
    in Sweden, 85–6, 92
Werner Plan, 40–1
World Bank, 28, 141
World Governance Indicators, 8, 10, 75,
    82, 106, 159, 178, 181